Catullus

BLACKWELL INTRODUCTIONS TO THE CLASSICAL WORLD

This series will provide concise introductions to classical culture in the broadest sense. Written by the most distinguished scholars in the field, these books survey key authors, periods and topics for students and scholars alike.

Published

Greek Tragedy
Nancy Sorkin Rabinowitz

Roman Satire
Daniel Hooley

Ancient History
Charles W. Hedrick, Jr.

Homer, second edition
Barry B. Powell

Classical Literature
Richard Rutherford

Ancient Rhetoric and Oratory
Thomas Habinek

Ancient Epic
Katherine Callen King

Catullus
Julia Haig Gaisser

In Preparation

Ancient Comedy
Eric Csapo

Sappho
Ellen Greene

Catullus

Julia Haig Gaisser

A John Wiley & Sons, Ltd., Publication

This edition first published 2009
© 2009 Julia Haig Gaisser

Blackwell Publishing was acquired by John Wiley & Sons in February 2007. Blackwell's publishing program has been merged with Wiley's global Scientific, Technical, and Medical business to form Wiley-Blackwell.

Registered Office
John Wiley & Sons Ltd, The Atrium, Southern Gate, Chichester, West Sussex, PO19 8SQ, United Kingdom

Editorial Offices
350 Main Street, Malden, MA 02148-5020, USA
9600 Garsington Road, Oxford, OX4 2DQ, UK
The Atrium, Southern Gate, Chichester, West Sussex, PO19 8SQ, UK

For details of our global editorial offices, for customer services, and for information about how to apply for permission to reuse the copyright material in this book, please see our website at www.wiley.com/wiley-blackwell.

The right of Julia Haig Gaisser to be identified as the author of this work has been asserted in accordance with the Copyright, Designs and Patents Act 1988.

All rights reserved. No part of this publication may be reproduced, stored in a retrieval system, or transmitted, in any form or by any means, electronic, mechanical, photocopying, recording or otherwise, except as permitted by the UK Copyright, Designs and Patents Act 1988, without the prior permission of the publisher.

Wiley also publishes its books in a variety of electronic formats. Some content that appears in print may not be available in electronic books.

Designations used by companies to distinguish their products are often claimed as trademarks. All brand names and product names used in this book are trade names, service marks, trademarks or registered trademarks of their respective owners. The publisher is not associated with any product or vendor mentioned in this book. This publication is designed to provide accurate and authoritative information in regard to the subject matter covered. It is sold on the understanding that the publisher is not engaged in rendering professional services. If professional advice or other expert assistance is required, the services of a competent professional should be sought.

Library of Congress Cataloging-in-Publication Data

Gaisser, Julia Haig.
  Catullus / Julia Haig Gaisser.
      p. cm. — (Blackwell introductions to the classical world)
  Includes bibliographical references and index.
  ISBN 978-1-4051-1889-7 (hardcover : alk. paper) 1. Catullus, Gaius Valerius—Criticism and interpretation. 2. Elegiac poetry, Latin—History and criticism. 3. Love poetry, Latin—History and criticism. I. Title.
  PA6276.G348 2009
  874'.01–dc22
                                                                            2008046987

A catalogue record for this book is available from the British Library.

Set in 10.5 on 13pt Galliard by SNP Best-set Typesetter Ltd., Hong Kong
Printed and bound in Malaysia by Vivar Printing Sdn Bhd

01 2009

For T.K.G.

Contents

List of Figures		viii
Preface		ix
1	Introduction: The Young Poet in Rome	1
2	Poetry Books	22
3	The Catullan Persona	45
4	What Makes It Poetry	72
5	Poetic Architecture	100
6	Songs for Mixed Voices: Allusions, Intertexts, and Translations	133
7	Receiving Catullus 1: From Antiquity through the Sixteenth Century	166
8	Receiving Catullus 2: England and America	194
Appendix 1 Catullus' Meters		222
Appendix 2 Glossary of Metrical and Rhetorical Terms		223
Bibliography		225
General Index		235
Index of Catullus' Poems		242

Figures

1	Ariadne in Pompeian Wall Paintings	156
2	Bacchus in Pompeian Wall Paintings	157
3	Title Page of *Les Amours de Catulle* (1713)	202
4	*Ave atque Vale* by Aubrey Beardsley	209
5	Lesbia and a Satyr by Véra Willoughby	211

Preface

This book is for people who like poetry—in any language. It is for those who like thinking about words and what happens when they are put together, how they sound, how they resonate both inside a poem and with other poems they have read. I hope that there will be something new in it for those who already know Catullus well, but I am thinking mostly of readers whose acquaintance is not so deep, or perhaps not deep at all. That would include students at every level, but especially undergraduates and graduate students, as well as faculty members coming to Catullus from fields like English or comparative literature, or classicists not specializing in Roman poetry. I am also thinking of non-academics—perhaps people who read Catullus once and liked him, or those who never read a word of Latin, but would like to include him in their poetic universe.

For all these readers I have tried to situate Catullus in his times, which are among the most exciting and interesting eras in Roman history. I have tried to bring his poetry to life, looking at it in as many ways as possible. There are chapters on the arrangement of the poems, the character or persona that Catullus presents in his poetry, his language and poetic structure, the ways his poetry draws on and resonates with earlier poetry, and finally, on the interpretations of his readers from antiquity to the present. My concerns above all are always literary and poetic, and I try to show the ways in which looking at meter or the persona or intertextuality or the approaches of other readers can help us to enjoy and find meaning (often multiple meanings) in the poetry.

Catullus' poetry presents two apparent barriers to the reader. Much (about a quarter) of it is obscene, and all of it is in Latin. I have confronted both of these facts head on and unapologetically in the belief that twenty-first century readers do not need to be protected from either.

Catullus' obscenity is not just a matter of "dirty words." Unlike most of the obscenity we hear in the media and daily life, it is not empty or gratuitous, but purposeful in the context and construction of each poem where it appears. Sometimes it is shocking, sometimes funny; but it is always meaningful. I translate and discuss obscene poems frankly throughout.

Catullus' Latin of course is fundamental. Poetry is a compound of thought and language. Its words matter, not only for their meanings, but also (and sometimes almost even more) for their sounds and rhythms and the patterns those sounds and rhythms make with other words. Each poem (or part of a poem) is presented first in Latin, then in translation, but I constantly refer to the Latin in discussion. In Chapter 4 ("What Makes It Poetry") I encourage even Latinless readers to read the Latin aloud, presenting a simplified account of pronunciation, meters, and sound effects and how they create meaning in the poetry.

I have included both footnotes and a bibliography of secondary sources in English because I think it is important to let readers interested in a particular point know where they can find out more. But I have not used the footnotes for discussion or to cite every conceivable item of bibliography. My purpose is to get readers started, not to finish them off.

The poems are quoted from the text of D.F.S. Thomson's *Catullus* (1997). All Latin is translated. Unless otherwise noted, the translations are my own.

I have greatly enjoyed working on this book. Catullus is a poet who amply repays reading, rereading, and rethinking, and I constantly found myself seeing things in his poetry I had not seen before, which I think is the greatest pleasure a poetry lover can have. The project has been aided and abetted by several good friends and colleagues. I am extremely grateful to Al Bertrand at Wiley-Blackwell for proposing it and to my editor Haze Humbert for patiently waiting for it to come to fruition. My thanks also go to Joseph Farrell, Susannah Brower, and Thomas Gaisser, each of whom read chapters and provided helpful comments. I owe a special debt of gratitude to David Ross, who generously read every chapter with an eagle eye and gave me the benefit of his learning and poetic insight.

1
Introduction: The Young Poet in Rome

> Romae vivimus: illa domus,
> illa mihi sedes, illic mea carpitur aetas.
> (Poem 68.34–5)

Catullus is the most accessible of the ancient poets. His poems (even the very long ones) convey an emotional immediacy and urgency that claim the reader's sympathy. The emotions themselves—love, sorrow, pleasure, hatred, contempt—are clear, direct, passionate, very much like our own, we are tempted to imagine. They are set out for us not in the abstract but in the real, historical world of late republican Rome. This Rome, evoked for us with a few light, sharp strokes, is a virtual character in the poetry, with its politicians, playboys (and girls), low-lifes, and fellow poets. Catullus' language seems for the most part as clear and direct as his feelings. His characteristic meter, the phalaecean hendecasyllabic, is relaxed, conversational, and memorable. He is learned (formidably so), but a first reader does not have to be equally learned in order to respond to him. Many of his poems are short—of fewer than 20 lines—so that even a novice Latinist can take them in at a sitting.

But Catullus' accessibility is deceiving. He draws us into his world and its emotional landscape so artfully that we think we know him much better than we do, rather like a seemingly open and guileless acquaintance we have known for a time and then realized we did not know at all. The emotional immediacy and factual details in Catullus' poems can make us forget that his poetry, like all poetry, is a fiction. The Catullus we see in the poems is a character or persona created by Catullus the poet, and we can never be sure where the one leaves off and the other begins. We will look more closely at the Catullan persona in chapter 3. In this chapter, however, we will consider what we can know about Catullus the poet, the maker (not the subject) of the poetry, and about the world in which he created his poems.

Fragments of a Biography

A few details of Catullus' life are recorded by ancient sources. The fourth-century writer Jerome mentions Catullus twice in his *Chronica* (a chronological list of historical dates). For 87 B.C. he says: "Gaius Valerius Catullus the lyric writer is born in Verona" (*Chronica* 150H); for 58 B.C.: "Catullus dies at Rome in the thirtieth year of his life" (*Chronica* 154H). But Jerome's dates cannot be right. Catullus mentions events of both 55 and 54, and he was still alive as late as August 54 (the date of his friend Calvus' prosecution of Vatinius, mentioned in poem 53).[1] Scholars generally accept the idea that Catullus died when he was twenty-nine or thirty. (Perhaps he did, even if dying young is a very "poetic" thing to do.) They adjust Jerome's chronology accordingly, dating Catullus' life to something like 84–54 or (more often) 82–52. But Jerome's testimony is important even though his chronology is inaccurate. He gives us at least approximate dates, identifies Catullus as a lyric poet (a point that is often disputed, as we will see), and places him in Verona and Rome, sites that resonate powerfully (and in different keys) in his poetry.

Jerome probably took his information on Catullus from a much earlier work on the lives of literary men called *De viris illustribus*, written by the biographer Suetonius around the beginning of the second century. This work is now lost, but Suetonius preserves another important biographical snippet in his *Life of Julius Caesar*. He uses the following anecdote about Catullus to demonstrate Caesar's eagerness to lay aside even legitimate grievances.

> Caesar did not hide the fact that Valerius Catullus had placed a permanent mark of infamy on him with his verses about Mamurra. But when Catullus apologized, he invited him to dinner on the same day, and continued to enjoy the hospitality of his father as he had been in the habit of doing. (*Life of Julius Caesar* 73)

Catullus wrote two poems attacking Caesar and his henchman Mamurra (29 and 57).[2] Suetonius (and Caesar) could have had both poems in mind, but 57 is especially virulent. It begins:

> Pulcre convenit improbis cinaedis,
> Mamurrae pathicoque Caesarique. (57.1–2)
> (The shameless faggots are well matched,
> Both queer Mamurra and Caesar too.)

The story in Suetonius is valuable evidence for the circulation of Catullus' poetry, for the verses on Mamurra must have been very widely known for Caesar to believe that he had received "a permanent mark of infamy." The story is also surprisingly informative about Catullus' family and social position. The essential point is that the Valerii of Verona had enough status and wealth and a sufficiently grand establishment to qualify as frequent hosts to a great man like Caesar. Italian tradition since the time of the Renaissance has located their property at Sirmione (ancient Sirmio) on a beautiful peninsula of Lake Garda near Verona. The tradition was inspired by archeological evidence (ruins of a great Roman villa of the first century A.D. are found on the site), but still more by Catullus' poem 31, in which he salutes Sirmio as his home and refers to himself as its master (*erus*). Modern scholars have agreed with the identification, and it has been suggested that the site was still in the family a century after Catullus' time when the villa was built.[3] Suetonius does not say when Catullus' apology and dinner with Caesar took place, but it would have been in the middle 50s during the Gallic wars when Caesar generally wintered in Cisalpine Gaul ("Gaul on this side of the Alps," i.e., northern Italy).[4] In any case, Catullus' father (whom the poet never mentions) was still alive at the time.

The most famous piece of ancient biographical information comes from Apuleius in the *Apology* (mid-second century). In response to the charge of using pseudonyms for the boys he addresses in his erotic poetry he says: "By the same token they should accuse Gaius Catullus because he used the name Lesbia for Clodia" (*Apology* 10). Apuleius' identification of Lesbia places Catullus' most famous subject and the poems about her in a particular social context, for Clodia was a member of one of the greatest and most ancient patrician families in Rome, the Claudii. The spelling of her name (Clodia, not Claudia) tells us that she was a sister of the infamous demagogue Publius Clodius Pulcher, who used the "popular" spelling. But it is not clear which sister she was.[5] Clodius had three sisters, all named Clodia, the feminine form of their *nomen*. Like most aristocratic women, they were differentiated either by the genitive form of their husband's name or by an ordinal number corresponding to their place in the birth order of female children (Prima, Secunda, Tertia, etc.). Thus, the three were Clodia Metelli (Clodia the wife of Metellus), Clodia Luculli (Clodia the wife of Lucullus), and Clodia Tertia, who was the third daughter born, but not the youngest of the surviving group (Clodia Luculli was the youngest). Clodia Metelli is generally identified as Lesbia, largely on the basis of Cicero's racy and slanderous portrait of her in his oration *Pro Caelio*. But she is not the only possible candidate. Little is known of Clodia Tertia, but Clodia Luculli lived at least as fast and loose as Clodia Metelli. All three sisters, but especially Clodia Metelli and Clodia Luculli, were rumored to have committed incest with their brother Clodius. The charge is reflected in Catullus' invective on "Lesbius pulcer" in poem 79, which begins:

> Lesbius est pulcer; quid ni? Quem Lesbia malit
>   quam te cum tota gente, Catulle, tua. (79.1–2)
> (Lesbius is pretty. Why not? For Lesbia would prefer him
>   to you with your whole family, Catullus.)

From the details provided by Jerome, Suetonius, and Apuleius we can begin to piece together the outlines of the poet's life. He was born in the 80s and died about thirty years later. He was of a wealthy and important provincial family in an area that had come fairly recently under Roman control. (The settlements in northern Italy between the Alps and the river Po were designated Latin colonies in 89 and their inhabitants, called Transpadani, "people on the other side of the Po," received a general grant of Roman citizenship only in 49.) He lived for some time in Rome and wrote poems to a patrician woman (Clodia) calling her by the pseudonym Lesbia. He died in Rome.

A few more pieces of the poet's biography can be gleaned from the poems themselves. Catullus tells us that he served in the *cohors* or entourage of Memmius in Bithynia (poems 10 and 28). He also says he didn't like it. Since Memmius is known to have been governor of Bithynia in 57–56, Catullus' complaints provide one secure date in his biography and poetry: poems 10 and 28 and the others referring to Bithynia (31 and 46) were written in 57–56 or later. His presence in Memmius' *cohors* helps to flesh out the picture of his social status we saw in Suetonius, for such positions were held by young men with excellent connections and political prospects. Being in a governor's *cohors* was not uncommon in Catullus' circle, nor was coming home disenchanted with it. Catullus' friends Veranius and Fabullus served in Piso's *cohors* in Spain (poems 12, 28, 47), and they seem to have enjoyed their experience no more than Catullus did. Their dissatisfaction, like Catullus', was financial: they had expected to make money out of the province and failed to do so. We get a glimpse of the expectations and frustrations of such young men in poem 10. (Catullus is reporting a conversation with his friend Varus and Varus' girlfriend.)

> Huc ut venimus, incidere nobis
> sermones varii: in quibus, quid esset
> iam Bithynia; quo modo se haberet;
> ecquonam mihi profuisset aere.
> Respondi, id quod erat, nihil neque ipsis
> nec praetoribus esse nec cohorti,
> cur quisquam caput unctius referret,
> praesertim quibus esset irrumator
> praetor, nec faceret pili cohortem. (10.5–13)
> (When we got there, various topics came up in our conversation—among them what Bithynia was like now, how it was doing, whether I had made any money out of it. I replied (and it was true) that neither the natives nor the praetors nor the entourage had any way to line their pockets—especially those whose praetor screwed them and didn't give a damn for his entourage.)

Catullus also speaks of a brother (otherwise unknown), whose death in Troy he laments in poems 65, 68, and 101. Poetically the brother is useful and important, providing an emotionally powerful foil to Lesbia, and representing the pull of Verona and familial love against that of Rome and eros. But the only thing we know about him is his death far from home, and that only from Catullus. Another detail that emerges from the poetry is mysterious in a different way. A dozen or so of Catullus' 116 poems can be dated, but none of the datable poems falls outside the short period 57–56 to 54.[6] The fact may or may not be significant. Perhaps he wrote all of the extant poems within a period of three or or four years, but it is also possible that the clustering of datable poems is a coincidence.[7]

A final piece of the poet's biography is so large that we might almost overlook it even though it overshadows all the rest. At some point Catullus went to Rome. We do not know when or why he did so, but there are some probabilities. It is likely that he arrived at some time in the late 60s or early 50s, perhaps with the intention of embarking on a political career. The career did not materialize, but he settled in Rome, anyway. A number of his poems are set in the territory of Verona, but it is Rome that he celebrates as his home, as in poem 68:

> . . . Romae vivimus: illa domus,
> illa mihi sedes, illic mea carpitur aetas. (68.34–5)
> (I live in Rome. That is my home,
> that is my place, there my life is spent.)

In the rest of this chapter we will consider what Rome was like—politically, socially, intellectually—for the young poet living there in the last decades of the Roman republic.

Politics

Rome in the 50s B.C. was a large, dirty, rich, violent, exciting city, the head of an increasingly far-flung empire that stretched from Asia Minor in the east to Spain in the west, taking in parts of north Africa on the way. Political strife had been a constant accompaniment to its great and still growing power, and in the 50s—the last full decade of the Roman republic—violence, social unrest, and the competition for political supremacy intensified. In 59 the three rival dynasts, Caesar, Pompey, and Crassus, formed an uneasy alliance (the so-called first triumvirate) that held together for the first half of the decade. The alliance on the part of Caesar and Pompey was sealed with the marriage of Caesar's daughter Julia to Pompey. The marriage made Caesar Pompey's father-in-law, a fact that provided irresistible fodder for political satirists. Catullus makes a jingle of it in the last line of poem 29:

> socer generque, perdidistis omnia? (29.24)
> (father-in-law and son-in-law, have you squandered everything?)

Each of the three stood to gain by their arrangement, but Caesar's prize turned out to be greatest: a special command in Transalpine Gaul. He waged a long and brutal campaign (58–51), brought Gaul under Roman control, and enriched himself and his friends. The three renewed their agreement in 56. Under the new agreement Pompey and Crassus became consuls in 55; Caesar's command in Gaul was renewed for five years; Pompey became governor of Spain and Crassus of Syria, which he used as a base to attack the Parthians. But this time the agreement could not hold. After Pompey's wife Julia died in 54 and Crassus and his army were massacred by the Parthians in 53, there was nothing to prevent Pompey and Caesar from becoming open enemies. The two jockeyed for supremacy for the rest of the decade, and events marched toward the civil war that began in 49 when Caesar invaded Italy with his Gallic legions.

Caesar, Pompey, and Crassus were the principals in the power struggles of the 50s, but there were also other players. Among the most important was Clodia's brother, Publius Clodius Pulcher.[8] Clodius had his own ambition: to control the city through the urban mob. To do so, he needed to become tribune of the *plebs*, which required renouncing his status as a patrician and transferring to the *plebs*. He achieved this feat in 59 with the connivance of the triumvirate, but for the most part he remained an independent operator outside their control. He won popular support by distributions of grain and used gangs of thugs to terrorize his opponents. In 58 he satisfied an old grudge against Cicero by getting him exiled in spite of Pompey's attempts to defend him, and he used his thugs to try to forestall efforts to recall him, breaking up assemblies and even besieging Pompey in his house. But Clodius' opponents had armed gangs of their own, and there were bloody battles between them. In 52 Clodius was murdered on the Appian Way by the gang of Pompey's supporter Milo. Rioting followed. Clodius' body was carried to the forum, where the fires of his funeral pyre destroyed the Senate House. In the aftermath Pompey was named sole consul, setting the stage for his confrontation with Caesar.

We cannot know how many of these events Catullus was in Rome to see or hear about. The date of his arrival in the city is unknown. He would have missed much of the excitement in 57–56 over Cicero's return from exile since he was in Bithynia with Memmius' *cohort*, and perhaps he did not live to know of Crassus' great disaster in 53 or Clodius' murder in 52. But he would have seen plenty of political turmoil all the same. Like everyone in Rome, he was aware of the violence in the streets and of the high-handed behavior of the great and powerful. As an intimate of Clodia, he would have had a privileged perspective on Clodius' activities. Major political figures appear in several of his poems: Caesar in 11, 29, 54, 57, and 93, Clodius in 79, Pompey in 29 and 113, Cicero in 49. Other figures less well known to us but famous at the time appear in many more.[9]

High Society

The Valerii Catulli of Verona were *domi nobiles* ("nobles at home"). (The term describes families rich and important in their native province who had not yet "arrived" socially and politically in Rome.) Catullus was sufficiently well connected to join a governor's entourage and to move in at least some of the higher circles of Roman society. His friend and fellow poet C. Licinius Calvus, for example, was a rising political orator from a prominent family: Calvus' father was a praetor, and a Licinius had been consul as early as the fourth century.[10] Catullus' lover Clodia (whichever Clodia she was) had even higher social credentials. As Cicero reminds Clodia Metelli in his oration *Pro Caelio*:

> Had you not seen that your father was a consul, had you not heard that your uncle, your grandfather, great-grandfather, great-great-grandfather, great-great-great-grandfather were consuls? (Cicero, *Pro Caelio* 34)

Catullus' ancestry could not compete with those of Calvus or Clodia, for he was probably descended from Italian or Roman settlers who had moved into Transpadane territory around the end of the second century, ordinary men who had done very well in their new surroundings, perhaps in commerce of some kind.[11] But he was no country bumpkin either. In the late republic, provincial families like his were in the process of rising to senatorial rank within a generation or two (his own family would accomplish the feat by the time of Tiberius in the early first century A.D.).[12] He had a splendid education, as the learning—especially the Greek learning—of his poetry attests. He had plenty of money, and whatever he chose to do with it, a family connection with Caesar. Above all, he had great literary talent and interests in tune with contemporary poetics, as we will see in the last section of this chapter.

Many modern scholars argue that Catullus' provincial origins made him an outsider in Roman society and that he was correspondingly anxious about his status.[13] Certainly the persona we meet in his poems is very much attuned to nuances of behavior, status, and even accent. In poem 44 he notes that some people might think his country house has the wrong address (in rustic Sabine territory as opposed to fashionable Tibur). In poem 12 he castigates someone gauche enough to filch a napkin at a dinner party. In poem 84 he mocks a certain Arrius who mispronounces his aitches. But similar comments can be found in his contemporaries, particularly in Cicero. Cicero, too, can be seen as socially insecure (he was a "new man," the first in his family to reach the consulship, and like Catullus, he came to Rome from elsewhere in Italy). The more important point, however, is that Roman society in general was alert to details of behavior, dress, and speech as markers of status. Men (for it was men who appeared in public settings) both closely observed each other for such markers and were careful to construct their own performance to confirm their place on the desired rung of the hierarchical ladder. It is safe to say that Catullus shared his society's preoccupation—he could hardly do otherwise. Allusions to status in his poetry demonstrate his interest (as well as the fact that he was a keen observer of social behavior). But they cannot show that his interest was different in kind or degree from that of his contemporaries. To put it another way: we cannot infer deep *personal* anxiety about his status from particular poems.

The markers of status in Roman society were various in kind. Some were obvious and definite: pedigree, wealth, political power. Others were intangible, the sum of selected personal qualities of behavior, speech, and appearance. Among the most important intangible markers was *urbanitas*, which we can translate as "urban sophistication"—but only so long as we remember that such terms are not universal and unchanging across societies or even over time in the same society. (Consider the difference between the "urban sophistication" of the *Thin Man* movies of the 1930s and that of *Seinfeld* or *Sex in the City* in the 1990s.) Elite Romans themselves saw *urbanitas* as indefinable: they knew it when they saw it.[14] Pressed for a definition of "an urban coloring" (*urbanitatis color*) in rhetoric, Cicero says: "I don't know. I only know that it exists" (*Brutus* 171). But the very indefinability of *urbanitas* was its strength. The people who had it knew what it was; their shared possession of it bound them together, as did their confidence that others could not fully understand or achieve it. Its power to exclude is nicely summed up in this definition by Michael Winterbottom: "*Urbanitas* was the code of attitudes and behaviour employed by the sophisticated ancient to make the outsider feel small."[15] As Winterbottom's words suggest, *urbanitas* was a composite of qualities. It included what was tasteful (*elegans*), witty (*facetus*), charming (*lepidus*), attractive (*venustus*), nice (*bellus*), and humorous (*festivus*). We will discuss some of these words in later chapters. For now the important point is the fluidity and relative vagueness of *urbanitas* and its components and their precariousness as social markers. A man's pedigree was stable, his wealth and political power perhaps somewhat less so; but *urbanitas* could be compromised in an instant by an ill-judged action or remark. In poem 22 Catullus shows us how fragile *urbanitas* is for the poet Suffenus[16]:

> Suffenus iste, Vare, quem probe nosti,
> homo est venustus et dicax et urbanus,

idemque longe plurimos facit versus.
. . .
haec cum legas tu, bellus ille et urbanus
Suffenus unus caprimulgus aut fossor
rursus videtur. (22. 1–3, 9–11)
(That Suffenus, Varus, whom you know well, is a charming and witty
and urbane fellow, and yet he makes by far the most verses.
. . .
When you read these things, that smart and urbane Suffenus now seems
an ordinary goatmilker or a ditchdigger.)

Although many markers of status operated across elite society, the Roman social world was not monolithic. It contained different circles whose attitudes, interests, and activities varied widely. The circle we meet in Catullus' poetry is young, well-off, pleasure-loving, and focused more on private concerns than on public responsibility.[17] In this respect they were at odds with traditional Roman values, which promoted worthwhile activity (*negotium*) on behalf of the state. Men were supposed to keep busy—in the army, in politics, in provincial administration, or even in commerce. But not everyone did. In the late republic there were plenty of privileged young men who used their wealth and position to suit themselves, perhaps dipping in and out of politics, perhaps dropping out of public life altogether, as Catullus seems to have done. Cicero likes to talk about such young men about town, his tone hostile or indulgent depending on the situation. In an oration against Catiline he portrays some of them as vicious and dangerous revolutionaries (*In Catilinam* 2.22–4), but in his defense of Caelius he takes a softer line: youth should be allowed its pleasures before it assumes the responsibilities of marriage, the forum, and the state (*Pro Caelio* 42). In both contexts he describes them as given over to a life of pleasure: love, all-night parties, dancing, and adultery.[18]

Catullus presents himself and his friends in a different light. Their *otium*, which means not "leisure" or "idleness" exactly, but perhaps something we could call "lack of *negotium*," or "lack of busy-ness," includes sensual pleasures and a certain amount of frivolity; but it is not merely a slothful refusal of gainful employment as Cicero and other traditionalists would see it, but rather a positive choice of private over public life. An important component in their choice is a shared commitment to poetry, whether writing it, talking about it, or criticising it. Catullus often shows poetry as an activity shared by members of the group: for example, in poem 14 Calvus sends Catullus a collection of terrible poems as a gift and Catullus threatens to retaliate; in 22 Catullus criticises Suffenus' poems to his friend Varus; in 35 he writes to Caecilius about one of Caecilius' poems; in 38 he asks Cornificius for a poem of consolation; in 50 he recalls writing poems for fun with Calvus when they were *otiosi* ("at leisure"). Poetry was the activity of their *otium*, but it was also serious business. Cicero speaks approvingly of the great Roman hero Scipio Africanus, who was said "even in *otium* to think about *negotia*" (*De officiis.* 3.1.1). We might say the same of the young men in Catullus, except that theirs was a different *negotium*: not matters of state but poetry.

Sexual Attitudes

To the social markers discussed in the last section we must add another, which some modern scholars consider the most important of all: masculinity.[19] In the rigidly hierarchical world of Roman society, masculinity represented not merely the possession of certain physical attributes, but status, domination, and power. Masculinity manifested itself in carriage, speech, actions, and conduct, but above all in the sexual act, its most basic demonstration of control. The dominance belonged to the one who penetrated another with his penis, whether he did so vaginally, anally, or orally (respectively, *futuere, pedicare, irrumare*); and the one penetrated, whether female or male, was considered submissive and lesser in power and status.[20] The essential point was not the sex of the person with whom a man performed a sexual act, but whether or not he was the penetrator. The ability to penetrate another was a demonstration of masculinity and power; submitting to penetration (or being forced to submit) was an act of softness (*mollitia*) and an acknowledgement of inferiority. For a male slave it was just another aspect of his servitude; for an adult male citizen it was humiliating and shameful. Women did not play an important role in this social calculus of dominance and submission. Of course they participated in sexual activity, whether willingly or unwillingly, and whether as wives, mistresses, prostitutes, or slaves. But since it was a given that they were the ones penetrated, they occupied the negative pole of the virility continuum: the penetrated male was said "to suffer the woman's role" (*muliebria pati*). The contest of masculinity was for men.

Dominance could be demonstrated by actual sexual acts, but also by verbal or physical aggression, threats of homosexual rape, and accusations of *mollitia* or of having endured oral or anal penetration.[21] Catullus' poetry contains many examples of masculine accusations and threats, the most famous being in poem 16.

> Pedicabo ego vos et irrumabo,
> Aureli pathice et cinaede Furi,
> qui me ex versiculis meis putastis,
> quod sunt molliculi, parum pudicum. (16.1–4)
> (I'll bugger you and stuff it down your throats,
> queer Aurelius and faggot Furius!
> who think from my verses, because they're
> a little soft, that I'm not quite modest.)

Furius and Aurelius have accused Catullus of being *parum pudicum* ("not quite modest"—i.e., "unmale" and submitting to penetration by another) because he writes poems that are *molliculi* ("a little soft") and *parum pudici*. He retaliates by threatening to demonstrate his masculinity by raping them anally and orally. The threat is heightened if we agree with Wiseman that the epithets *pathice* and *cinaede* are proleptic or anticipatory and that Furius and Aurelius will be *made* pathic and "unmale" by his rape.[22] Catullus' masculinity will be asserted by his act, while theirs will be diminished or destroyed. Since phallic aggression was a display of power, the exercise of domination and control could be represented metaphorically as a sexual act.[23] In both poem 10 and poem 28 Catullus characterizes Memmius, the praetor with whom he served in Bithynia, as an *irrumator* (literally, someone who penetrates his "partner" orally). In 28 the language is graphic:

> O Memmi, bene me ac diu supinum
> tota ista trabe lentus irrumasti. (28.9–10)
> (O Memmius, when I was on my back you took your time and stuffed my mouth well and long with that whole beam of yours.)

Memmius had greater power and status than Catullus and let his subordinate know it, and Catullus describes his contemptuous domination in sexual terms. The metaphor in his description is not dead or even faded, but as potent as Catullus' Memmius, taking its force from the deep-seated connection between social standing and aggressive masculinity.

No label of effeminacy or homosexuality was attached to a man who penetrated another male, for as we have seen, his masculinity depended on his being the penetrator, not on the sex of the person he penetrated. But there were clearly understood laws about the status and character of his partners.[24] Free-born citizen boys were off-limits, as were free-born girls, married women, and slaves used without their owner's consent. Foreigners, one's own slaves, and citizens of either sex who had engaged in prostitution were fair game. A slave in Plautus' comedy *Curculio* explains the rules to his young master: "Make love to anything you like, as long as you keep away from the wife, the widow, the virgin, young men, and free-born boys" (lines 37–8).

Within these limits the elite male could do as he pleased, but the conduct of elite women was closely scrutinized. The Roman matron was protected by law and custom from rape or seduction, but if her virtue was suspect, she was subject to punishment by her husband or family that—in theory, at least—might include even death.[25] At the least, however, she became vulnerable to slander and humiliation. The reputation of Clodia Metelli was such that Cicero felt free to treat her publicly with vicious contempt. In *Pro Caelio*, his speech in defense of her former lover M. Caelius Rufus, he calls her "a woman not only noble but notorious" (*Pro Caelio* 31), alludes insinuatingly to the rumors of her relations with Clodius ("her husband—I meant to say her brother—I always make that mistake;" *Pro Caelio* 32), and refers to her as *amicam omnium*, which we might translate as "everyone's very good friend" (*Pro Caelio* 32). Modern scholars have correctly cautioned against uncritical belief in Cicero's characterization of Clodia.[26] But his account is still valuable—not so much for its portrait of the historical Clodia as for the insight it provides into contemporary attitudes. In his sketch of the immoral behavior of a supposedly hypothetical woman (intended to be recognized as Clodia) we get a contemporary glimpse of decadent high life and its likely social consequences for a woman too publicly engaged in it.

> I say nothing now against this woman [Clodia]. But just suppose there were someone unlike her who made herself available to everyone, who always had an openly declared lover, into whose garden, house, seaside villa every lecher went back and forth at will, who even kept young men and compensated for their fathers' stinginess with her own generosity; suppose a widow were living freely, a bold widow were living shamelessly, a rich widow extravagantly, a lecherous widow like a whore, would I consider anyone who greeted her a little too freely an adulterer? (*Pro Caelio* 38)

New Poets and Poetry

Catullus arrived in Rome in time to become a major figure in a group of poets engaged in a new kind of poetry. The poets were young, like

Catullus; and like him, they differed from many of their predecessors in being financially independent, which meant they could suit themselves about what and how they wrote. Modern scholars generally call them "neoteric" or "new poets." The term is convenient although it does not appear in the works of the poets themselves.[27] The poetry they wrote was largely influenced by the Greek poets of third-century Alexandria, combining the ideas of the Alexandrian scholar-poet Callimachus with traditional Roman forms and adding new stylistic devices and themes to the Roman repertoire.[28] To the modern reader it seems to have an air of freshness and novelty, but so little Latin poetry survives from the late second and early first century that we cannot be sure to what extent the neoterics were breaking with their predecessors rather than building on their work and taking it in new directions. Roman poets had been imitating Greek and even Alexandrian models for generations. To take just one example, around 85 B.C. the young Cicero made a Latin translation of Aratus' quintessentially Alexandrian poem *Phaenomena* (on the constellations); his translation shows many features of archaic poetic style, but also many stylistic devices more commonly associated with the neoterics and the poets of the Augustan age.[29] But the new poets, even if they were not entirely "new", seem both to be more intensely focussed on Alexandrian poetics than their predecessors had been, and to share ideas about literary style and subject matter to a greater degree.

For us Catullus is the important figure in the group. He is, after all, the one whose poetry survives. But we have to remember that the survival of any ancient work is largely a matter of luck—Catullus himself survived the middle ages in a single manuscript that could have been lost or destroyed at any point in a thousand years, as we will see in Chapter 7. The other neoterics are known to us from several sources: from a few fragments quoted by later writers, from references in Catullus, from their influence on later poetry, and from the historical record. The most important were C. Licinius Calvus and C. Helvius Cinna.

Calvus (born in 82 and dead by 47) was nearly Catullus' exact contemporary, and—to judge by the ways and the number of times Catullus mentions him—his closest friend among the neoterics. Catullus shows himself and Calvus teasing each other with gifts of the works of terrible poets (poem 14) and playing with different meters for amusement (50), but he also laughingly celebrates Calvus' oratorical prowess (53) and writes a consolation for the death of Calvus' beloved Quintilia (96). This last poem gives us a glimpse into the way in which the neoterics liked to play with the same subjects, bouncing their ideas and themes back and forth.³⁰ Calvus had written a lament for Quintilia, of which only two fragments survive.³¹ (Quintilia seems to be the speaker in both.)

> cum iam fulva cinis fuero (Calvus, fragment 15 Courtney)
> (when I shall soon be yellow ash)
> forsitan hoc etiam gaudeat ipsa cinis (Calvus, fragment 16 Courtney)
> (perhaps the very ash may rejoice even in this)

This verse and a half (which might or might not go together) is all we have of what might have been a much longer poem. (We have them at all only because they were quoted by a later grammarian to show that Calvus treated the noun *cinis*, "ash," as feminine although it is usually masculine.) The meter is elegiac couplet, traditional for laments and grave inscriptions.³² Catullus' reply is the same meter.

> Si quicquam mutis gratum acceptumve sepulcris
>   accidere a nostro, Calve, dolore potest,
> quo desiderio veteres renovamus amores
>   atque olim missas flemus amicitias,
> certe non tanto mors immatura dolori est
>   Quintiliae, quantum gaudet amore tuo. (96)

(If anything pleasing or welcome can come about for the silent dead from our grief, Calvus, from the painful longing with which we revive old loves and weep for friendships once thrown away, certainly Quintilia does not grieve so much at her early death as she rejoices in your love.)

Too little of Calvus' poem remains for us to see exactly how Catullus answers it, but some points are clear. Both poets have taken as their theme Quintilia's death and her pleasure in Calvus' love even after death. Catullus answers Calvus' "perhaps" (*forsitan*) with his own "certainly" (*certe*) and echoes Calvus' *hoc . . . gaudeat* with *gaudet amore tuo*, which he makes the climax of his poem. Quintilia is the speaker in Calvus. Catullus wittily silences her in his own first line (note the phrase "silent dead," *mutis sepulcris*) and makes himself the speaker. With the change he takes Calvus' theme in a different direction—lamenting with him and consoling him at the same time.

Cinna was probably a few years older than Catullus and Calvus. His date of birth is unknown, but he died under famous circumstances in 44. He was torn to pieces at the funeral of Julius Caesar by the angry mob in mistake for a different Cinna (L. Cornelius Cinna), who was known to be one of Caesar's enemies.³³ Like Catullus, Cinna was from Cisalpine

Gaul, and poem 10 suggests that he was in Memmius' entourage in Bithynia with Catullus in 57–56. (In 10.27–30 Catullus has to admit that the litter bearers he claimed to have brought from Bithynia were really Cinna's.) But Cinna also seems to have been in Bithynia much earlier, for he is usually thought to have acquired the Greek poet Parthenius of Nicaea as booty after the defeat of Mithridates and brought him back to Rome.[34] The date would be either 73 or 66/65 (Mithridates suffered defeat on both occasions). Cinna's acquisition of Parthenius had important consequences for Latin poetry. Parthenius did not introduce Alexandrian poetry to Rome as scholars once believed, but he almost surely had a great influence on Cinna and through him on the other neoterics. He certainly also influenced Cornelius Gallus and Vergil in the next generation.

Parthenius' learned style and poetic tastes seem to have left their mark especially on Cinna's most famous poem, *Zmyrna*, of which only a few fragments are preserved.[35] The work, which was so difficult that it soon required a commentary, told the story of the heroine Zmyrna and her incestuous union with her father that produced the beautiful Adonis. Catullus celebrates it in poem 95.[36]

> Zmyrna mei Cinnae nonam post denique messem   1
>   quam coepta est nonamque edita post hiemem,
> milia cum interea quingenta *Atrianus in*[37] uno
> . . .
> Zmyrna cavas Satrachi penitus mittetur ad undas,   5
>   Zmyrnam cana diu saecula pervolvent.
> At Volusi annales Paduam morientur ad ipsam
>   et laxas scombris saepe dabunt tunicas.
> Parva mei mihi sint cordi monimenta <*sodalis?*>,[38]
>   at populus tumido gaudeat Antimacho. (95)   10

(The *Zmyrna* of my friend Cinna, published at last, nine harvests and winters after it was begun—although meanwhile the man of Atria [has written] five hundred thousand [verses] in a single [year]—*Zmyrna* will be sent to the deep channeled waters of the Satrachus; future ages, whitehaired, will long unroll *Zmyrna*. But the *Annales* of Volusius will die right at the river Po and will often furnish loose wrappers for mackerel. Let the small works of my [friend] be dear to my heart, but let the rabble take pleasure in swollen Antimachus.)

Catullus' poem is a literary manifesto of the neoteric program, which it presents in the form of contrasts.[39] It opposes careful writing to sloppy writing, distant rivers to local ones, literary immortality to ignominious obscurity, short works to long, an informed audience to an ignorant one, and—above all—good poets to bad. Cinna worked on *Zmyrna* for nine years, Catullus tells us, while the man of Atria (Volusius) produced half a million verses in a single day or month or year.[40] Cinna's work will travel as far as the river Satrachus in Cyprus (Zmyrna's home) and be read for generations, but Volusius' Annals will perish at his native Po, and its sheets will be used for fish wrap. Catullus caps the argument with a statement of his own taste, again in the form of an opposition: his friend's short poems are dear to him; the mob can have the notoriously long-winded Greek poet Antimachus.

Cinna's *Zmyrna* was a tale of bizarre and criminal love. Such stories were popular with Hellenistic poets, and Parthenius had a good supply of them: in the next generation he produced a prose collection of plot summaries he called *Erotica Pathemata* ("Misfortunes in Love") to provide material for the poetry of Cornelius Gallus. Stories of this kind were often the subject of poetic narrative in a genre modern scholars call "epyllion" ("miniature epic"). The epyllion seems to have been the essential neoteric genre: a poem in dactylic hexameter, the meter of epic, but on an "unepic" subject, a story of unhappy love with emphasis on a heroine and her emotional condition. We have fragments of Cinna's *Zmyrna* and Calvus' *Io*, and know the names of a few possible epyllia by other poets. But Catullus' poem 64 is the only surviving example from this period. The poem tells the stories of two sets of lovers, embedding one within the other: the story of Theseus and Ariadne is framed by the marriage of Peleus and Thetis. It is discussed in Chapter 6.

The neoteric poets also shared other genres. If it is fair to hazard a guess from the tiny number of neoteric fragments, Calvus and Catullus seem to have been closest in their choice of genres. In addition to epyllia, both poets composed epithalamia (marriage songs), wrote love poetry, and attacked Caesar and his friends with invective. The most general feature of neoteric poetry, however, was its preoccupation with poetic style. We shall have more to say about Catullus' style in later chapters. For now it is enough to note that style was important on both the macroscopic and the microscopic level: poetry had to be elegant, "urbane," polished, and carefully wrought, and it needed to demonstrate minute attention to structure, vocabulary, word order, and rhythm. Poets conforming to these ideals were praised, as Catullus praises Cinna for the *Zmyrna* or Cinna praises Aratus for the *Phaenomena* (fragment 11 Courtney) and glorifies Valerius Cato for *Dictynna* (fragment 14 Courtney).

Failures like Suffenus and Volusius were convicted of both a literary and a social sin: lack of *urbanitas*.

> At vos interea venite in ignem,
> pleni ruris et inficetiarum
> annales Volusi, cacata carta. (36.18–20)
> (But as for you, come into the fire,
> full of rusticity and clumsiness,
> Annals of Volusius, shitty sheets.)

Conclusion

We know much more about the times he lived in than we do about Catullus himself. For Catullus we have only a few secure facts: that he was born near Verona around 84 B.C. to a wealthy and well-connected family, that he served on the staff of a provincial governor in 57/56, that he was a major figure in the group of poets who set Roman poetry on a new course in the late Republic, that he insulted Caesar (and was forgiven for it), that he had an affair with Clodia, that his brother died, and that he himself died at around the age of thirty. Catullus lived in one of the most exciting and interesting periods in Roman history, the end of the Roman Republic; and his poems, so far as we can tell, are all to be dated to its last decade. His poetry is deeply imbedded in that time and place—in its politics, society, sexual mores, and literary ideas—and we need to know his world as well as we can if we are to understand a single poem. Nevertheless, it is important to remember that although his poems reflect his time, they do not chronicle it. And conversely, that although knowing about his time gives us access to his poetry, it does not explain it or let us see into the inmost heart of Catullus himself.

Understanding Catullus' historical context is an essential beginning, but it is only a beginning. In the rest of this book we will be concerned with the context but also—and primarily—with the literary aspects of his poetry.

Notes

1 Gruen, "Cicero and Licinius Calvus," 218–21.
2 Mamurra is attacked by himself under the obscene nickname Mentula ("Prick") in several epigrams: poems 94, 105, 114, 115. For *mentula* as

obscene, see Adams, *The Latin Sexual Vocabulary*, 9–12. Here and elsewhere I follow Richlin in translating it as "prick" (*The Garden of Priapus*, 18).
3   Wiseman, "The Masters of Sirmio." Wiseman is followed by Thomson in his commentary on 31 and Skinner, *Catullus in Verona*, xxi-xxii.
4   Wiseman, "The Masters of Sirmio," 335 n. 3l.
5   See Wiseman, *Catullan Questions*, 50–60.
6   Wiseman, "Catullus, His Life and Times," 167.
7   Wiseman considers it "not absurd" to date all the poems between 57 and 54 ("Catullus, His Life and Times," 167). Skinner believes that the clustering suggests "that Catullus' working life in Rome was relatively brief" and that poems not referring to events in the capital may have been written elsewhere (*Catullus in Verona*, xxi).
8   See Tatum, *The Patrician Tribune: Publius Clodius Pulcher*.
9   For example: Memmius (governor of Bithynia) in poems 10 and 28; Vatinius (an important ally first of the triumvirate and later of Clodius, and subsequently prosecuted by Calvus) in 14, 52, and 53; Piso (governor of Spain) in 28 and 47; Mamurra (Caesar's henchman) in 29, 57, 94, 105, 114, 115. For Vatinius see Gruen, "Cicero and Licinius Calvus," 217–21. Piso is unidentified; Wiseman suggests that he might be L. Piso Frugi ("Catullus, His Life and Times," 163). Catullus also mentions contemporaries who were active in both literature and politics: most notably Calvus (14, 50, 53, 96) and Cinna (10, 95, 113). For the identification of historical figures mentioned in the poems, see Neudling, *A Prosopography to Catullus*.
10 Gruen, "Cicero and Licinius Calvus," 215.
11 Wiseman, *Catullus and His World*, 107–10.
12 Wiseman, "The Masters of Sirmio," 343–6.
13 E.g., Tatum, "Friendship, Politics, and Literature," 494; Fitzgerald, *Catullan Provocations*, 9–10; Wray, *Catullus and the Poetics of Roman Manhood*, 45–6.
14 For a good modern discussion, see Fitzgerald, *Catullan Provocations*, 88–93.
15 Winterbottom in a review of Ramage, *Urbanitas. Ancient Sophistication and Refinement. Classical Review* 26 (1976): 59.
16 Catullus does not use the word *urbanitas*; in addition to 22, *urbanus* appears at 39.8 and 10 (the Spaniard Egnatius is not *urbanus*, and neither is his habit of smiling at the wrong time) and very interestingly at 57.3 (where Caesar and Mamurra are tainted with equal stains, the one an "urban" stain, the other a stain from Formio).
17 Segal, "Catullan 'Otiosi': The Lover and the Poet."
18 *In Catilinam* 2.22–4; *Pro Caelio* 35 (accusations made against Caelius, but tacitly accepted by Cicero).
19 See, esp., Skinner, *Sexuality in Greek and Roman Culture*, 192–7, 212–14; Edwards, *The Politics of Immorality in Ancient Rome*, 63–84.

20 Wiseman, *Catullus and His World*, 9–14.
21 Richlin, *The Garden of Priapus*, 220–2.
22 Wiseman, "Catullus 16," 14–15.
23 Wiseman, *Catullus and His World*, 11; Skinner, *Sexuality in Greek and Roman Culture*, 196.
24 Fantham, "*Stuprum*: Public Attitudes and Penalties for Sexual Offences in Republican Rome"; Skinner, *Sexuality*, 199–200.
25 A famous passage from Cato the elder is often quoted: "If you caught your wife in adultery you could kill her with impunity according to law, but she would not dare lay a finger on you if you committed adultery, nor is it the law" (Cato, *Orat.* 222, Malcovati). In fact, however, there are no known examples of husbands or fathers killing the adulterous wife or daughter. Divorce was the usual solution. See Edwards, *The Politics of Immorality*, 41. Female adultery became a criminal offence under Augustus' marriage laws of 18 B.C. (Fantham, "*Stuprum*," 267; Skinner, *Sexuality*, 206–7).
26 Skinner, "Clodia Metelli," with earlier bibliography. For a complementary treatment, see Wiseman, *Catullus and His World*, 15–53.
27 Scholars have taken the word "neoteric" (literally, "younger" or "more recent") from Cicero in a letter to his friend Atticus (50 B.C.). After a verse parodying the style of contemporary poetry, he says: "Peddle this spondaic line as your own to anyone you like of the *neoteroi* ('more recent [poets]')" (*Letters to Atticus* 7.2.1).
28 There is a very large bibliography on this subject. Among the most important discussions are Quinn, *The Catullan Revolution*, 19–26; Fordyce, *Catullus. A Commentary*, xviii-xxii; Lyne, "The Neoteric Poets"; Clausen, "Callimachus and Latin Poetry" and "Catullus and Callimachus"; Hinds, *Allusion and Intertext*, 74–83. See also Courtney, "The New Poets" in *The Fragmentary Latin Poets*, 189–91, as well as his discussions of individual poets.
29 Kubiak, "The Orion Episode of Cicero's *Aratea*."
30 For such a poetry game between Catullus and Calvus in poem 50, see Chapter 6, pages 139–42; Burgess, "Catullus c. 50: The Exchange of Poetry."
31 See Courtney, *The Fragmentary Latin Poets*, 207–9.
32 For Catullus' meters, see Chapter 4. Fragment 15 can be the first half of either a hexameter or a pentameter; fragment 16 is a pentameter.
33 The story is told by Plutarch (*Life of Brutus*, 20). See Wiseman, *Cinna the Poet*, 44–58.
34 The Byzantine encyclopedia *Suda* says in its entry for Parthenius: "He was taken as booty by Cinna when the Romans defeated Mithridates; then he was set free because of his learning."
35 The fragments of Parthenius have been edited with a commentary and translation by Lightfoot, *Parthenius of Nicaea*. For an older edition and translation, see Gaselee in the Loeb volume of *Daphnis and Chloe*

and Parthenius. For *Zmyrna*, see Cinna, fragments 6–8 in Courtney, *The Fragmentary Latin Poets*, 218–20.

36 In some texts, including Mynors', 95.9–10 are separated from 95 and printed as 95b. Thomson includes the verses with 95. See also Goold's edition and Courtney (*The Fragmentary Latin Poets*, 230).

37 The manuscripts and most modern editions read *Hortensius*. I print *Atrianus in*, following Courtney's suggestion (*The Fragmentary Latin Poets*, 231). *Atrianus* ("man of Atria," a town on the Po) points to Volusius, mentioned by name in line 7. For discussion, see Courtney and Solodow, "On Catullus 95."

38 Angle brackets indicate an addition by the editors.

39 For more on poem 95 as a demonstration of neoteric principles, see Clausen, "Callimachus and Latin Poetry," 188–91.

40 In the translation I have supplied "year" for the word agreeing with *uno* that would have appeared in the missing verse 4.

2

Poetry Books

        Cui dono lepidum novum libellum
        arida modo pumice expolitum?
        Corneli, tibi: namque tu solebas
        meas esse aliquid putare nugas
        iam tum, cum ausus es unus Italorum   5
        omne aevum tribus explicare cartis
        doctis, Iuppiter, et laboriosis.
        Quare habe tibi quidquid hoc libelli,
        qualecumque quod, <o> patrona virgo,
        plus uno maneat perenne saeclo.   10
                    (Poem 1)

(To whom shall I give my charming new little book, just polished with dry pumice? To you, Cornelius. For you used to think my trifles were something even at the time when you alone of the Italians dared to unroll all past time on three sheets—learned ones, by Jupiter, and full of hard work. So keep my little book, such as it is and for what it's worth. And may it remain enduring, o patron maiden, for more than a single age.)

This poem, placed at the beginning of Catullus' book, announces his literary program, explaining his aesthetic principles and telling us what to expect in the poetry that follows. The program is not set out as a manifesto of abstract ideas. Rather, it emerges as a concrete demonstration from the poem itself. Each detail of structure, theme, language, and technique illustrates Catullus' conception of poetry and how it should be written. The poem, like many in Catullus, possesses a high degree of what we might call poetic economy. In only ten verses Catullus describes his book (*libellus*), dedicates it to Cornelius Nepos (and tells us why), describes Nepos' literary work, and hopes that his own *libellus* will last "for more than a single age." These ideas follow each other easily and naturally, almost casually, but the underlying structure is anything but casual. Everything revolves around the two figures of Catullus and Nepos, their books, and their literary and perhaps personal friendship.

Cornelius Nepos (ca. 110–24) was a generation older than Catullus. Like Catullus, he was a Transpadane who had moved to Rome and devoted himself to literature. His own writing, however, was in the field of biography and history rather than poetry. Catullus makes Nepos and his *Chronica*, a universal history, the centerpiece, although not the exact center, of his poem. The section on Nepos and his history (lines 3–7) is framed, not quite symmetrically, by two short passages on Catullus and his *libellus*: two verses at the beginning of the poem and three at the end. Catullus treats Nepos' *Chronica* as the counterpart of his own poetry book. He describes both in terms of their physical form (the papyrus roll), but his language refers as much to aesthetic as to physical qualities. The aesthetic qualities are those revered by Catullus and his fellow neoterics. He describes his own book roll as a small one (*libellus* is a diminutive); it is carefully polished, charming, and new. Nepos' book is in three rolls (three long "sheets" of papyrus), which also display neoteric features: they are "learned and full of hard work." Nepos' work is bigger than Catullus'—three rolls to Catullus' one; but he too has the gift of literary economy: he has "unrolled all past time on three sheets." Also like Catullus, he has done something new. The Greeks had been writing universal history for a long time, but Nepos was "alone of the Italians" in doing so.

But Catullus' program poem, so seemingly transparent and straightforward, is also problematic, for it presents the reader with two complex and controversial questions fundamental to the understanding of Catullus and his poetry. First, what is Catullus' view of both Nepos and his work? Second, what is the relation of poem 1 to the collection as a whole? Both questions are bound up with the theme of this chapter: the poetry book as both a physical artifact and an artistic entity. In what follows we will consider how literary works in Catullus' time were circulated and promoted, what his poetry book (or books) might have contained, and what aesthetic possibilities the poetry book presented to both poet and reader.

Circulating Poetry

The *libellus* of poem 1 was a papyrus roll, carefully fashioned especially for Nepos as the presentation copy of Catullus' poems. But each poem in the collection would have gone through several previous steps before taking its final form and position in the book. Catullus jotted down his first ideas and drafts, not on a papyrus roll, too cumbersome and expensive for everyday use, but on small hinged tablets (called *codicilli* or *pugillares* or *tabellae*), the usual vehicle for notes and other casual writing.[1] Many images of such tablets are preserved in Pompeian wall painting.[2] They were hinged wooden frames containing a reusable writing surface, usually of wax, which could be inscribed with a metal stylus and easily smoothed out or erased for corrections or new writing. The tablets were often double, but they could also contain several leaves.[3]

Catullus mentions such tablets in poems 42 and 50. In poem 42 an unnamed girl has his tablets and won't give them back. Did she take the tablets to tease him? Did he send her a poem on them? Catullus, his focus all on the girl and the return of the tablets, leaves us to wonder. In poem 50 he shows the tablets in use:

> Hesterno, Licini, die otiosi
> multum lusimus in meis tabellis,
> ut convenerat esse delicatos:
> scribens versiculos uterque nostrum
> ludebat numero modo hoc modo illoc,
> reddens mutua per iocum atque vinum. (50.1–6)
> (Yesterday, Licinius, having nothing to do,
> we fooled around a lot on my tablets
> since we had agreed to be frivolous,
> each of us writing little verses
> played now in one meter, now in another,
> going back and forth in jest over the wine.)

The vignette brilliantly brings the scene to life: Catullus and his friend Calvus (Licinius), leaning over a set of waxed tablets, quickly writing (and perhaps scratching out) their verses in turn, playing off each other's ideas and experimenting with different meters, spicing their game with laughter and wine.

Catullus and Calvus seem to be using tablets as scratch paper in their poetic play, but they would have used tablets also for their serious verses—writing, rubbing out their mistakes, and rewriting until they achieved a draft that suited them. At this point it was usual for a poet to send his draft—whether on tablets or carefully written out on papyrus—to a friend for comments and criticism.[4] Catullus' poem 35 may be a response to such a request for comment from his friend Caecilius, who has sent him a poem on the goddess Cybele. The response, if that is what it is, seems a little critical. Catullus calls Caecilius' poem "venuste/ . . . incohata" ("charmingly begun," 35.17–18), which seems to imply that it needs more work. We do not know whether Caecilius reworked his poem or not, but the next step for a poet who *did* listen to the criticisms of his first readers was to revise his work and either read it to a small group of friends or send copies to them for criticism. The procedure was probably very much like the one followed by the younger Pliny as he tried to perfect his speeches a hundred and fifty years later.

> First of all, I go through my work myself; next, I read it to two or three friends and send it to others for comment. If I have any doubts about their criticisms, I go over them again with one or two people, and finally I read the work to a larger audience. . . . I do not invite the general public, but a select and limited audience of persons whom I admire and trust. (Pliny, *Letters* 7.17, Penguin translation)

After the process of revision and testing the waters was complete, the author would at last allow his friends to let others read and copy the work. At this point it was considered public and allowed to circulate. In the republican period, at least, circulation was essentially a personal and private matter, with a work moving through "a series of widening concentric circles" from the author to a close friend or two, to more close friends, to friends of friends, and finally to readers who might be unknown to the author.[5]

If the work had a dedicatee, courtesy demanded that he be sent a copy before it was released.[6] Accordingly, we can be sure that Nepos was the first "official" reader of poem 1 and the *libellus* it introduced. Individual poems within the *libellus* had undoubtedly been made public earlier and circulated independently. Eight of the first fourteen poems, for example, are addressed to various friends and acquaintances, who probably saw them before they were collected into a book.[7] But the *libellus* was made for Nepos—not for his sole enjoyment since the work was available to others once Catullus had released it, but to honor him and his friendship with the poet.

The point is important since Catullus' praise of Nepos in poem 1 is sometimes seen as ironic. Today Nepos is not highly regarded as either a historian or a literary stylist: one critic even goes so far as to call him an "intellectual pygmy."[8] Since Nepos was no Catullus, the argument goes, Catullus' words must be sarcastic or ironic, or at the very least, obviously insincere. Various compelling arguments have been made against this view.⁹ But the system of ancient book circulation also argues against it. Catullus' book was not mass-produced. It might be copied many times, but there was only one presentation copy, made specifically for Nepos as a personal gift from the poet. We may suspect that Catullus was teasing Nepos a bit—the line "learned, by Juppiter, and full of hard work" has a playful ring to it—but an *ironic* dedication would have been both discourteous and pointless under the circumstances. It would have been particularly out of place in a poem in which Catullus is thanking Nepos for his earlier high estimation of his poetry. "You used to think my trifles were something," he says in line 4. The vague language makes it clear only that Nepos was an early reader of Catullus' poetry, but we might suspect that he was also one of the *first* readers, a friend trusted to comment on some of Catullus' drafts as they moved through the process from composition to general circulation.

Whatever his exact role, Nepos had read and praised Catullus' poetry in the past. But in poem 1 Catullus is also looking to the future, wishing that his book "may remain enduring for more than a single age." The fulfillment of that wish is in the hands of someone specified in line 9. Unfortunately, however, the text of the verse is uncertain and the person's identity is disputed. The text at the head of this chapter is that printed in most editions, with line 9 reading: *qualecumque quod, <o> patrona virgo.* With this reading, Catullus is invoking a Muse: *<o> patrona virgo* ("o patron maiden"). But the *o* is a later supplement. It was inserted in the Renaissance to correct a fault in the meter, which lacked a syllable. Some modern scholars, however, have argued that the missing syllable is not the only difficulty in the line and that the patron invoked by Catullus should be Nepos rather than the Muse. Various readings have been proposed to accommodate this idea. One of the most common is *qualecumque quidem patroni ut ergo*: "whatever it is worth indeed, so that because of its patron (it may remain enduring for more than a single age)."¹⁰ The textual question is not settled and is unlikely to be. It is worth bringing up here for two reasons: first, to point out that Catullus' text is full of such problems, and that they significantly affect the interpretation of the poems: second, because it focuses our attention on the process by which Catullus' work or that of any other Roman author might be expected to survive.

Catullus did not write for money—in his time the commercial book trade in our sense of the word barely existed, and any books that *were* sold brought no financial profit to their authors. But he had a writer's desire for another kind of profit: literary immortality. He wanted others to read and admire his poetry, and to do so long after his death. Perhaps artistic inspiration and literary merit alone might keep his book alive. If the reading <o> *patrona virgo* in line 9 is correct, Catullus is claiming to rely on just such qualities, provided by the supernatural assistance of the "patron maiden" or Muse. But in actuality he undoubtedly also looked to human agency and the practical support of his friends. Nepos, whether or not he appears in line 9 as *patronus*, would have been such a friend—making sure that Catullus' poems were read at his dinner parties, having the *libellus* copied for other friends and acquaintances, and generally publicizing Catullus' work.[11] No doubt Catullus' poetry was also promoted by fellow poets like Calvus and Cinna. Catullus' own endorsement of Cinna's *Zmyrna* (poem 95), discussed in chapter 1, is a masterful example of just such literary promotion.

The literary fame that Catullus and other ancient poets aspired to was more limited than we might imagine, accustomed as we are to mass literacy and the printed book. His potential contemporary audience consisted of well educated elite men (and some women) with literary interests—an audience measured not in thousands but in a few hundreds at most. But his actual audience was probably somewhat smaller, for not everyone had a taste for poetry that was both highly sophisticated and made no claims to be instructive or morally edifying. Catullus was in the literary *avant-garde*, and his work might well have been rejected as frivolous and self-indulgent by those who preferred more conventional literary fare. Cicero, for one, probably disdained it. He spoke contemptuously of neoteric poetry, and he is supposed to have said that "even if his lifetime were doubled, he would not have time to read lyric poets."[12]

Contents of the Libellus

When Nepos unrolled the papyrus of his dedication copy, he found an album of Catullus' poems, but we cannot be sure that what he saw was identical with our present collection. To put it another way, although poem 1 functions as the introduction in modern texts of the poems, we do not know what it introduced in the book that Catullus presented to his friend. The question is important for the history of the text, but still more for literary reasons, as we will see in the next section. If we knew that our text was Catullus' "charming, new little book," we could attribute its arrangement to the poet himself and look for his artistic patterning in the placement of poems. The subject of authorial arrangement is one of the most hotly contested areas in Catullan studies and will probably remain so.[13] It raises important questions about the early history of Catullus' poems, about the ancient poetry book and the artistic unity of its contents, and about the intersection of aesthetic considerations, ancient ways of reading, and the facts of ancient book production.

A modern reader opening a text of Catullus will find 113 poems totaling around 2300 verses.[14] The poems fall into three sections of different metrical and formal character. In the first group are poems 1–60, often called the polymetrics. The longest of these (poem 10) has 34 verses; most are much shorter. The poems are in various meters (hence the term polymetrics), most typically the phalaecean hendecasyllable, and they are addressed to an assortment of friends, lovers, and enemies. Their themes are equally various: love, politics, poetry, friendship, invective. The second group (poems 61–68) contains Alexandrian and neoteric works in several meters: two epithalamia or wedding songs, the bizarre and haunting poem on Attis in the equally bizarre and haunting galliambic meter, Catullus' epyllion, poem 64, and four elegies. The third group (poems 69–116) consists of epigrams. It is metrically homogeneous (all the poems are in elegiac couplets), but thematically various; the themes range from love and grief to obscene invective. The three parts of the collection are unequal in length: the polymetrics have 848 verses, the Alexandrian and neoteric works, 1121, and the epigrams 320.[15] The whole collection is a small one. In the Oxford Classical Text, its standard vehicle, the printed text requires only 104 pages in a slender volume barely half an inch thick and only slightly larger than a popular paperback.

But this collection, so easily housed in a small modern printed edition, would require a very large papyrus, if we can judge from two papyrus fragments of Roman poetry from close to Catullus' time: the Gallus papyrus (ca. 50 B.C–ca. 20 B.C.; and a fragment of the *Carmen de bello Aegyptiaco* (31 B.C. to A.D. 79).[16] If the full text of Catullus were written in the style of the Gallus papyrus, it would require a papyrus roll of 11.62 meters (38 feet); written like the *Carmen de Bello Aegyptiaco*, it would require 15.85 meters (52 feet).[17] In either case the bookroll would be a hefty one. At a length of 11.62 meters it would make a cylinder thicker than a wine bottle; at 15.85 meters the cylinder would be a little smaller than a coffee can.[18] Papyrus heights were variable, but it is reasonable to assume that our hypothetical wine bottle or coffee can would have been about 28 centimeters (11 inches) tall.[19] Such a bookroll would not be out of the question, but it would be at the very upper end of the size range for papyri housing ancient literary texts.[20] Other Latin poetic books from the time of Catullus to the early Augustan period are much shorter and would have required correspondingly smaller bookrolls. The books of the *De Rerum Natura* by Catullus' contemporary Lucretius range from 1092 to 1455 verses. Single books of poetry in the generation after Catullus typically contain between 700 and 1000 verses. Vergil's *Eclogue*s, for example, has 829 verses, book 1 of Propertius 706. Individual books of the *Aeneid* range between 705 and 952 verses.

There is a further complication: some of Catullus' poetry clearly circulated separately.[21] Ancient authors refer to poetry that has not survived, and modern editors print three fragments not included in the manuscripts but quoted by ancient sources. Moreover, some poems that do appear in our text seem to have had an independent existence. The most conspicuous example is poem 62, the shorter of Catullus' two epithalamia. This poem is the only work of Catullus to have left its traces in the middle ages: it was included in a ninth-century florilegium or anthology, where it is entitled *Epithalamium Catulli*. It was also cited in the second century by Quintilian, who referred to it by the title *Epithalamium* (*Institutiones Oratoriae* 9.3.16). The separate appearance of poem 62 in the medieval anthology suggests that it circulated independently; the use of a title both in the anthology and by Quintilian confirms it, since poems within collections were apparently not cited by title.[22]

Taken together, the physical evidence of the papyri and the signs of independent circulation strongly suggest that our present text is not identical with the book Catullus sent to Nepos. That a single roll ever accommodated all of the extant poetry is possible but improbable, and if such a roll existed it seems inconceivable that Catullus called it a *libellus* ("little book"). It is much more likely that Catullus presented Nepos with a smaller number of poems—perhaps the polymetrics or some number of them. Nepos had admired Catullus' *nugae*: *namque tu solebas / meas esse aliquid putare nugas* ("you used to think my trifles were something"), Catullus reminds him. Some or all of the polymetrics would constitute a *libellus* in keeping with the tone of the dedication and of appropriate length for a bookroll of unpretentious but elegant poetry. The other poems could have circulated in an unknown number of books. Scholars sometimes think of three books corresponding to the three sections of the modern text (1–60, 61–8, 69–116), each of which would be a convenient size for a papyrus roll; but there are other possibilities. We have already suggested that poem 62 circulated separately. Poem 64, the epyllion linking the wedding of Peleus and Thetis with the affair of Theseus and Ariadne, probably had its own book as well. According to the multi-book hypothesis, the several rolls would have been brought together at some time in the fourth century or a little earlier when the literary works of antiquity were being transferred from the roll to the codex (book with pages). This model accounts for the fact that some of Catullus' poems have not survived or exist in only tiny fragments: the rolls containing them were already lost or unavailable at the time when someone transcribed the first codex of the poems, the ancestor of our text.

All of these ideas presuppose that Catullus' poems, whether in one book or several, existed in a more or less fixed form from the time of their composition until the age of the codex. But that might not have been the case. We know that Catullus created a *libellus* specifically for Nepos and intended for subsequent wider circulation, and it seems likely that he composed poetry in other books as well. But we do not know what happened next. After five hundred years of the printed book we are accustomed to the mass production and standardization of texts and take it for granted that a book once written stays put—that its contents remain as the author arranged and intended them. But this was not necessarily so in antiquity, particularly in the case of short or shortish poems on diverse themes like those of Catullus. We must remember that ancient books were individually produced, very often to order. The corollary is that readers and book owners could exercise a degree of influence over their contents. It is clear from recent papyrus discoveries that Greek epigram collections could be excerpted, modified, and reordered to the taste of individual readers.[23] Personal anthologies of poetry could, and did, exist—and not only in the Greek world. Catullus himself provides evidence for just such collections.[24] In poem 14 he promises to retaliate against Calvus for giving him an album of terrible poets:

>   di magni, horribilem et sacrum libellum!
>   . . .
>   nam, si luxerit, ad librariorum
>   curram scrinia; Caesios, Aquinos,
>   Suffenum, omnia colligam venena,
>   ac te his suppliciis remunerabor. (14.12, 17–20)

(Great gods, an awful and cursed little book!. . . . When dawn comes I'm going to run to the shelves of the booksellers. I'll collect the Caesii, Aquini, Suffenus—all the poisonous stuff—and I'll pay you back with these punishments.)

Calvus and Catullus compiled their *libelli* from the works of several different bad poets, but readers could also create an anthology from the work of a single good poet. They could select and arrange poems in personal collections just as modern music lovers download songs and create their own playlists or albums. Also like modern music collectors, they could either simply assemble their selections or arrange them with attention to artistic detail.

One or more ancient readers could have created personal anthologies of Catullus' poems at any time from Catullus' lifetime until the available books of his poems were copied into a codex centuries later. We do not know that any part of our present collection is descended from such a compilation, but the possibility cannot be ruled out either. The thought is an uncomfortable one for readers who believe that they can perceive the artistic genius of Catullus in the shape of the collection as well as in individual poems. But it is also intriguing to imagine that the arrangement of some parts of the collection might represent a silent artistic collaboration between the poet and a perceptive ancient reader. Such a creative response to Catullus' poetry could have its own interest and validity.

Reading the Collection

Catullus' poetry had appeared in several forms by the time it made its way to the codex that was the ancestor of our present text. Some poems, at least, would have circulated independently in both oral and written form before being gathered either into the *libellus* he gave to Nepos or into other books. To take just one example, the poems attacking Caesar and Mamurra (29 and 57) must have enjoyed a wide and malicious circulation by themselves before being brought into a collection. It seems likely that others, like poems 62 and 64, were issued in separate *libelli*. We cannot know how many *libelli* there were altogether or whether Catullus himself issued and arranged all the poems in the order we have them today. Two essential points, however, are certain. First, what we have is a *collection* and demands to be read as such. Second, the arrangement of the poems is ancient, going back at least to the time when the poems were transferred from roll to codex.

A poem by itself differs from a poem in a collection as a single flower differs from a flower in a bouquet or garland.[25] The one is a discrete or isolated entity; the other is part of an ensemble with which it exists in a mutual relationship, each interacting with and enhancing the other. And since the garland or collection has that relation with each of its constituent elements, and each element with all the others, the ensemble has a greater potential for meaning and beauty than the sum of its parts. But our analogy of the bouquet is imperfect. Unlike a bouquet, a poetry collection is not fixed but dynamic; each of its elements is complex, with its constituent themes both shaping the individual poem and resonating with the multiple themes of other poems across the collection. Seen in this light, the poetry collection is more like a kaleidoscope. When its parts are looked at in different ways—by changing one's starting place, say, or privileging some themes over others—the pieces regroup and fall into a different array. This dynamic and changing design requires the collaboration of the reader, whose mind perceives elements in a poem, makes connections between them, and notices the shifting patterns of thought that emerge when the elements from different poems are brought together.[26] To describe the process in another way, poems in a collection "demand to be read in terms of one another."[27]

It is hardly going too far to suggest that Catullus' poetry contains 113 examples of this collective demand, but here we can look at only three: poems 70, 72, and 85. First 70:

> Nulli se dicit mulier mea nubere malle
>   quam mihi, non si se Iuppiter ipse petat.
> Dicit: sed mulier cupido quod dicit amanti,
>   in vento et rapida scribere oportet aqua. (70)
> (My woman says that she would rather marry no one
> than me, not if Jupiter himself should ask her.
> She says, but what a woman says to an eager lover
> should be written on the wind and rushing water.)

"She says," "she says," "she says." With each repetition Catullus hammers home a distrust of words and promises, all blown away with the wind in the last line. He gives us two characters: himself ("the eager lover") and the *mulier*, whose promises trip so easily off the tongue. She is unnamed, but already the poem is reaching out to others in the collection: no matter how hard we try to read the epigram in isolation, we know that she has to be Lesbia. A moment ago I said there were two characters, but actually there are three, for we must also count the hypothetical Jupiter of line 2, dismissed in the woman's claims but still felt as a potential and powerful rival somewhere in the wings. The threat of the rival subtly increases in the second couplet when we learn what the woman's words are worth. It increases still more if we allow ourselves to stray outside the collection to feel the influence of the epigram of Callimachus that Catullus is using as a model.

> Kallignotos swore to Ionis that he would never love
> anyone, male or female, more than her.
> He swore, but it's true, what they say: the vows
> of lovers never reach the ears of the gods.
> Now he burns for a boy, and the poor girl
> (as they also say) is out in the cold.
> (Callimachus, *Epigram* 11, Nisetich translation)

By themselves Catullus' four lines imply that the woman's words will prove to be untrue. But if we read his epigram against Callimachus', we are certain of it, and that he will be "out in the cold" as surely as poor Ionis.[28] That is, Catullus has not only imitated Callimachus' epigram but evoked it, and the evocation supplies the conclusion to his own poem. (I will have more to say about this phenomenon in Chapter 6.)
Now poem 72:

Dicebas quondam solum te nosse Catullum,
   Lesbia, nec prae me velle tenere Iovem.
Dilexi tum te non tantum ut vulgus amicam,
   sed pater ut gnatos diligit et generos.
Nunc te cognovi: quare, etsi impensius uror,   5
   multo mi tamen es vilior et levior.
Qui potis est, inquis? quod amantem iniuria talis
   cogit amare magis, sed bene velle minus. (72)
(Once upon a time you used to say that you knew Catullus alone,
Lesbia, and that you did not wish to hold even Jupiter in
   preference to me.
I cherished you then not as an ordinary man cherishes a mistress,
but as a father cherishes his sons and sons-in-law.
Now I know you. And so although I burn more passionately,
you are much cheaper and less important to me.
How can this be, you ask? Because a hurt like that
forces a lover to love more but to like less.)

The opening couplet invites us to read poems 72 and 70 together, for it presents the same cast of characters (the lover, a woman, and the hypothetical Jupiter), linked by the woman's claim to favor the lover over Jupiter. But not everything is the same. This time the lover and the woman are called Catullus and Lesbia, and Lesbia is not just the subject but the addressee. The very first word, *dicebas*, is a reproach: "you used to say." Like *dicit* in 70, it implies an antithesis between words and actions; the past tense suggests that her claim—even before we hear it—is known to be false. She claimed that Catullus was her only sex partner (*nosse* in this context means "know sexually"[29]), and we already know that her assertion was a lie. But Lesbia's faithlessness is the starting point, not the climax of 72. After beginning like poem 70, the epigram goes off in a different direction and other elements enter the picture, which from now on shows only Catullus and his feelings. The added elements combine with the ideas of the first couplet to form a pattern of contrasts between past and present in the two halves of the poem. The past (1–4) was the time of Lesbia's claims and Catullus' devotion. The present (5–8) finds everything changed: "now I know you," he tells her (5); and the knowledge both fires his sexual passion and lessens his esteem.

At the heart of the epigram is one of Catullus' most important themes: the attempt to combine familial and erotic love. In the first section it is clear that the relationship between Catullus and Lesbia was sexual (the verb *nosse* guarantees it), but Catullus' feelings were not only sexual. "I cherished you then," he tells Lesbia, not as an ordinary man cherishes a mistress, but as a father cherishes his sons and sons-in-law" (3–4). For the modern reader the phrase "sons and sons-in-law" strikes a jarring note (we expect "sons and daughters"). But the sons-in-law are there for a purpose: to make it clear that the father in the simile is caring not merely for his children but for the future of his family line, represented by the power of his sons and sons-in-law to beget his descendants. This generative power is inherent in the words *gnatos* and *generos*, both etymologically derived from the same root as English "generate" and "generation" and Latin *gens* ("family" or "clan"). The trio of father, sons, and sons-in-law is all male. By evoking it Catullus powerfully demonstrates his past feelings for Lesbia: he was bringing her into what for a male Roman was the very core of his family, the tightly bound group of kinsmen that represented its essence and continuity.

We turned away from poem 70 a moment ago since it seemed to have no more to contribute to our reading of 72, but that was too hasty. Ideas do not move in just one direction in a poetry collection; the poems contribute reciprocally to each other's meanings. If we can read 72 in the light of 70, we can also read 70 in the light of 72.

Let us look again at the woman's claim in 70: "My woman says that she would rather marry (*nubere*) no one than me" (70-1-2). The meaning of her claim depends on the meaning of *nubere*, which we can take in two different ways. If we see it in the light of 72.3–4, it looks like a reference to the theme of familial love. Marriage certainly belongs to the complex of ideas associated with the family, and it is a recurrent theme in many of Catullus' poems. But if we read it against Lesbia's corresponding declaration at the beginning of 72, a different idea presents itself. *Nubere*, like *nosse*, often bears a sexual meaning; it can be used as a euphemism for sexual intercourse.[30] A sexual reading of *nubere* brings the openings of the two epigrams even closer together. In 70, then, the woman says that Catullus is the only man she wants to have sex with; in 72 Lesbia used to say that he was the only man she *was* having sex with. The sexual sense of *nubere* is dominant in 70, but even so the word cannot be separated completely from its literal meaning, "to marry." It retains an affective nuance that resonates with the family theme not only in 72, but also elsewhere in the collection.

Poem 72 concludes with a return to Lesbia, who seems to have asked for an explanation: "How can this be, you ask?" But the explanation only rephrases Catullus' earlier expression of his conflicting emotions. The hurt she has inflicted has made him love her more but like her less.

And now poem 85:

> Odi et amo. Quare id faciam, fortasse requiris.
>   Nescio, sed fieri sentio et excrucior.
> (I hate and I love. Perhaps you ask why I do this.
> I do not know, but I feel it happening and I am in torment.)

Poem 72 is in these lines, but all that remains of it is the final couplet, as if its ideas had been torn out of their longer context. Here the emotional conflict laid out in 72 is distilled to its basic components, hate and love. The request for an explanation seems to come out of nowhere, with no clue to the identity of the questioner. Perhaps Catullus is addressing himself, perhaps the reader. It hardly matters, for the focus is all on the poet, his divided emotions, and his pain. In 72 he offered an explanation that was no explanation at all. Here, he simply gives up: "I don't know."

The elements we have identified in poems 70, 72, and 85 appear in other poems in the collection, and if we had included them in the discussion, we would have found additional connections and a different and still richer set of resonances. Some of the Lesbia poems with similar elements are 8 (the contrast between past and present), 37 and 58 (Catullus' love and Lesbia's degradation), 75 (personal disdain combined with sexual passion), 109 (Lesbia's promises).

Unrolling the Book

In the preceding section we treated the collection like the modern page turners we are, picking out and lingering over poems here and there that seem to speak to each other. But this is not the way that ancient readers would have had their first experience with the collection. They would have come to each of the poems in sequence as they worked their way through the bookrolls containing them, following the collection as it moved, slowly or quickly, before their eyes. The medium in which the poems appeared affected—and directed—the way in which they read and interpreted them.[31]

We can take a book off the shelf and open it to any page we like. But an ancient reader opening a book had to start at the beginning. He (or more rarely she) would hold the book in the right hand and pull it open with the left, exposing one or more columns of text. Then with the left hand the reader would reroll the portion just read, unrolling the papyrus with the right hand to show new columns of text. The process would be similar to, but probably much slower than, what we call "scrolling down" on a computer screen. The papyrus reader would also have more than one column in the field of vision at a time (probably two or three) while we see only one on our computers. As a column disappeared on the left into the rerolled papyrus, a new one would emerge into sight on the right; and the reader could form a continuous and changing impression of the text.

With second and third and subsequent readings, the reader could discern thematic patterns across the collection, but without losing the initial impression made by reading the poems in sequence, in their linear succession on the papyrus roll.

The opening sequence as it appears in our present collection is a good place to see what patterns emerge when we read the poems in order. Modern scholars are in general agreement in considering poems 1–11 or 1–14 an artistically ordered ensemble. Some would identify this array as a separate *libellus* arranged by Catullus or even as the *libellus* he gave to Nepos, but let us leave that point aside for the moment and concentrate simply on seeing the poems in succession. We will look at poems 1–14 first and then consider the shorter ensemble of poems 1–11.

poem 1: the dedication to Nepos
poem 2: address to the girl's sparrow
poem 3: the death of the girl's sparrow
poem 4: the speaking yacht
poem 5: the first kiss poem to Lesbia (give me a thousand kisses, then a hundred)
poem 6: Catullus wants to celebrate Flavius and his girlfriend
poem 7: the second kiss poem to Lesbia (you ask how many kisses I want)
poem 8: Catullus tries to renounce his love
poem 9: Catullus welcomes Veranius home from Spain
poem 10: Catullus is embarrassed by Varus' girlfriend
poem 11: Catullus renounces his girl
poem 12: the napkin thief
poem 13: Catullus invites Fabullus to dinner and offers him his girl's perfume
poem 14: Calvus and his gift of terrible poetry

As we scroll through the sequence we find an alternation between amatory poems and poems to or about Catullus' male friends, and the immediate impression is of two distinct worlds: the private world of the poet and the woman he loves and the social world of the young man about town and his contemporaries.

The love poems appear in a sequence that suggests a narrative of the affair.[32] In 2 and 3 the story begins, hinting at intimacy and a desire for it in the playful poems on the sparrow that may—or may not—present a *double entendre*.[33] It reaches a high point in the joyous celebration of love in 5, the first kiss poem, and in 7, the second kiss poem, where the joy is slightly more muted. The story then becomes darker: the unhappiness of Catullus' first attempt at renunciation (8) is succeeded by the bitterness of what seems to be his final good-bye in the second (11). In the end (13), all that Catullus has left of the girl is her perfume, which he will use as a table perfume at dinner with a friend.[34]

The story that we have just traced is that of Catullus and Lesbia, as every reader of Catullus knows; but the surprising fact is that Lesbia's name appears only in the kiss poems, 5 and 7. Elsewhere the woman is simply *mea puella* ("my girl"). Just as in the case of poem 70 discussed in the previous section, what we know, or think we know, about Catullus has influenced our reading of the poems, supplying the name Lesbia even where Catullus has withheld it. Again the poems have demanded to be read in terms of one another, and we have given in to that demand. But let us pull back for a moment and try to put ourselves in the place of an ancient reader opening the bookroll of Catullus' poems for the first time. Imagine that our hypothetical reader knows nothing of Catullus' great romance. She (or more often he) opens the roll, seeing first the dedication to Nepos and then the two sparrow poems. *We* know that the sparrow belongs to Lesbia, but the reader has never heard of her. The sparrow is clearly connected with love: sparrows are the birds of Venus, and this one is obviously on very close terms with someone Catullus calls *mea puella*. In poem 2 it plays in her lap, and in poem 3 it has died, making her weep. The poems are erotic and sentimental at the same time, but in themselves they do not suggest a serious love affair or deep emotional involvement on the part of the poet. We can imagine the reader pondering them, perhaps eagerly unrolling the book to see what comes next, only to come upon poem 4, on the speaking yacht, a curious poem whose subject and tone are miles away from the girl and the sparrow. Then at last poem 5 comes into sight. The first line presents Lesbia:

> Vivamus, mea Lesbia, atque amemus (5.1)
> (Let us live, my Lesbia, and let us love.)

Mea Lesbia ("*my* Lesbia"). The address is also an endearment, and the girl is now present for the first time as a concrete emotional reality. She is also addressed in poem 7 ("you ask how many of your kisses, Lesbia, are enough for me and more than enough," 7.1–2). The effect of the name Lesbia in 5 and 7 is both retrospective and prospective. The first-time ancient reader seeing the poems in sequence would know now what we have known all along: that *mea puella* in the sparrow poems was Lesbia. And the reader would know her again when she appeared in poems 8, 11, and 13.[35] Lesbia makes such a strong impression, in fact, that the first-time reader might be as surprised as we are to go back and discover that in the narrative of the opening sequence she is named only in the kiss poems and that she does not appear by name again until poem 43.

The poems to friends, on the other hand, present not a story, but a state of being, the life that Catullus shares with his male contemporaries, which provides both a contrast with the amatory poems and a context for them. In poem 1 Catullus dedicates his book to Nepos. In 4 he invites his friends to hear the story of a yacht that has traveled from Bithynia to a clear Italian lake; the journey suggests his own homeward journey from serving on the staff of Memmius. In 6 he urges Flavius to reveal the details of his sexual affair. The poem falls between the two kiss poems and adopts a different stance from its neighbors: explicit realism in contrast to their romanticism, and prurient curiosity in contrast to their defiance of curious outsiders. In 9 Catullus welcomes Veranius home from Spain; the poem seems to balance poem 4, on the return of the yacht from Bithynia. Poem 10 is a humorous social vignette in which Catullus is embarrassed when Varus' girlfriend catches him in a lie; like poem 6, it presents a more realistic pair of lovers than Catullus and Lesbia. In 12 Catullus attacks the man who has stolen the napkin Veranius and Fabullus had sent to him from Spain. In 14 Catullus blames Calvus for his gift of awful poetry.

Closer inspection would reveal further detailed patterning in the run of poems from 1 to 14, but the main lines are clear. The ordering shows and for the most part keeps separate the two realms of the poet's life: private and public, love and friendship. The two are brought together only in 11 and 13, the last amatory poems in the sequence. In 11 Catullus instructs Furius and Aurelius (who may or may not be his friends) to take a message of dismissal to Lesbia. In 13 the Lesbia theme is absorbed into the friendship theme when Lesbia lingers as only a fragrance in the air at the convivial dinner to be shared by Catullus and Fabullus. Two poems on poetry, 1 and 14, frame the sequence.

The shorter ensemble of poems 1–11 preferred by some scholars reads a little differently. The poems of course are the same, but the array itself presents a different aspect. Ending the sequence with 11 takes the array out of the frame formed by the two poems on poetry, makes Catullus' dismissal of Lesbia its climax and finale, and changes the balance between the worlds of love and friendship so that the emphasis rests firmly on the Lesbia narrative. The love story looks different too. If we stop at 11, the narrative ends with the crash of a powerful and angry rupture rather than with a quiet evocation of her absent charm.

Modern readers will choose between these two sequences and the stories they tell according to their own preferences and artistic criteria. But what about our ancient counterparts? No one knows whether the ancient reader reached the end of a roll (and hence the end of a book) at poem 11 or poem 14 or somewhere else in the collection, and no one can be entirely sure even that the sequence (whether 1 to 11 or 1 to 14) was arranged by Catullus himself. But we do know that the arrangement not only of the sequence but of the larger collection is ancient. This point was mentioned earlier. Now it is time to look at it more closely.

The arrangement of the collection was set in its present form no later than the time when the poems were transferred from roll to codex, probably in the fourth century A.D. but perhaps earlier. Although it is conceivable that whoever oversaw that transition changed the order in which the poems appeared in their individual rolls or books, it is far more likely that the rolls were simply copied into the codex just as they were. This would mean that the order within the rolls was left essentially unchanged, although one or more poems beginning or ending a given roll might have been lost or mutilated by the time it came to the scribe of the codex (the ends of bookrolls were especially vulnerable to loss and damage). The rolls themselves might not have been copied in any canonical order, but either as they came to hand or according to the preferences of whoever commissioned the codex. Some books, as we saw earlier, never made their way into the codex at all.

This reconstruction suggests that the arrangement of large portions of the collection is much older than the transfer to codex. The corollary is that sequences of poems in an original or very early order survive in our present text, even if their starting or stopping points are not always obvious now. We have been focusing on the opening sequence, but other groups of poems also display interesting structural and thematic patterning. To give just a few examples: poems 14b to 26 present a series of obscene invectives attacking Furius and Aurelius and other targets; poems 61–64 and 65–68 deal in various ways with marriage; the poems in elegiac meter (65–116) are framed by programmatic references to Callimachus in 65 and 116; in poems 69–77 attacks on Rufus and Gellius punctuate a series of epigrams on Lesbia's unfaithfulness.[36] Some (perhaps all) of these arrangements may have been designed by Catullus himself; but in any case their patterning is in tune with the aesthetics of poem arrangement found in both Alexandrian and Augustan poetry books—that is, in the books of both Catullus' Greek literary models and his immediate Roman successors. These principles of arrangement include many of the characteristics we have already observed in the case of the opening sequence. The devices include: framing an array with poems (often program poems) on similar themes, *variatio* or variation of tone and theme, juxtaposing poems on similar themes (as in poems 2 and 3 on the sparrow), alternating poems on one theme with those of another (as poem 6 interrupts the kiss poems 5 and 7 and as poems 9, 10, and 12 alternate with the renunciations of Lesbia in 8, 11, and 13).[37]

Readers and Listeners

The person unrolling the papyrus and construing its words could be a solitary reader, enjoying the poetry in a quiet place and reading silently.[38] This is the picture that immediately comes to mind, for it is the way that we think of reading and generally practise it. But it was not the only, or even the most common, model of reading in antiquity. The Romans could and did read to themselves from personal copies of literary works, but they were also read to by others, whether at dinner parties or privately at home.[39] In convivial settings the reader might be the author himself or (more likely) a slave trained as a *lector* ("reader"); at home the reader would be a slave. Many in Catullus' audience would have enjoyed his poetry in all three ways, sometimes reading privately, sometimes listening in a group, sometimes listening by themselves. But whether visually or aurally, they would have perceived the poems in the same way—sequentially, as the book that contained them was unrolled.

However the audience received them, the oral component of the poems was always important—much more than it is for us. Reading aloud was an essential element of elite education. This description by a famous teacher called Dionysius the Thracian tells us what it entailed.[40]

> Reading is the correct performance of poetic or prose texts. The reader must assume the appropriate persona, take account of the metre, and adopt the appropriate speaking voice. The first of these enables us to appreciate the quality of the text which is being read; the second, the craftsmanship; the third, the thought behind the text. Thus, we read a tragic text in heroic style, a comic text in a natural style; an elegiac text is read with charm, an epic text with vigour; a lyric poem is read melodiously, a pathetic text with restrained grief. A reading which fails to observe these requirements destroys the poetry and makes the reader's performance ridiculous. (Dionysius Thrax, *De grammatica* 2. Quinn translation)

An author who read his work in public would have been trained in correct delivery from his schooldays. The slave or other professional *lector* would have to reach a similar standard in order to satisfy a knowledgeable and critical audience. In either case the person who read a text to others was an oral interpreter, a performer who expressed its tone and sense as well as its words and meter. But solitary silent readers would also have been trained in reading aloud. Attuned to oral performance, they would be ready to appreciate aural effects and verbal music in the text before them.

For performing and solitary readers alike the bookroll was in effect a script in which they might identify and interpret the character or persona of the poet.

Notes

1. But tablets were also used for legal documents and family records. See Roberts and Skeat, *The Birth of the Codex*, 12.
2. One of the most famous paintings, sometimes entitled "Sappho," shows a young woman holding a stylus in one hand and a set of closed tablets in the other. Another shows a man and his wife, the man holding a papyrus roll and the woman a stylus and open tablets. For color photographs, see Grant, *The Art and Life of Pompeii and Herculaneum*, 82 ("Sappho") and 83 (man and wife); Ward-Perkins and Claridge, *Pompeii A.D. 79*, fig. 17 (man and wife).
3. These tablets are of course the antecedent of the codex, or book with pages. See Roberts and Skeat, *The Birth of the Codex*.
4. My account follows the invaluable discussion of Starr, "The Circulation of Literary Texts in the Roman World." See also Quinn, "The Poet and his Audience in the Augustan Age," 88–91.
5. Starr, "The Circulation of Literary Texts," 213. For the negligible role of bookshops in Catullus' time, see 219–23.
6. Starr cites passages from Cicero's letters demonstrating the importance of this point (ibid., 218).
7. Poems 5, 6, 7, 9, 11, 12, 13, 14.
8. Horsfall, "Cornelius Nepos," 116.
9. For example, Wiseman in *Clio's Cosmetics*, 154–74; Tatum, "Friendship, Politics, and Literature," 485–8.
10. For a full discussion with earlier bibliography, see Gratwick, "*Vale, Patrona Virgo*: The Text of Catullus 1.9." Gratwick suggests *Quare habe tibi quidquid hoc libelli, / qualecumque <ali>quid. Patro<ci>ni ergo* (306), translating: "Therefore have as your own whatever this book adds up to; something for what it is worth. In witness of your advocacy, etc."
11. See Gratwick, "*Vale Patrona Virgo*," 307. The literary relationship of Cicero and Atticus may be a useful analogy for that between Catullus and Nepos. Cicero both sent Atticus his drafts for criticism and relied on him to publicize and promote his work; see Starr, "The Circulation of Literary Texts."
12. Cicero makes slighting references to the neoterics in *Letters to Atticus* 7.2.1, *Orator* 161, and *Tusculanae Disputationes* 3.45. Seneca reports his comment on lyric poetry in *Epistulae* 49.5.

13 See Skinner, "Authorial Arrangement of the Collection," for a summary of the scholarship.
14 The last poem is numbered 116, a legacy of the mistaken addition of three poems to the collection by Marc-Antoine de Muret in his 1554 edition. The poems, later numbered 18, 19, and 20, were removed by Lachmann in the nineteenth century, but the numbering was left unchanged, leaving a confusing gap between poems 17 and 21. See chapter 7, p. 187.
15 Some scholars would divide the collection differently, placing the elegies (65–8) with the epigrams. This division produces sections of roughly equal length: 1–60 (848 verses), 61–4 (795 verses), 65–116 (646 verses).
16 For the Gallus papyrus, see Anderson, Parsons, and Nisbet, "Elegiacs by Gallus from Qasr Ibrim," plates IV–V. For *Carmen de Bello Aegyptiaco* (PHerc 817), see Lowe, *Codices latini antiqui* III.385; and Scott, *Fragmenta Herculanensia*, plates A–H.
17 For the calculations, see Gaisser, *Catullus and his Renaissance Readers*, 277 n. 16.
18 According to the calculations of Johnson (*Bookrolls and Scribes in Oxyrhynchus*, 150), a papyrus roll 10 meters long would have a diameter of 7.4 centimeters (the diameter of a wine bottle); one 15 meters long would have a diameter of 9 centimeters.
19 Johnson has found a range of 25 to 32 centimeters for Greek literary papyri in Oxyrhynchus ("Pliny the Elder and Standardized Roll Heights in the Manufacture of Papyrus," 47 n. 4. My calculations for the length of the papyrus assumed a column height of 25 centimeters (See note 17 above.)
20 Johnson's statistics for Oxyrhynchus show 15 meters. as the top of the "normative span" (*Bookrolls and Scribes*, 149, 151). Older sources argue for a maximum length closer to 11 meters. See, e.g., Kenyon, *Books and Readers in Ancient Greece and Rome*, 54.
21 For an excellent detailed discussion, see Butrica, "History and Transmission of the Text," esp. 17–22.
22 Ibid., 18–19.
23 Hutchinson, "The Catullan Corpus," 207–9; Barchiesi, "The Search for the Perfect Book," 337–9.
24 As Hutchinson has pointed out ("The Catullan Corpus," 207).
25 For the collection vs. the single poem, see Gutzwiller, "The Literariness of the Milan Papyrus," esp. 277; Fraistat, "Introduction," *Poems in their Place*, esp. 8; Miller, *Lyric Texts and Lyric Consciousness*, 52–77
26 Here and elsewhere my discussion is much influenced by the ideas of reader-response criticism. For a good introduction, see Iser, "The Reading Process."
27 Miller, *Lyric Texts and Lyric Consciousness*, 74.
28 Or perhaps we should say: he will be "as much out of the picture as Ionis." Nisetich has given a free translation of Callimachus' last line. The Loeb

       translation reads: "of the poor girl, as of the Megarians, there is neither word nor count."
29 See Adams, *The Latin Sexual Vocabulary*, 190; *Oxford Latin Dictionary* under *nosco* 12.
30 Adams, *The Latin Sexual Vocabulary*, 160.
31 See Van Sickle, "The Book-Roll and Some Conventions of the Poetic Book," 5–6.
32 Segal, "The Order of Catullus, Poems 2–11; Hubbard, "The Catullan *Libellus*."
33 See chapter 7, pp. 170, 181–2, 184–5.
34 Hubbard, "The Catullan *Libellus*," 225.
35 For a formulation of the process of continual reinterpretation in terms of reader-response theory, see Iser, "The Reading Process," esp. 53–5.
36 For discussion and bibliography, see Hubbard, "The Catullan *Libelli* Revisited"; Skinner, "Authorial Arrangement of the Collection."
37 Santirocco, *Unity and Design in Horace's Odes*, 7–11; Skinner, "Authorial Arrangement of the Collection," 39.
38 The old idea that the ancients did not read silently was refuted forty years ago by Knox, "Silent Reading in Antiquity." See also Johnson, "Toward a Sociology of Reading in Classical Antiquity."
39 Wiseman, *Catullus and His World*, 122–9; Johnson, "Toward a Sociology of Reading in Classical Antiquity."
40 Dionysius was a Greek from Alexandria who taught in Rhodes in the late second century B.C. His treatise, *Technē grammatikē*, had a great influence in late republican Rome. See Quinn, "Poet and Audience in the Augustan Age," 102–4.

3

The Catullan Persona

> nam castum esse decet pium poetam
> ipsum, versiculos nihil necesse est.
> (Cat. 16.5–6)

The character of Catullus portrayed in the poems is vivid, sympathetic, and realistic, so attractive and so full of passionate emotion that generations of readers have believed in its sincerity, thinking that they know Catullus as he really was. But the character is a fiction. Although we are invited by Catullus' use of the first person to assume that whatever the "I" in the poems experiences or feels is a real part of his biography and emotional life, that "I" is not the historical Catullus but a construct or literary identity created by the text. Critics call this identity a *persona* ("mask"), a term derived from the ancient theater, in which actors wore masks (*personae*) appropriate to the roles they played.[1] The term refers to a character or role assumed by the author, and the idea of performance is never far away. As Paul Veyne neatly observed of Catullus: "Catullus took his own name, Catullus, as his stage name."[2] The performative aspect of Catullus' poetry, and of all Roman poetry, is enhanced by the fact that it was often literally performed by being read aloud, whether by the poet himself or by a professional *lector*. The performance of literature took place in a wider culture oriented to acting and display. Orators performed their works in public. Politicians and other members of elite society, aware of close scrutiny by friends and foes alike, suited their behavior, dress, and gestures to the character and effect they wished to convey. Roman culture as a whole, as we saw in chapter 1, had its basis in performance, whether of wealth, status, power, culture, or masculinity.

The persona, then, is not identical with the poet, and we cannot construct Catullus' physical or emotional biography from his poetry. That does not mean, however, that there is nothing of the poet himself in the persona or that the persona is false, only that we as readers cannot be sure where the persona leaves off and the poet begins. The Muses in Hesiod say, "We know how to to tell many lies like the truth, and we know how to tell the truth when we please" (*Theogony*, 27–8). A reader can never be sure of the difference. Even avowedly autobiographical poetry is to some extent fictional. Robert Lowell, who is often described as a confessional poet, said of his autobiographical poems:

> They're not always factually true. There's a good deal of tinkering with fact. You leave out a lot, and emphasize this and not that. Your actual experience is a complete flux. I've invented facts and changed things, and the whole balance of the poem was something invented.[3]

"Your actual experience is in flux," as Lowell points out. Ezra Pound made a similar point writing on the poems he called *Personae*:

> In the "search for oneself," in the search for "sincere self-expression," one gropes, one finds some seeming verity. One says "I am" this, that, or the other, and with the words scarcely uttered one ceases to be that thing.[4]

The poet, even one who wants to, cannot make a perfectly accurate self-portrait, since life, experience, and the perception of it are always changing. But the reader's life, experience, and perception are always changing too. Both the literary work and the character of its author seem different to us at different moments. As Lowell says of his writing, we in our reading "emphasize this and not that." In the different lights of different readings the familiar features of the poet take on a new cast. The portrait changes still more when it is perceived by different readers, of different times and cultures.

The subject of this chapter is Catullus as he comes to life in his poetry, not the real life Catullus. The two undoubtedly intersected and overlapped at various points, but we will never know which ones. The Catullus of the poems is the only one that we will ever know, and we must be reconciled to the fact not only that every reader will see him differently but that each reader will see him differently at different times. My starting point is the absolute believability of the Catullan persona, which I think is far greater than that of other ancient poets. We are not convinced that we know Horace's inmost character when we read the *Odes* or that we understand the deepest feelings of Propertius, Tibullus, and Ovid when we read their elegies. But we do believe in Catullus; every poem seems the product of genuine and spontaneous emotion and demands a corresponding response from us. Readers are persuaded that they understand Catullus, that on some level he is just like them, not only identifying with Catullus, but identifying Catullus with themselves.

In what follows we will look at the persona in action, paying attention to different aspects of his behavior, emotions, and language in several poems. We will try to see how the poet has created him, what he is like, and what responses he evokes. In order to distinguish between the poet and his persona, throughout this chapter I will reserve the name Catullus for the persona or the speaker of the poems, calling his creator the poet or Catullus the poet.

Acknowledging the Persona: Poem 16

In the verses quoted as the epigraph of this chapter Catullus presents what has become a famous dictum on the relation between the poet and his poetry:

> nam castum esse decet pium poetam
> ipsum, versiculos nihil necesse est. (16.5–6)
> (For it is right for the true poet to be chaste
> himself, but not necessary for his verses to be so.)

The lines have often been interpreted as a complete disavowal of any connection between the character of the poet and the content of his verses, but that is not quite what they are, as we can see by comparing them with the famous imitations of them by Ovid and Martial. Ovid says, "My life is chaste; my Muse playful" (*vita verecunda est, Musa iocosa mea. Tristia* 2.354). Martial proclaims, "My page is naughty; my life pure" (*lasciva est nobis pagina, vita proba.* Martial 1.4.8). The claims of Ovid and Martial are unambiguous: both admit to writing racy verses, and both assert that their own lives are chaste and pure. Catullus, by contrast, presents only a general statement of propriety introduced by the impersonal word *decet* ("it is right"). He neither reveals nor claims anything about his own life and character. This is an important point, and we will return to it presently. First, however, we must look at the poem as a whole.

Pedicabo ego vos et irrumabo, 1
Aureli pathice et cinaede Furi,
qui me ex versiculis meis putastis,
quod sunt molliculi, parum pudicum.
Nam castum esse decet pium poetam 5
ipsum, versiculos nihil necesse est;
qui tum denique habent salem ac leporem,
si sunt molliculi ac parum pudici,
et quod pruriat incitare possunt,
non dico pueris, sed his pilosis 10
qui duros nequeunt movere lumbos.
Vos, quod milia multa basiorum
legistis, male me marem putatis?
pedicabo ego vos et irrumabo.
(I'll bugger you and stuff it down your throats,
queer Aurelius and faggot Furius!
who think from my verses—because they're
a little soft—that I'm not quite modest.
For it is right for the true poet to be chaste himself,
but not necessary for his verses to be so;
they only have wit and charm
if they are a little soft and not quite modest,
and can stir up sexual excitement—
I don't mean for boys, but for these hairy old men
unable to move their stiffened loins.
You, because you have read of many thousands
of kisses, do you think me hardly a man?
I'll bugger you and shove it down your throats.)

Like many of the poems, 16 has a circular structure. The idea that frames it (lines 1–4 and 12–14) has its basis in the Roman conception of masculinity, as we saw in chapter 1. Furius and Aurelius have accused Catullus of being *parum pudicum* ("not quite modest"—i.e., "unmale" and submitting to sexual penetration by another) because he writes poems that are *molliculi* ("a little soft"). He retaliates by threatening to demonstrate his masculinity by raping them anally and orally.

Furius and Aurelius are shown as guilty of what used to be called the biographical fallacy. In their reading, tender or emotional poetry must be the product of an effeminate poet. Their interpretation is abetted by the double meaning of *mollis* ("soft"), which can be used either in a literary sense to describe tender love poetry or in a sexual sense to describe a man who lets himself be penetrated by another. Furius and Aurelius do not say that Catullus himself is *mollis* or *molliculus* ("a little soft")—the diminutive would make him even more effeminate—although they imply it. Instead, we get the phrase *parum pudicum* ("not quite modest"), which means the same thing but also suggests moral (or at least social) disapproval. The verses that have inspired their accusation are the ones on "many thousands of kisses." Readers working sequentially through a modern text will think first of poems 5 and 7, the kiss poems to Lesbia, and especially of 5, in which Catullus uses the phrase "many thousands" (*milia multa*). (The poet's contemporaries might have read the poems in the same sequence, although the point is uncertain, as we saw in chapter 2.) But 5 and 7 are not the only possibilities. In poem 48 Catullus tells the boy Juventius:

> usque ad milia basiem trecenta
> nec mi umquam videar satur futurus (48.3–4)
> (I would go on kissing up to three hundred thousand
> nor ever think I'd had enough.)

Furius and Aurelius could have been thinking of either 48 or 5 and 7 or both. Their point was not who the poet wanted to kiss but that he wrote so extravagantly about kissing. Perhaps they claimed that he was too "soft" and impotent to describe (or accomplish) anything more than kissing,[5] or perhaps they simply considered a preoccupation with kisses sentimental and overly demonstrative. In either case, for them Catullus the poet of kisses was something less than a man.

Catullus makes two replies to their allegations. Both are programmatic in that they concern the natures of poetry and the poet. The first is the threat in the frame: Catullus' promise to demonstrate that his soft verses are no reflection of his ("real") hard masculine self. The second is what we might call the argument of the poem, introduced by the famous lines on the proper character of the poet. The opening of the argument is subtly different from the assertion in the frame: not that Catullus' character cannot be read from his poems, but that a poet and his verses operate under different codes. The poet ought to be chaste himself, but his verse does not have to be. The word "chaste" here does not mean that the poet should be celibate or even that he should not consort with men, only that he should not be the one penetrated. It means, that is, that the poet should not be what Furius and Aurelius have accused Catullus of being: *parum pudicum*. It must be noted again, however, that Catullus has not told us whether he is actually chaste or not, only that a true poet should be. But his verses have no such requirement. In fact, as he notes in lines 7–11, they have charm and wit only if they are *unchaste* (*si sunt molliculi ac parum pudici*, line 8) and can arouse boys and exhausted old men alike. If Catullus is referring to the kiss poems (and I think he is), the titillating poetry he has in mind is not necessarily explicit or obscene, merely powerful enough to arouse the reader.

In poem 16 the speaker acknowledges the existence of the persona and lets us think that we are seeing the real self of Catullus the poet. In the frame he asserts that his soft verses do not reflect his softness as a man. In the argument he disclaims a necessary likeness of character between a poet and his poetry. But he is only playing with the mask, not taking it off. In the argument, he *suggests* that he is chaste, but when we read the fine print we see that he has not actually said so. In the frame he presents us with a riddle or paradox. If poetry does not necessarily reflect the truth about the poet, should we believe in his threats to Furius and Aurelius, which are expressed in a poem? Here is how Batstone puts it:

> Can we let Catullus assert that only his *molliculi versiculi* are poetic creations and that his manly threats of buggery are true expressions of self?[6]

The poet has teased us. His mask is still firmly in place and we will never know for sure what is behind it—or how many masks there might be between us and himself.

But if we cannot see behind the mask, we can still look at the mask itself, the persona presented in the poem. The Catullus we see in 16 is a poet of tender verses. He is touchy about his masculinity and ready to defend it with sexual aggression. He takes the calling of poet seriously. He has also been badly misunderstood by men who do not deserve his respect. Furius and Aurelius are either guilty of effeminacy (*mollitia*) or soon will be, when he gets through with them. In either case their status and masculinity are suspect. If we read the way they are presented here against their scornful depiction in nearby poems, they appear even more disreputable. In poem 11 they are sent as errand boys to deliver Catullus' farewell to Lesbia. In 15 and 21 Aurelius is accused of wanting to defile Catullus' boy Juventius (as yet unnamed); in 23 and 26 Furius is ridiculed for his poverty, and in 24 Catullus is outraged that Juventius seems to have been won by him.

Some of the features of the Catullan persona in 16 appear across the collection, especially aggressiveness and the sense of being misunderstood or undervalued by people unworthy of him.⁷ By themselves these characteristics would not evoke great sympathy from readers, but combined with other more attractive qualities evident in other poems they help to present him as a complex and nuanced personality. Two of these more attractive qualities are at least hinted at in 16. The first is his passionate emotion, just barely suggested in the mention of poems on thousands of kisses. The second is a concern for traditional Roman values evoked by the vocabulary of line 5, where the emotionally loaded words *castum*, *decet*, and *pium* ("chaste," "it is right," "true") give the poet's calling (and by association Catullus himself) an air of moral seriousness. Catullus has it both ways with "chaste": in the context of the poem as a whole it has a specialized sexual meaning; next to *decet* and *pium* it retains its aura of old fashioned virtue.

"The Braggart" (A Social Comedy): Poem 10

A different side of the Catullan persona appears in poem 10. The opening lines set the scene:

> Varus me meus ad suos amores
> visum duxerat e foro otiosum. (10.1–2)
> (My friend Varus had taken me from the forum to see his girlfriend when
> I had nothing better to do.)

The speaker is a young man about town. He was at a loose end (*otiosus*) in the forum, killing time in a place proverbial for worthwhile activity (*negotium*), when his friend Varus removed him to a more congenial locale, the house of his girlfriend. In only two lines the poet has drawn us into the world and genre of Roman comedy, presenting a cast and setting that we could find in Plautus or Terence. The idle young protagonist (the Catullan persona), his crony, and the girlfriend make up the familiar cast. The setting is equally familiar: the house of the girlfriend on stage, with the forum (representing the world of work) offstage in one direction and the harbor (representing arrivals and departures) offstage in the other.⁸ Catullus and Varus have just come from the forum; the harbor will be suggested presently (lines 7–8) by the mention of Catullus' recent return from Bithynia. We are about to witness a comedy of manners, or as modern critics might describe it, a social performance of *urbanitas*.⁹ But we do not hear and see the actors directly as in an actual play. The action is filtered through the narrative of the principal actor, the persona, who is by no means an objective narrator. The character of the persona is revealed as much by the way he tells his story as by the story itself.

Here is how the comedy unfolds. At a glance, our young man about town sees what Varus' girl is:

> scortillum, ut mihi tum repente visum est,
> non sane illepidum neque invenustum. (10.3–4)
> (a little tart, as I saw at once, yet certainly not without charm or unappealing.)

The word *scortillum*, which I have translated "little tart," may have been coined by the poet, for it appears only here. It has an air of whimsical affectation; the description as a whole conveys the narrating persona's attitude of mannered condescension. In the ensuing conversation (briefly discussed in chapter 1) Varus and the girl ask Catullus what Bithynia was like and whether he had made any money there. He tells them the truth, that it was a horrible place and he didn't make a dime. The governor under whom he served was a bastard and screwed his entourage (lines 12–13). But surely, they insist, he at least brought back some litter bearers; that's where they come from, after all. This is the point at which Catullus gets himself into trouble.

> ego, ut puellae
> unum me facerem beatiorem,
> "non" inquam "mihi tam fuit maligne,
> ut, provincia quod mala incidisset,
> non possem octo homines parare rectos." (10.16–20)
> (To make myself out to the girl as especially well off, I said, "I didn't do so badly that, just because I drew a bad province, I couldn't get eight tall men.")

It's a lie, of course, as the narrator admits in an aside (lines 21–23). But both the lie itself and his complaint against the governor of Bithynia (identified in other poems as Memmius) tell against him, as scholars have noted.[10] Catullus is indignant because Memmius did not allow his entourage to enrich themselves in Bithynia, but if Memmius kept a tight rein on his underlings, he was on the high ground both morally and legally: governors and their staffs were not supposed to loot their provinces.

Catullus claims to have eight litter bearers. If he actually did, he would be seen as effete and extravagant. Litters were for women or the elderly and infirm, not for able-bodied young men. An eight-man litter suggests an eastern potentate, or a corrupt Roman trying to behave like one—like Verres, the notorious governor of Sicily, prosecuted in 70 by Cicero. (One of Verres' excesses, according to Cicero, was "being carried around in an eight-man litter like the kings of Bithynia," *Verr.* 2.5.27.)

But Catullus' grandiosity is soon punctured.

> hic illa, ut decuit cinaediorem,
> "quaeso" inquit mihi, "mi Catulle, paulum
> istos commoda; nam volo ad Serapim
> deferri." (10.24–27)

(At this point the girl, like the shameless tramp she was, says to me, "Please, dear Catullus, lend them to me for a little while. For I'd like a ride to the temple of Serapis.")

In a twinkling, the "little tart" indulgently described at the beginning has turned into something far worse: *cinaediorem* ("shameless tramp"). The word (a comparative of *cinaedus*, "lewd") is hard to translate. A *cinaedus* is a male sexually penetrated by other males (compare 16.2, where it is translated "faggot"), sometimes a male prostitute. But the word also refers to a lewd (male) dancer. I do not know of another instance where it is applied to a woman. I think that the narrator uses it here not only to demean the girl but to suggest enticement on her part: she was guilty of entrapment, inveigling him into a grandiose lie and then pulling the rug out from under him. Both the language she uses to Catullus and her proposed destination characterize her as a "working girl." Her familiar address ("please, dear Catullus") sounds like the wheedling of a professional, and the shrines of Egyptian gods like Serapis were popular with prostitutes. Confronted with her request, Catullus can only backpedal in embarrassment.

> "Mane," inquii puellae,
> "istud quod modo dixeram me habere,
> fugit me ratio: meus sodalis—
> Cinna est Gaius—is sibi paravit.
> verum, utrum illius an mei, quid ad me?
> Utor tam bene quam mihi pararim.
> Sed tu insulsa male et molesta vivis,
> per quam non licet esse neglegentem. (10.27–34)

("Hold on," I said to the girl. "About what I said I had just now—I misspoke. My friend—Gaius Cinna, that is—got them for himself. But what does it matter to me whether they're his or mine? I use them as well as if I'd got them for myself. But you're awfully stupid and tiresome not to let a man be careless.")

Catullus' concluding words to the girl contradict his initial description. At first he thought her "not without charm or unappealing" (*non . . . illepidum neque invenustum*), but now he calls her "stupid and tiresome (*insulsa . . . et molesta*). Except for *molesta*, all these words belong to the language of social performance, the behavior praised or blamed by the devotees of *urbanitas*.[11] The girl's social performance, we could say, has not lived up to expectations. According to Catullus, she has acted inappropriately by gauchely exposing his lie, showing that contrary to appearance, she does not know how to behave in sophisticated company.

But the failed social performer is really Catullus. In the comedy we have just witnessed, the girl is cast as the clever and venal courtesan, but Catullus also plays a stock role, that of the foolish braggart who gets his comeuppance and takes it badly. He has mastered the language, but not the behavior of *urbanitas*, and his pose of blasé sophistication ends in ruins. His churlish attack on the girl for a lack of *urbanitas* only emphasizes his own. The way he tells the story reveals that he has not learned his lesson. In recalling the event, far from showing the wry detachment scholars have sometimes attributed to him, he demonstrates the same pretentious self-importance that got him into trouble in the first place.

Combining the comic characters of idle youth and self-deceiving boaster, the persona in poem 10 is foolish and unreflective, trying to appear better off and more important than he is, and blaming someone else for the embarrassment he has brought on himself. These qualities, like the belligerence and aggressiveness of poem 16, are unappealing, but the persona tries to disarm us by telling the story on himself and by taking us into his confidence as if we were his friends.[12] In one self-deprecating aside he candidly reveals the reason for his lie (he wanted to impress the girl). In another, he humorously exaggerates his real financial condition (he didn't have a single slave who could lift so much as the broken leg of an old bedstead).[13] Charming and confidential, the narrating persona expects the reader's sympathy. Whether he gets it depends on the reader. Those who judge him from the standpoint of cultural studies are not won over. For them he is a disagreeable embodiment of a hierarchical and patriarchal society and the woman is his victim.[14] Others may be more indulgent, acknowledging his unattractive traits, but somehow persuaded by the artful poet to like him anyway.

Poem 10 is all about performance. Shaped as a Roman comedy, it presents its contemporary characters from late republican Rome in familiar roles from the ancient genre. The principal actor in this play of "modern" manners is the Catullan persona, already a performer. ("Catullus," we remember, is the stage name of the poet.) Even more than most of Catullus' poems, it is performed by whoever reads it. As modern readers we perform it in our minds, reading and interpreting it like a script, but in antiquity an oral reader would have performed and interpreted it for an audience. The layers of performance and impersonation would have multiplied when the reader was the poet himself, performing as the persona "Catullus," to whom he had awarded the additional mask of a stock character in a Roman comedy.

Lesbia's Lover: Poem 8

Catullus the poet has always been most famous for the poems in which he chronicles a love affair with a woman called Lesbia. The picture of the lover that emerges from these poems is the poet's most memorable creation, a persona tormented, passionate, and committed to an unattainable woman who does not deserve his devotion. He tells us a little about Lesbia: that she is beautiful and witty, charming, promiscuous, and married. He reports a few of her words and actions.[15] But it is not what Lesbia says or does that creates the impression of her personality, and not the "facts" of her life and appearance. It is her lover's emotional response. Looking at her through the feelings of the Catullan persona, we are led to see her as he does: vivid, captivating, and ultimately depraved. The focus is not on Lesbia herself, but on Catullus reacting to her. He is shattered by Lesbia's promiscuity, but never seems to understand his own culpability as an adulterous lover. He is occasionally happy or cautiously hopeful in his doomed and illicit relationship, but far more often in despair or torn between obsession and disgust, not so much expressing his emotions as cataloging and trying to understand them.

In this section we will look at the persona of Lesbia's lover in poem 8, with brief excursions to poems 5, 37, 58, and 87. Lesbia is unnamed in poem 8, but she is identified by the way that Catullus speaks of her as clearly as by a fingerprint.[16]

Miser Catulle, desinas ineptire,
et quod vides perisse perditum ducas.
Fulsere quondam candidi tibi soles,
cum ventitabas quo puella ducebat
amata nobis quantum amabitur nulla.   5
Ibi illa multa cum iocosa fiebant,
quae tu volebas nec puella nolebat,
fulsere vere candidi tibi soles.
Nunc iam illa non vult; tu quoque inpote⟨ns noli⟩,
nec quae fugit sectare, nec miser vive,   10
sed obstinata mente perfer, obdura.
Vale, puella. Iam Catullus obdurat,
nec te requiret nec rogabit invitam.
At tu dolebis, cum rogaberis nulla.
Scelesta, vae te! quae tibi manet vita?   15
Quis nunc te adibit? Cui videberis bella?
Quem nunc amabis? Cuius esse diceris?
quem basiabis? Cui labella mordebis?
At tu, Catulle, destinatus obdura.

(Unhappy Catullus, stop being foolish, and consider lost what you see is lost. Once the sunny days shone bright for you when you would go where the girl led, loved by us as no girl will ever be loved. Then, when lots of love play went on, which you wanted and the girl did not refuse, truly the sunny days shone bright for you. Now she refuses; you refuse, too, weakling, and don't chase a girl who runs away, or be unhappy, but harden your heart and endure. Stand fast. Good-bye, girl. Now Catullus is standing fast, and he won't seek you out or ask you against your will. But you will be sorry, when you are not asked at all. Wretch, woe upon you! What life awaits you? Who will go to you now? To whom will you seem pretty? Whom will you love now? Whose girl will they say you are? Whom will you kiss? Whose lips will you bite? But you, Catullus, keep your mind made up, stand fast.)

The poem is a dramatic monologue in two parts with a short coda. In the first part (lines 1–11), Catullus addresses himself. He recalls past happiness, admits that Lesbia is through with him, and orders himself to repudiate her: "Harden your heart and endure. Stand fast." In the second part (lines 12–18), he addresses the absent Lesbia. He resolutely says good-bye, tells her that she will be sorry, wonders who will love her now, and with this last idea slips into an increasingly vivid fantasy as he pictures her with another man. In the coda (line 19), he pulls himself up sharply: "But you, Catullus, keep your mind made up, stand fast."

I have called the poem a dramatic monologue. Actually, it is a *comic* monologue, for in its language, style, and content it evokes the typical speech of a vacillating lover in comedy.[17] Scholars have pointed to parallels between Catullus' speech and those of several comic lovers, but the poet's model is generic rather than specific.[18] As in poem 10, he is typecasting. There the stock character was the comic braggart, here the lovesick youth. The young lover in comedy is foolish, gullible, and irresolute, alternating between joy and despair, both equally ill-founded. He is designed to win a laugh or at least a smile from an audience that has seen his ilk many times before. The speaker of poem 8, however, is more complex. The shape of his monologue is essentially comic, particularly from the end of the first part through the coda (lines 11–19): firm instructions to self ("stand fast"), a claim of resolve ("now Catullus stands fast"), progressive and inadvertent undermining of resolution, and repetition of the original instruction ("stand fast"). The sequence, and especially the device of the comic build-up demonstrated in the imaginary speech to the girl, is duplicated in countless comedies from Plautus to the modern sit-com. But the persona himself is not wholly, or even predominantly comic. There are serious elements in his monologue that complicate and darken the picture, especially phrases and thoughts that resonate with those in other Lesbia poems. Such repetitions and echoes, as we saw in chapter 2, allow the ideas in one poem to be felt in another, creating shared patterns of meaning.[19]

The monologue is full of echoes. The "sunny days (*soles*) that once shone bright" (lines 3 and 8) poignantly evoke the sunshine (*soles*) of happier days in the first kiss poem (5.4). There "suns could set and rise again." Here that brightness is gone for ever, for, as Quinn points out in his commentary, the perfect tense of the verb *fulsere* ("shone") has the sense sometimes found with the perfect of something that is "over and done with."[20] The kisses that Catullus imagines Lesbia giving to someone else (line 18) also resonate with the kisses in poem 5 that he imagined for himself. Seen in isolation, the line "whom will you kiss? whose lips will you bite?" (*quem basiabis? cui labella mordebis?*) is the comic climax of the lover's speech. But when it is read against the joyous effusion of "give me a thousand kisses, then a hundred" (*da mi basia mille, deinde centum*, 5.7), the verse draws attention to what the lover has lost and takes on a darker tone.

Catullus' claim in line 5 that Lesbia was "loved by us as no girl will ever be loved" (*amata nobis quantum amabitur nulla*) reaches out to at least three poems. The sentiment appears in almost exactly the same words in poem 37, in a slightly different form in 87, and with still greater variation in 58.

In poem 87 the idea appears in an address to Lesbia:

> Nulla potest mulier tantum se dicere amatam
>   vere, quantum a me Lesbia amata mea es.[21]
> Nulla fides ullo fuit umquam in foedere tanta,
>   quanta in amore tuo ex parte reperta mea est. (87)

(No woman can truly say that she has been loved so much, my Lesbia, as you were loved by me. No fidelity was ever so great in any compact as was found on my side in love of you.)

The two couplets are strictly parallel in form—each beginning with *nulla* ("no") and structured around forms of the same correlatives: *tantum . . . quantum* ("so much . . . as"), *tanta . . . quanta* ("so great . . . as"). They are equally parallel in content. The second couplet restates, or perhaps it would be better to say, rephrases and explains the idea of the first, spelling out Catullus' conception of love. For him love is a compact (*foedus*), a formal and binding contract that requires fidelity (*fides*) to its terms from both parties. The terms *foedus* and *fides* are part of the language of male aristocratic friendship, its code of social commitment.[22] The code was deeply felt and its language carried great emotional force. By using it for his love of Lesbia, Catullus treated it—and her—with the kind of moral seriousness that Roman men aspired to, not in erotic relationships, but in their most solemn dealings with each other. But Lesbia was not equally serious, as Catullus' silence about her response reveals. Her part of the compact went unfulfilled; perhaps she did not even see (or care) what Catullus was offering to her.

In poem 37 the idea "loved as no girl will ever be loved" appears in Catullus' obscene attack on the oversexed patrons of a low tavern, a dive also frequented by Lesbia.

> Puella nam mi, quae meo sinu fugit,
> amata tantum quantum amabitur nulla,
> pro qua mihi sunt magna bella pugnata
> consedit istic. (37.11–14)

(For my girl, who fled my embrace, the one loved as no girl will ever be loved, for whom I have fought great battles, has set up shop there.)

Lesbia, to put it plainly, is prostituting herself.[23] Her clientele, it seems, are the dive's regulars—"creeps," as Catullus says, who "sit in a line, a hundred or two hundred strong."²⁴ In this context, the thought, "loved as no girl will ever be loved," points up the contrast between Catullus' devotion and Lesbia's careless depravity. The contrast and emotions are similar in poem 58:

> Caeli, Lesbia nostra, Lesbia illa,
> illa Lesbia, quam Catullus unam
> plus quam se atque suos amavit omnes,
> nunc in quadriviis et angiportis
> glubit magnanimi Remi nepotes. (58)

(Caelius, our Lesbia, that Lesbia, that Lesbia Catullus loved above all, more than himself and everyone dear to him, now in crossroads and alleys skins the descendants of great-hearted Remus.)

But here both the contrast and the emotions are intensified. Catullus loved Lesbia (the past tense is important) not only more than any woman would ever be loved, but more than he loved himself and his whole family—that is, not just erotically, but on the deeper plane of devotion a Roman reserved for his closest kinsmen.²⁵ Lesbia's present depravity is pictured in correspondingly stronger terms. Now she is on the street, and her actions are described with a shocking obscenity. (*Glubit* is a gutter word, meaning to pull back the foreskin of a penis before intercourse or other sexual activity.)²⁶

The contrast between Catullus' devotion and Lesbia's sexual depravity explicit in 37 and 58 is expressed more subtly in poem 8, so subtly in fact that we could easily miss it. In 8 there are no taverns or alleys, no obscenities, and no overt references to prostitution. But the idea is nonetheless present in the imaginary address to Lesbia, and it shows up all the more clearly in the light of 37 and 58. Catullus sketches it with a few light strokes. In line 15 he addresses Lesbia as *scelesta* ("wretch"). The strongly negative adjective is used only once elsewhere in the poems, and there too of someone we could call a sexual offender: a lecher Catullus suspects of having designs on his boy Juventius (15.15).²⁷ The repeated verb "ask" (*rogabit,* 13; *rogaberis,* 14) is almost a technical term in the sense "ask (for sex)" or "proposition."²⁸ In line 16 ("who will go to you now?"), the verb *adibit* is a euphemism meaning "go to for sex."²⁹

In all four poems (8, 37, 58, and 87) an essential contrast between Catullus and Lesbia is established by the claim, "loved as no girl will ever be loved," and its variations, but because both the treatment and the intensity of the contrast change from poem to poem, each presents the persona and his emotions a little differently. In poem 87 the contrast is only implicit, irresistibly suggested by the silence that follows the statement of Catullus' feelings. We can hear his unexpressed reproach as clearly as if he had shouted it in our ear: "But you did not love me back; you did not honor our compact." In poems 8, 37, and 58 the contrast is spelled out, intensifying as Lesbia's depravity is depicted in ever stronger terms—obliquely and euphemistically in 8, frankly in 37, and obscenely in 58, where (not coincidentally) it is countered by the most powerful description of Catullus' devotion. In poem 87, the persona is hurt and reproachful, as we have seen. In 8 he is unhappy and irresolute, in 37 enraged and on the attack, in 58 full of moral outrage.

The persona of poem 8 has inspired contradictory responses, striking readers as either foolish or (more often) pathetic. In fact he is both. If poem 8 were the only Lesbia poem preserved to us, we would have to read both it and the persona primarily in terms of Roman comedy, and the speaker's claim on our sympathy would probably be no stronger than that exercised by the young comic lover. But poem 8 does not exist in isolation. It shares ideas and language with several other Lesbia poems, and the echoes resonate with each other from poem to poem, always bringing some of their context with them. The result is what I have called a shared pattern of meaning—a fuller and more complex conception than that evident in any single poem. The persona of Lesbia's disappointed lover created in this way is profoundly serious: he is someone who longs to put his erotic love on the same plane as his commitment to the highest Roman moral values of friendship and devotion to kin. When the woman he tries to bring into this world of deeply felt masculine values rejects his devotion and turns to other men, his pain is intense. In poem 8 the poet has placed this tormented persona in an uncongenial genre, assigning him the lines of a comic monologue; as a consequence, the feelings of the persona and the format of his script pull against each other, creating a powerful emotional tension. To put it another way, the speech of the persona is formally comic, but his anguish is real.

Juventius' Lover: Poems 24 and 99

Catullus claims an eternal and undying passion for Lesbia and bitterly resents her promiscuity, but he is by no means sexually faithful himself. In poem 32 he issues an obscene invitation to Ipsitilla[30] for a midday rendezvous. In 41 he is outraged that the ugly Ameana has demanded so much for her sexual favors ("Doesn't she ever look in the mirror?" he asks in disbelief). In 110 he castigates Aufillena, who has taken her fee but failed to deliver. Far more important than any of these, however, is the boy Juventius, who is treated almost as a counterpart of Lesbia herself. Like Lesbia, Juventius has a cycle of poems devoted to him.[31] He is named in only four (24, 48, 81, and 99), but his presence in a poem, like hers, is clear even when his name is withheld. Like Lesbia, he is unfaithful. Catullus' sexual relationship with him, like that with Lesbia, is morally and socially illicit. Lesbia is off limits because she is a married woman, Juventius because he is a free-born, probably aristocratic youth.[32]

This last point requires some discussion since we do not know who Juventius was, or even if he really existed. All we have is his name, but that tells us all we need to know. The name is aristocratic, for there was a patrician family of Iuventii, which had been of consular rank for a hundred years.[33] Juventius may well have been a member of it; if not, the designation Juventius might be a pseudonym for a real person or a fictitious name for an imaginary one. What is important, however, is that the poet has used a name that *suggests* that he was a Roman aristocrat and that by so doing he has deliberately placed the persona in an illicit affair that mirrors his relationship with Lesbia. The poet could have achieved this effect by using any patrician name, but the name Juventius is suggestive and descriptive—what is sometimes called a "speaking name"; for it is etymologically related to the word *iuvenis* ("youth"), which perfectly fits his role as the young darling of Catullus' attentions.

In this section we will look at the persona of Catullus as Juventius' lover in several poems, but with particular attention to 24 and 99. The discussion will examine his emotions and the ways in which he is presented, comparing his personality and responses with those of his persona as Lesbia's lover.

Like his counterpart Lesbia, Juventius appears in the collection before he is actually named.[34] The reader first meets Lesbia in poems 2 and 3, where she is called simply *mea puella* ("my girl").[35] Juventius appears first in poems 15 and 21 with the corresponding designation, *meos amores* ("my darling").[36] In both cases the ordering of the poems (which is ancient, but may or may not be that of the poet himself) prepares the reader for the introduction of the loved one by name. The sparrow poems, 2 and 3, create interest in the unnamed girl before she appears as Lesbia in the first kiss poem (5). Poems 15 and 21 work a little differently, providing background information on Juventius and his milieu. In both poems Catullus obscenely attacks the sexually predatory Aurelius, threatening to rape him either orally (21) or anally (15) if he carries out his designs to seduce the boy designated only as *meos amores*. Thus, even before we are introduced to him by name in poem 24, we know that Juventius is both sexually vulnerable and the object of Catullus' jealousy.

Here is poem 24.

> O qui flosculus es Iuventiorum,
> non horum modo, sed quot aut fuerunt
> aut posthac aliis erunt in annis,
> mallem divitias Midae dedisses
> isti, cui neque servus est neque arca,
> quam sic te sineres ab illo amari.
> "Quid? non est homo bellus?" inquies. Est:
> sed bello huic neque servus neque arca.
> Hoc tu quam lubet abice elevaque:
> nec servum tamen ille habet neque arcam. (24)

(O you who are the tender flower of the Iuventii, not only of the present generation, but of all those that have been or will be afterwards in future years, I'd rather you'd given the riches of Midas to that man who has neither slave nor money box than allow yourself to be loved by him like this. "What? Isn't he a stylish fellow?" you will ask. He is: but this stylish fellow has neither slave nor money box. Dismiss and make light of it as you please: he still has neither slave nor money box.)

Catullus presents himself as Juventius' advisor, and his pose is ironic throughout. His first words both name and describe Juventius: "O you who are the tender flower of the Juventii." The words *flosculus . . . Iuventiorum* not only present Juventius as a very choice member of his family (*flosculus*, like English "flower" often means "the best" or "the finest"), but also pun on the common phrase *flos iuventae* ("flower of youth"), which refers to the beauty of a downy-cheeked boy in his late teens—the time of his greatest attractiveness to older male lovers.[37] This very special boy, it seems, is wasting his charms on a stylish but impoverished lover, one who possesses "neither slave nor money box," as Catullus reminds him three times. This insolent lover is not Aurelius, as one might suspect from Catullus' worries in poems 15 and 21, but Furius, his equally detestable friend.[38] (Furius' poverty is the subject of poem 23, and he is unmistakably identified with Juventius' destitute lover by its first line: "Furius, who has neither slave nor money box.").[39]

As in poems 10 and 8, the persona is cast in a stock comic scene—in this case the one in which a *lena* (bawd or procuress) advises a young prostitute to abandon a poor lover in favor of a rich one.[40] The scene was a favorite with poets, and we find it also in the elegies of Ovid and Propertius in the next generation.[41] Poem 24 parodies and inverts this comic situation. Juventius is cast as the prostitute; Furius plays his impoverished but purportedly stylish (*bellus*) lover; and Catullus takes the role of the bawd. This is not how it is supposed to be. According to convention, the prostitute is a poor but honest working girl, the poor man her faithful lover, and the venal bawd a danger to their happiness. Macleod called the poem an "outrageous infringement of the conventions of poetic love."[42] And so it is. All of the roles in this topsy-turvy comedy are ugly ones. The most important part, of course, is that of the angry Catullus, cruelly sarcastic at Juventius' expense. He plays the bawd—not straight, but as an act of ferocious irony intended to degrade the boy and show him for the prostitute Catullus considers him to be.

Catullus takes a different line in poem 81, in which he finds fault with another of Juventius' lovers. This one is not *bellus* and insolent, but an out-of-town bumpkin. He is even unattractive: "an outsider paler than a gilded statue" (*hospes inaurata pallidior statua*, 81.4). The word *inaurata* ("gilded") may be a pun on the name of Juventius' suitor Aurelius, the target of poems 15 and 21; and the phrase as a whole may hint that the lover has a taste for oral sex.[43] (Pallor is often adduced as a result of the habit; in poem 21 Aurelius is charged with being a devotee.[44]) The persona is as critical of Juventius' taste in this poem as he is in 24, but his predominant emotion is different—not anger, but a painful mixture of indignation and jealousy. His feelings emerge in the final couplet, where he reveals his real objection to Juventius' lover:

> qui tibi nunc cordi est, quem tu praeponere nobis
> audes, et nescis quod facinus facis. (81.5–6)

(the one who is now dear to your heart, whom you dare to prefer to me, and you do not know what crime you commit.)

Poem 48 is the only poem in the Juventius cycle in which Catullus is not angry, jealous, or unhappy. Instead, he wishes for thousands of kisses.

> Mellitos oculos tuos, Iuventi,
> siquis me sinat usque basiare,

> usque ad milia basiem trecenta;
> nec mi umquam videar satur futurus,
> non si densior aridis aristis
> sit nostrae seges osculationis. (48)

(If someone would let me keep kissing your honey-sweet eyes, Juventius, I would go on kissing up to three hundred thousand, and I would never think I'd had enough, not if the harvest of our kissing was thicker than ripe ears of grain.)

Catullus' emotional enthusiasm here is comparable to that in the kiss poems to Lesbia, but it is both more muted and less complex. In the Lesbia poems the kisses are a reality. Catullus is asking for them, to be sure, but we know that Lesbia will kiss him and he will kiss her back, over and over again. As he says in poem 5:

> da mi basia mille, deinde centum,
> dein mille altera, dein secunda centum,
> deinde usque altera mille, deinde centum;
> dein, cum milia multa fecerimus,
> conturbabimus (5.7–11)

(Give me a thousand kisses, then a hundred, then another thousand, then a second hundred, then another thousand, then a hundred, then when we have made many thousands, we'll mix them up)

But in poem 48 all the verbs are subjunctive; the kisses are wished for, but perhaps will never be a reality. In poems 5 and 7, kissing Lesbia is linked to other themes: the shortness of life in 5, adulterous loves in 7, and the disapproval of the curious in both. In 48 Catullus is single-minded and undistracted, focussed on kissing alone.

Kissing is also the subject of poem 99.

> Surripui tibi, dum ludis, mellite Iuventi,   1
>   saviolum dulci dulcius ambrosia.
> Verum id non impune tuli: namque amplius horam
>   suffixum in summa me memini esse cruce,
> dum tibi me purgo nec possum fletibus ullis   5
>   tantillum vestrae demere saevitiae.
> Nam simul id factum est, multis diluta labella
>   guttis abstersti mollibus articulis,
> ne quicquam nostro contractum ex ore maneret,
>   tamquam commictae spurca saliva lupae.   10
> Praeterea infesto miserum me tradere amori

> non cessasti omnique excruciare modo,
> ut mi ex ambrosia mutatum iam foret illud
> saviolum tristi tristius elleboro.
> Quam quoniam poenam misero proponis amori, 15
> numquam iam posthac basia surripiam. (99)

(I stole from you while you were teasing, honey-sweet Juventius, a little kiss sweeter than sweet ambrosia. But I did not get away with it unpunished. For I remember being nailed to the top of a cross for more than an hour while I apologized to you and could not for all my tears diminish a bit of your fury. For as soon as it was done, you washed your lips with many splashings of water and wiped them off with your dainty fingers, in case any contagion from my mouth remain, like the filthy spittle of a pissed-on whore. Besides, you did not hesitate to hand me over, wretched, to cruel love and to torture me in every way, so that changed from ambrosia that little kiss was now more bitter for me than bitter hellebore. Since this is the penalty you hold over my wretched love, I'll never steal kisses any more.)

In this poem Catullus relates his humiliation by Juventius. (He also relates it *to* Juventius—an important point that will concern us presently.) The poem is artfully symmetric. Its first and last words are different tenses of the same verb, *surripio* ("steal"), and it is framed by two opposite descriptions of the same kiss: the phrase *saviolum dulci dulcius ambrosia* ("a little kiss sweeter than sweet ambrosia,") in line 2 is perfectly matched by *saviolum tristi tristius elleboro* ("a little kiss more bitter than bitter hellebore") in line 14. The symmetry is purposeful, a framing structure that makes Juventius' furious action in response to the stolen kiss (7–10) not only the centerpiece but the exact center of the poem.

When he wiped off Catullus' kiss as if it was "the spittle of a pissed-on whore," Juventius delivered a powerful insult, for his action (at least in Catullus' interpretation of it) likened Catullus' mouth to that of a prostitute accommodating her clients with fellatio.[45] The insult "unmanned" the persona in two ways: both by the allegation of passive oral sex and by the comparison to the lowest kind of *female* prostitute. In poem 48 Catullus hoped for three hundred thousand kisses, but in the end he seems to have got only one, and to have paid a terrible price for it in pain and humiliation. Juventius led him on, for that seems to be the point of *ludis* in line 1, which I have translated as "tease."[46] When Catullus eagerly took the bait, he fell into Juventius' trap and laid himself open to abuse. We might think that such treatment would keep him away from

Juventius for ever, and the reference to hellebore in line 14 suggests as much, since the ancients considered love a form of madness and hellebore was used to treat insanity. On this reading, one could see the persona as "cured" of his passion by the bitter hellebore of that fatal kiss. But perhaps not. We have to remember that Catullus is relating and interpreting this past event *to Juventius*, who certainly knows all about it. Is he reminding Juventius of the episode in hopes of receiving an apology and perhaps even a genuine offer of unpunished kisses, or simply to break off with him? There is no way to tell.

The persona of Catullus in the Juventius poems is quite different from the one in the Lesbia poems. His emotions are not necessarily less intense, but they are not the same emotions, nor should we expect them to be; for love, even erotic love, varies depending on its object and circumstances. Both Lesbia and Juventius are unattainable and both treat Catullus badly: Lesbia by betraying him in every alley in Rome, and Juventius by cruelly rebuffing him. Neither seems to understand that Catullus and his emotions deserve special consideration. Lesbia does not care for more than a sexual passion, and Juventius treats Catullus with no more regard than he would any other admirer—perhaps less, given his preference for Furius and Aurelius.

With Juventius the persona is in familiar erotic territory, playing the older lover in pursuit of a desirable and fickle boy. Although Juventius' social status gives the relationship an illicit flavor, affairs with eligible boys were both a common feature of Roman society and a stock subject of ancient poetry.[47] Such affairs, however passionate, were by nature ephemeral, lasting at best only as long as the boy was in the attractive "flower of his youth." The Catullan persona is jealous of his rivals and longs to keep Juventius safe from them. In poem 15, for example, he utters a moving and emotional plea to Aurelius: "if you've ever desired with all your heart / to keep something chaste and innocent, / please preserve my boy in decency."[48] But he never expresses the desire for a long-lasting love affair.

The love affair with Lesbia is something new, or at least the persona tries to make it so. He tries to transform it from an essentially sexual affair into something else: an erotic relationship lived in accordance with the ideals of aristocratic friendship. To put it another way, Catullus tries to bring Lesbia and their affair into a region of moral seriousness and commitment created and valued (if not always lived up to) by aristocratic men. In his last words on Lesbia (the last lines in the last Lesbia poem) he prays for just such an affectionate union:

> ut liceat nobis tota perducere vita
>   aeternum hoc sanctae foedus amicitiae (109.5–6)

(May it be possible for us to maintain for all our life this eternal compact of holy friendship.)

This prayer (which one cannot imagine being made for his affair with Juventius), like the persona's other hopes for Lesbia, is destined to fail. Everything we know about Lesbia tells us that she will never live up to an "eternal compact of holy friendship." But Catullus' aspirations are immoral as well as impossible. His relationship with Lesbia is adulterous, and the compact he proposes, its lofty ring notwithstanding, flies in the face of all traditional morality, a fact he never acknowledges.

Conclusion

In this chapter we have looked at the Catullan persona as a defender of his masculinity (poem 16), as a social performer (10), and as the lover of both Lesbia (8) and Juventius (24 and 99). But these are not his only roles. Catullus appears in other poems as an affectionate friend, grieving brother, self-conscious neoteric poet, angry foe, and political satirist.[49] His various aspects are not separate, like the different parts played by an actor who is cast as the lover in one play or the villain or fall-guy in another. They are diverse but complementary components of a single personality, which possesses a depth and complexity not found in the persona of any other ancient poet. This personality is both appealing and realistic. The Catullan persona is appealing in the intensity of his feelings, his powerful affection for his friends and brother, and his evocation of serious Roman values, but also, and perhaps even more, because he wins our sympathy. He grieves for his brother. He is disappointed in Lesbia and spurned by Juventius. His friends sometimes let him down. His distress, which always seems undeserved, makes us care about him all the more, but it also increases his realism and believability since his losses and disappointments could be our own. The impression of realism is also created in other ways. The persona's diverse emotions, reactions, and experiences make him seem many-sided and authentic, and so do his obvious flaws. Catullus is not always admirable. He can be aggressive and belligerent, as we saw in poem 16. He is prone to self-pity, both in some of the Lesbia poems and in some of his addresses to friends (poems 30, 73, and 77 are good examples). He can be blind to his own failures, as in poem 10 when he tells a lie that reflects badly on him and then attacks the girl for catching him in it, or, most notably, in the Lesbia poems in which he fails to see his love affair as the adultery it is. His lack of self-awareness perfectly exemplifies the human failing he describes in the famous conclusion of poem 22. There, after telling how the wretched versifier Suffenus thought of himself as a splendid poet, he comments:

> nimirum idem omnes fallimur, neque est quisquam
> quem non in aliqua re videre Suffenum
> possis. suus cuique attributus est error;
> sed non videmus manticae quod in tergo est. (22.18–21)

(Of course we all make the same mistake, and there is no one whom you cannot see as a Suffenus in something. Everyone has his own failing assigned to him, but we do not see the part of the knapsack that hangs on our back.)

The Catullus we meet in the poems is a fiction, although he cannot be entirely fictitious. It is unbelievable that the historical Catullus would have circulated poetry to his contemporaries about a character called Catullus who was completely unlike himself or that he would have placed this Catullus in situations unlike anything in his own life. The persona undoubtedly has points—perhaps many points—in common with the poet. But we cannot go farther than that, and it would be unproductive to try. The important point is the poet's achievement in creating the persona: the Catullus we find in the poems is a first-person protagonist as vivid and fully realized as a character in a novel. As we will see in chapter 8, the fact has led many later readers to construct narratives from the poems, some writing what they consider to be biographies of the poet, others using the poems as the basis for actual novels.

Notes

1 There is a large bibliography on persona theory. Among the most useful are Edmunds, *Intertextuality and the Reading of Roman Poetry*, 63–82; Elliott, *The Literary Persona*; Veyne, *Roman Erotic Elegy*, esp. 31–49; Nappa, *Aspects of Catullus' Social Fiction*, esp. 15–43.
2 Veyne, *Roman Erotic Elegy*, 174.
3 Seidel, "Interview with Robert Lowell," 17. The passage is quoted in a slightly abbreviated form by Elliott, *The Literary Persona*, 55.
4 Quoted from Elliott, *The Literary Persona*, 8.

5   This is Wiseman's argument: "Catullus 16."
6   Batstone, "Logic, Rhetoric, and Poesis," 152.
7   For example, Catullus is aggressive in poems 37, 42, 56, 116, misunderstood or undervalued in poems 30, 38, 73, 77.
8   Duckworth, *The Nature of Roman Comedy*, 79–86.
9   For social performance, see Krostenko, *Cicero, Catullus, and the Language of Social Performance*, 233–90. For *urbanitas*, see chapter 1 above, pp. 9–10.
10 For the lie, see Skinner, "*Ut Decuit Cinaediorem*: Power, Gender, and Urbanity in Catullus 10," 9–14. For the complaint, see Braund, "The Politics of Catullus 10: Memmius, Caesar and the Bithynians."
11 Krostenko, *Cicero, Catullus, and the Language of Social Performance*; Ross, *Style and Tradition in Catullus*, 104–12.
12 For the poet's manipulation of the reader, see Pedrick, "*Qui potis est, inquis?* Audience Roles in Catullus," esp. 196–201. See also Skinner, "*Ut Decuit Cinaediorem*," 10–11.
13 Lines 21–3.
14 Skinner reads the encounter with the girl "as a paradigm of class and gender oppression" ("*Ut Decuit Cinaediorem*," 10). Her reading has been followed and amplified by Fitzgerald (*Catullan Provocations*, 173–9) and Nappa (*Aspects of Catullus' Social Fiction*, 86–93).
15 The list is surprisingly short. She had a sparrow for a pet and cried when it died (poems 2 and 3). She asked Catullus how many kisses he wanted (7). She used to be willing but now she isn't (8). She acted like a whore (11, 37, 58). She promised to make a sacrifice to Venus and Cupid if Catullus would be reconciled with her and stop attacking her in his poetry (36). She had an illicit rendezvous with him in the house of Allius (68). She said that she preferred him to Jupiter (70, 72). She preferred her brother to Catullus (79). She constantly criticized him (83, 92). She promised reconciliation and eternal love (107, 109).
16 See also chapter 2, pp. 32–3, 37–8, for the way in which the reader is led to supply the name Lesbia even when the poet withholds it.
17 Wheeler, *Catullus and the Traditions of Ancient Poetry*, 227–30; Skinner, "Catullus 8: The Comic 'Amator' as 'Eiron'." Examples of language familiar in comedy include: *miser* (1), *quod vides perisse perditum ducas* (2), *miser vive* (10), *scelesta* (15). See Fordyce, *Catullus. A Commentary*, 111–12.
18 Scholars most frequently cite Plautus, *Truculentus*, 759–69, and *Bacchides*, 520–5; neither is very close. The closest parallel to the style and structure of poem 8 is from Menander (*Samia*, 325–56); see Thomas, "Menander and Catullus 8." Menander's vacillating character, however, is an old man, not a young lover.
19 See chapter 2, pp. 32–6.

20 Quinn, ed., *Catullus: The Poems*, 117. The classic example of this use is in Vergil's *Aeneid* in the account of the sack of Troy: *fuimus Troes, fuit Ilium* ("we are no longer Trojans, Troy no longer exists," *Aeneid* 2.325).
21 I have printed *es*, following Thomson's text. (Mynors prints *est*.)
22 For an excellent account of the language of social obligation, see Lyne, *The Latin Love Poets from Catullus to Horace*, 23–38. The vocabulary is found mostly in the epigrams; see chapter 4, pp. 96–7.
23 For the quasi-technical force of *consedit* ("set up shop"), see Wiseman, *Catullus and His World*, 150.
24 *continenter . . . sedetis insulsi/ centum an ducenti* (37.6–7). The translation is Goold's (*Catullus*, 81). Catullus imagines a similarly large number of lovers for Lesbia at 11.18: *simul complexa tenet trecentos* ("she holds three hundred at a time in her embrace").
25 The same idea is used in 72.3–4; see chapter 2, p. 34.
26 Adams, *The Latin Sexual Vocabulary*, 168.
27 For *scelestus* as abusive, see Thomas, "Menander and Catullus 8," 313–14.
28 The classic example of this meaning is Ovid's ironic *casta est, quam nemo rogavit* ("the chaste woman is the one no one has propositioned," *Amores* 1.8.43).
29 Adams, *The Latin Sexual Vocabulary*, 176.
30 I follow Mynors' text in printing *Ipsitilla*, but the name (if it is a name) is uncertain. Thomson prints *ipsimilla*, which would be a diminutive of *ipsa* ("self").
31 Most scholars would agree that poems 15, 21, 23, 24, 48, 81, and 99 belong to the cycle. Poems 16, 26, and 40 are also possible candidates.
32 For Roman attitudes about eligible and ineligible sexual partners, see chapter 1, pp. 12–13.
33 Wiseman, *Catullus and His World*, 130.
34 For Lesbia's appearance in poems 2 and 3 before she is identified in poem 5, see chapter 2, pp. 37–8.
35 2.1; 3.3; 3.17.
36 *Commendo tibi me ac meos amores* (15.1); *pedicare cupis meos amores* (21.4).
37 For the phrase, see Fantham, *Stuprum*, 273.
38 The pair seem virtually interchangeable. For the poems in which they are mentioned, see page 50 in this chapter.
39 *Furi, cui neque servus est neque arca* (23.1).
40 Macleod, "Parody and Personalities in Catullus," 297–8. The closest parallel in Roman comedy seems to be Plautus, *Asinaria* 505–44; see O'Bryhim, "Catullus 23 as a Roman Comedy," 143.
41 Ovid, *Amores* 1.8; Propertius 2.5.
42 Macleod, "Parody and Personalities in Catullus," 298.

43 The taste was considered vile and degrading, both because its practitioners were regarded as unmale and soft (*mollis*) and because oral contact with the genitalia of either sex was considered filthy. See Richlin, *The Garden of Priapus*, 26–9, 68–70.
44 Aurelius in 21 is "the father of hunger" (*pater esuritionum*, 21.1), and Catullus worries that he will give Juventius a taste for the habit: "Now I grieve because my boy may learn from you to hunger and thirst (*Nunc ipsum id doleo, quod esurire / a te mi puer et sitire discet*, 21.10–11).
45 This is the point of *commictae* ("pissed-on"), since in vulgar and obscene contexts urine and semen were often assimilated. See Adams, *The Latin Sexual Vocabulary*, 142; Richlin, *The Garden of Priapus*, 150.
46 Richardson, "*Furi et Aureli, comites Catulli*," 95.
47 Richlin, *The Garden of Priapus*, 220–6; "Not before Homosexuality," esp. 533–9; Williams, *Roman Homosexuality*, 72–7, 183–8.
48 . . . *veniam peto pudenter / ut, si quicquam animo cupisti / quod castum expeteres et integellum, / conserves puerum mihi pudice* (15.2–5). The translation is Goold's (*Catullus*, 51).
49 Some examples follow (the list does not claim to be complete). It should also be noted that the persona in a given poem may have several aspects. *Affectionate friend*: 9, 12, 13, 46, 47. *Grieving brother*: 65, 68, 101. *Neoteric poet*: 14, 22, 35, 36, 50, 95. *Angry foe*: 25, 33, 37, 39, 77, 80, 88–91, 103, 116. *Political satirist*: 29, 43, 57, 79, 93, 94, 105, 114, 115.

4

What Makes It Poetry

> numero modo hoc modo illoc.
> (Poem 50.5)

Words become poetry not only by what they say but by how they say it, for poetry is an indissoluble compound in which content and form join together to create meaning beyond what either could communicate alone. So far in this book we have been concerned almost entirely with content: Catullus' subjects and themes, the nature of his book, the various aspects of his persona. Now it is time to look at form, the verbal art by which he gives shape to his ideas and turns them into poetry. Form matters to any poet, but it mattered to Catullus especially. Exquisite technique was a hallmark of neoteric poetry, and Catullus was a neoteric master, a meticulous craftsman who paid minute attention to every element of poetic style, from diction and rhythm to word order, structure, and verbal play.

All of these elements were perceived aurally, for ancient poetry was meant to be heard, not just seen. Catullus expected his poetry to be read aloud, and he knew that his audience would notice and appreciate its verbal effects and stylistic art. Roman readers were experienced listeners. They were also accustomed to reading aloud themselves since correct and expressive reading was an important part of their education. They could and did read silently, but the habits of aural perception and oral performance were so deeply ingrained that even as silent readers they would have listened for the cadences and structure of poetry with a sort of inner ear, much as singers can look at a score and mentally "hear" the songs expressed by the words and notes on the page. As moderns we have largely lost this inner poetic ear, for we tend to see rather than hear our poetry. We might or might not try to imagine its sounds as we read it to ourselves. Performing and hearing the music of poetry, even in English, do not come naturally to most of us, and aurally perceiving verbal art in Latin may seem doubly difficult. But it is essential to make the attempt: reading Catullus only with the eye is like studying the libretto of an opera without listening to the music.

In this chapter we will try to read Catullus with the sound turned on. We will consider his meters and verbal music and the registers of his language, always with our eye (and ear) tuned to artistic effect. What follows is not a technical treatise but a simple (and highly simplified) introduction intended as an encouragement to be aware of the aural qualities and the rhythmic and verbal mastery at the heart of Catullus' work. Such awareness, of course, is best achieved by reading the poems aloud—preferably over and over—paying close attention to the words and listening for their melody.

Sounding out Catullus

Correct pronunciation of the Latin words is basic to hearing Catullus' poetry. Latin pronunciation is straightforward.[1] It follows a few fairly simple rules by which we may be able to approximate the sound of the poetry even if we cannot exactly reproduce it.

There are no silent letters, and pronunciation of the same letters or letter combinations is consistent. In Latin there is nothing like the manifold and confusing pronunciation of English *ough* (thr*ough*, thor*ough*, *ough*t, en*ough*).

With a few exceptions consonants are pronounced roughly as in English. Exceptions and points to be noted are shown in Table 1.

The vowels provide more difficulty, both because long and short vowels are sounded differently and because our pronunciation of the long vowels is unlike that of the Romans. The pronunciation is shown in Table 2. (Long vowels are indicated with a long mark, thus: ā = long a.)

Pronunciation in Latin or any language is not just a matter of putting sounds together but of *how* they are put together, both in words and in combinations of words. In this broader sense pronunciation involves both accent (stressed and unstressed syllables) and rhythm (some syllables take longer to pronounce than others). Accent and rhythm, essential elements of ordinary speech, are intensified in poetry. In Latin poetry, meter is based on a highly regularized form of rhythm. As we will see in detail in the next section, Latin meters are patterns of long and short syllables.

Table 1: Points to be noted in the pronunciation of Latin consonants

c   always hard like *c* in *curl*
g   always hard like *g* in *gut*
gn   probably nasalized and pronounced like *gn* in *hangnail*[a]
        magnus ("great") would be pronounced *mangnus*.
h   does not count as a consonant, only as an aspirate, a little puff of air.
        In the combinations *ch*, *ph*, *th* the initial sound (*c*, *p*, *t*) predominates;
        h provides only aspiration and emphasis.
i   sometimes consonantal and pronounced like English "y"
        iam ("now") would be pronounced *yam*.
qu   like *qu* in *quit*[b]
r   trilled with the tip of the tongue
s   always voiceless like *s* in *sit*
v[c]   like English *w*
double consonants (like the two *l*'s in *puella*, "girl") are both pronounced.

[a] Allen, *Vox Latina*, 23.
[b] The analogy is permissible but imperfect since English *qu* represents two sounds (*k*, *w*), and Latin *qu* is considered "a single labio-velar consonant." Allen, *Vox Latina*, 18.
[c] The letter *v* represents a consonantal *u*, which is often printed in scholarly texts. Thus, the word "man" can be spelled *vir* or *uir*, but in either case the first letter is pronounced like *w*.

    A Latin word contains as many syllables as it has vowels or diphthongs. Word accent follows a simple rule. It falls on the next to last syllable (penult) if that syllable is long or if the word has only two syllables (like *puto*, "think"). Otherwise it falls on the third to last syllable (antepenult). A syllable is long if it contains a long vowel or diphthong or if it is closed. Diphthongs are obvious, but long vowels must be learned by observation. In this chapter all long vowels are indicated with a macron or long mark (¯) above the letter. Quantities are also marked in Latin dictionaries. A syllable is closed if it ends with a consonant. In syllabification a single consonant goes with the following vowel, leaving the preceding syllable open; if there are two consonants, division takes place between them and the preceding syllable is closed.[2] Thus in the name *Catullus* the first syllable, *Ca-*, is open and the second, *-tul-*, is closed and thereby long; the accent falls on the next to last syllable: *Catúllus*. In the name *Lesbia*, the first syllable is closed (*Les-*), the second open (*-bi-*); since the *i* is short, the syllable is short, and the accent falls on the third to last syllable: *Lésbia*. The final syllable of any word may be open or closed; it is closed

Table 2: Pronunciation of Latin vowels and diphthongs

Vowels

a	like *a* in *about*
ā	like *a* in *father*
e	like *e* in *pet*
ē	like *a* in *plate*
i	like *i* in *pit*
ī	like the vowels in *feet*
o	like *o* in *pot*
ō	like *o* in *home*
u	like *u* in *put*
ū	like the vowels in *fool*
y[a]	like the vowels in *moo*

Diphthongs (two adjacent vowels sounded as one)

ae	like *ai* in *aisle*
au	like *ow* in *how*
ei	like *ei* in *reign*
eu	as short *e* combined with long *u*
oi or oe	like *oy* in *boy*
ui	like *ooey* in *gooey*

[a] The letter "y" appears in Latin only to represent a Greek upsilon (υ) as in *mnemosynum* ("souvenir," 12.13).

if it ends with a consonant and the following word begins with a consonant, open if the following word begins with a vowel. Note that the quantity of the vowel in a closed syllable may be long or short; closure does not affect it. (The *u* in *Catullus* and the *e* in *Lesbia* are both short; their syllables are long.) The words in the first two lines of poem 5 are pronounced and accented as follows.

> Vīvā́mus, mea Lésbia, átque amḗmus
> rūmṓrḗsque sénum sevēriṓrum.
> (Let us live, my Lesbia, and let us love,
> and [discount] the gossip of strict old men)

If one word ends in a vowel, and the next begins with a vowel, the result is called *hiatus* ("gaping"). English avoids some kinds of hiatus by adding a consonant (thus: "a baby", but "an infant"), but the solution in Latin verse is to *elide* (suppress) the final vowel of the first word. In the first verse above, for example, hiatus occurs both between *Lesbia* and *atque* and between *atque* and *amēmus*. The suppressed vowels (elisions) are shown in parentheses: *vīvāmus, mea Lesbi(a) atqu(e) amēmus*. The last three words would be pronounced: *Lesbi- atqu- amēmus*. Hiatus also occurs between a word ending in a vowel and one beginning with an *h* since *h* does not count as a consonant; the two words are elided, as in *intere(ā) haec* ("meanwhile, these things," 101.7). Since final *m* was weakly pronounced, hiatus was also felt if a word ending in *m* preceded a word beginning with a vowel; both the *m* and the preceding vowel were elided as in *sal(em) ac lepōrem* ("wit and charm," 16.7). If *es* or *est* ("you are," "he, she, it is") is the second word in hiatus after either a vowel or *m*, its *e* is suppressed; in this case the process is called *prodelision*. Examples of all three types of elision (between vowels, of final *m* before an initial vowel, and prodelision) are found in the first couplet of poem 87 (the whole poem is translated and discussed on p. 58 in chapter 3). The elisions are indicated with parentheses here and throughout this chapter.

> Nulla potest mulier tantum sē dīcer(e) amātam
> vērē, quant(um) ā mē Lesbi(a) amāta mea (e)s.

(No woman can truly say that she has been loved so much, my Lesbia, as you were loved by me.)

Elision is an important part of the poet's tool kit. It is used not only to avoid hiatus (its primary function), but also both to drop insignificant syllables (that is, syllables not needed for intelligibility) and to create evocative sound effects. In the couplet above, the final *e* of *dīcere*, the *um* of *quantum* and *e* of *est* are all easily dispensed with; without them the sense is still clear and the expression is sharper and more economical. The *a* in *Lesbia* is not necessary either (the syllables *Lesbi-* are enough to identify her), but the elision also creates the sound *Lesbi-amāta*, running together the words "Lesbia" and "loved." Catullus makes a more striking play on Lesbia's name in the first two lines of poem 58:

> Caelī, Lesbia nostra, Lesbi(a) illa,
> illa Lesbia

"Caelius, our Lesbia, that Lesbia, that Lesbia . . ." The name appears three times, the second time in an elision (*Lesbi-illa*) that turns it into a diminutive and an endearment by making the pronoun *illa* sound like a diminutive suffix. In the next line the order is reversed: *illa Lesbia*. The reversal is artful and emphatic in itself, but it also creates an echo of the endearing *illa*: *Lesbi-illa illa*. In poem 3 Catullus describes Lesbia's sparrow: *circumsiliēns mod(o) hūc mod(o) illūc* ("hopping about, now here, now there," 3.9). The elided words *mod- hūc mod- illūc* are onomatopoetic, wittily suggesting the hopping of the little bird. In poem 27 Catullus calls Postumia: *ēbriōs(ā) acin(ō) ēbriōsiōris* ("drunker than the drunken grape," 27.4). The elisions create a wonderfully slurred, tipsy sound: *ēbriōs- acin- ēbriōsiōris*. In poem 5 Catullus points out that nature is cyclical ("suns can set and rise again"), but human life is not: "we, when once our brief life has set, must sleep one never-ending night."[3]

> nōbīs, cum semel occidit brevis lux,
> nox est perpetu(a) ūna dormienda. (5.5–6)

The elision of *a* in *perpetua* in the second line makes that one night still longer and more unbroken. Hear the mournful *oo* sound created by joining the *u* in *perpetua* with that in *ūna*: *perpetu-ūna*.

Meters and Music

English meter is based on word accent or stress; its rhythms are patterns of stressed and unstressed syllables. Latin meter works differently.[4] It is quantitative, not accentual, and its rhythms are patterns of long and short syllables, not accented and unaccented ones. Strictly speaking, long syllables should be held or pronounced for a longer period of time than short syllables, not more strongly stressed or accented. But the distinction is not always easy to maintain, both since the ears of English speakers are more attuned to accentual than to quantitative rhythms and because the Latin language itself is strongly accentual. To put it another way, Latin meter is quantitative, but Latin words are pronounced with a stress accent. The poets often exploited this contradiction, particularly in certain meters, using a clash between the quantitative meter and the natural word accent to produce a complex rhythmical counterpoint.

A list of the poems in each of Catullus' meters is given in Appendix 1. In this section we will look at a few of the most frequent or important ones. In describing meters the conventional notation is – for a long syllable, ∪ for a short syllable, and × for a syllable that may be either long or short. It is important to note that in most meters the last syllable in the line is counted as long, regardless of its actual quantity.

Phalaecean Hendecasyllable

Catullus' most famous and characteristic meter is the phalaecean hendecasyllable, a light and graceful eleven-syllable line found in about two-thirds of the polymetrics (poems 1–60). It seems to have been a favorite meter of the neoterics. The pattern is described thus: × × – ∪ ∪ – ∪ – ∪ – –. The line usually opens with two long syllables in the shape called a spondee (– –), but Catullus sometimes uses ∪ – (an iamb) or – ∪ (a trochee) instead. Since the metrical beat and word accent often coincide, the verse produces a naturalistic, conversational effect. The basic rhythm will usually take care of itself if one pays close attention to word accent, vowel length, and elision. Poems 5, 27, and 58 discussed in the previous section are in hendecasyllables. Here are the first two verses from poem 3, on the death of the sparrow. The scansion (metrical pattern) and word accent are marked.

$$\bar{-}\,\bar{-}\quad\overset{/}{-}\,\overset{/}{\cup}\,\cup\,-\quad\overset{/}{\cup}\,-\,\cup\,\overset{/}{-}\,-$$
Lūgēt(e), ō Venerēs Cupīdinēsque
$$\overset{/}{-}\,\overset{/}{-}\,-\quad\overset{/}{\cup}\,\cup\,-\quad\overset{/}{\cup}\,-\,\cup\overset{/}{-}\,-$$
et quantum (e)st hominum venustiōrum:

(Mourn, o Venuses and Cupids / and all you men of finer feeling!)[5]

The meter looks more complicated than it is. A reader pronouncing the verses several times will start to recognize and feel certain patterns in the line. Two of the most striking are the sequences – ∪ ∪ – (as in *ō Venerēs* and *-um-st hominum*) in the middle and ∪ – – (as in *-inēsque* and *-iōrum*) at the end. There is generally (but not always) a word break after the fifth or sixth syllable (in these lines after the sixth). As a consequence, the end of the line naturally attracts certain word shapes and favors a characteristic kind of diction (diminutives, comparatives, genitive plurals). Memorable words like *Cupīdinēsque* and *venustiōrum* and formulas like *meae puellae* or *meōs amōrēs* gravitate to the end of the verse. Catullus sometimes playfully coins racy or obscene words for this position, like *cinaediōrem* ("shameless tramp," 10.24)[6] or *futūtiōnēs* ("fuckifications," 32.8). He also creates interesting sound effects by omitting or eliding over the word break, as in two of the verses we looked at in the previous section: *nox est perpetu(a) ūna dormienda* (5.6) and *ēbriōs(ā) acin(ō) ēbriōsioris* (27.4).

Sapphic Strophe

Catullus uses the sapphic strophe (named after the Greek poet Sappho) only twice, but in extremely important poems: 11, a powerful renunciation of Lesbia, and 51, the famous translation of a poem of Sappho that some critics have wanted to see as his first poem to Lesbia.[7] The stanza consists of four verses: three eleven-syllable lines in the pattern – ∪ – × – ∪ ∪ – ∪ – – and a short fourth line in the shape – ∪ ∪ – –. Here is the first stanza of poem 51.

$$- \cup\ -\ -\ -\ \cup\ \cup-\ \cup\ -\ -$$
Ille mī pār esse deō vidētur
$$- \cup\ -\ -\ -\ \ \cup\ \cup-\cup\ -\ -$$
ille, sī fās est, superāre dīvōs,
$$- \cup\ -\ -\ -\ \cup\ \cup-\ \cup\ -\ -$$
quī sedēns adversus identidem tē
$$- \cup\ \cup\ -\ -$$
spectat et audit

(That man seems to me to be equal to a god.
That man, if it is allowed, seems to surpass the gods,
who sitting opposite, again and again
watches and hears you.)

In this meter, as in the hendecasyllable, correct pronunciation makes the rhythm apparent, and certain patterns soon make themselves felt. The most noticeable cadence is that in the fourth line: – ∪ ∪ – –. This verse often contains striking expressions giving a sense of closure, as in the third stanza of 51, where Catullus describes the way in which seeing and hearing Lesbia snatches away all his senses:

$$- \ \cup\ -\ -\ -\ \cup\ \cup-\ \cup\ -\ -$$
lingua sed torpet, tenuis sub artūs
flamma dēmānat, sonitū suōpte
tintinant aurēs, geminā teguntur
$$- \ \cup\ \cup\ -\ -$$
lūmina nocte. (51.9–12)

> (But my tongue is numb, a thin flame runs down
> into my limbs, my ears ring with
> their own noise, my eyes are covered
> with twin night.)

I have translated *lūmina* in the last verse as "eyes," but its first meaning is "lights"; in the singular the word often connotes the light of life as opposed to the darkness of death. We cannot get all these ideas into English, but Catullus brings them before us in two words: *lūmina nocte* ("light, night"). In poem 11 the poet denounces Lesbia's promiscuity:

> null(um) amāns vērē, sed identid(em) omni(um)[8]
>   īlia rumpēns (11.19–20)
> (loving no man truly, but over and over again
> breaking the balls of all)

Here of course the striking phrase is *īlia rumpens* ("breaking the balls"). Another distinctive cadence can be heard at the ends of the long lines, which often have a word break after the fifth or sixth syllable. The rhythm of the phrase after the break may be either ∪ ∪ – ∪ – – as in 51.9–11 (*tenuis sub artūs, sonitū suōpte, gemina teguntur*) or ∪ – ∪ – – as in 51.1 and 51.3 (*deō vidētur, identidem tē*).

Iambics

Catullus makes frequent use of iambics, the second most common meter in the polymetrics. Iambic rhythm is close to the cadence of speech (it was the ordinary meter of Roman comedy). Like hendecasyllables and sapphics, it is relatively easy to read aloud. An iamb in its purest form takes the shape ∪ –. They are measured in groups of two, thus: ∪ – ∪ –. Such a group is called a metron ("measure"). A spondee (– –) can be substituted for the first iamb in the metron. Catullus uses pure iambic trimeter (with no substitutions) in poems 4 and 29; the line in each case consists of six iambs.[9] Here is the first line of poem 4 (the scansion and word accent are marked; the vertical line | shows the division between metra.)

$$\cup\;\acute{-}\;\cup\;\acute{-}\;|\;\cup\;\acute{-}\;\cup\;\acute{-}\;|\;\cup\;\acute{-}\;\cup\;-$$
Phasēlus ille, quem vidētis, hospitēs (4.1)

(That boat which you see, friends)

And the first two verses of 29, one of the poems attacking Caesar;

$$\acute{\cup} \; - \; \acute{\cup} \; - \; | \; \cup \; \acute{-} \; \cup \; \acute{-} \; | \; \cup \; \acute{-} \; \; \cup \acute{-}$$
Quis hoc potest vidēre, quis potest patī,
$$\acute{\cup} \; - \; \cup \; \acute{-} | \cup \; \acute{-} \; \; \cup \; \acute{-} | \cup \; \acute{-} \; \cup \acute{-}$$
nis(i) impudīcus et vorax et āleo (29.1–2)

(Who e'er could witness this, who could endure
Except the lewdling, dicer greedy-gut?)[10]

Pure iambics are rare. They are hard to write, and the unvarying alternation of short and long syllables becomes monotonous after a line or two. But the meter suits both 4 and 29. In 4 it evokes the rocking of a boat, and in 29 it has the sing-song quality of a scurrilous street chant.[11] Catullus uses another form of iambic trimeter much more frequently: choliambic (also called scazon or "limping" iambic). This meter allows substitutions and resolutions at two regular points in the line. The first and second metra may begin with either an iamb (∪ –) or a spondee (– –); the third metron always ends with a spondee.[12] The line may be represented thus (the vertical line | shows the division between metra): × – ∪ – | × – ∪ – | ∪ – – –. The verse is called limping because the three long syllables at the end of the line create a dragging effect. This effect is particularly emphasized in Catullus' attempt to renounce Lesbia in poem 8 (the whole poem is translated and discussed in chapter 3). Here are 3 verses from Catullus' self-address:

$$\acute{\cup} \; - \; \; \cup \; \acute{-}|- \; \; \acute{-} \; \; \cup \; \acute{-}|\cup \; \; \acute{-} \; \; \acute{-} \; \acute{-}$$
sed obstinātā mente perfer, obdūrā.
$$\acute{\cup}- \; \; \cup \acute{-}|\cup \; \; \acute{-} \; \; \; \; \cup \acute{-}|\cup \; - \; \; \acute{-} \; \acute{-}$$
valē, puella. iam[13] Catullus obdūrat,
$$\acute{-} \; \; \acute{-} \; \cup \; \acute{-}|- \; \; \acute{-} \; \; \cup \; \acute{-}|\cup \; - \; \; \acute{-} \; \acute{-}$$
nec tē requīret nec rogābit invītam. (8.11–13)

(But harden your heart and endure. Stand fast.
Good-bye, girl. Now Catullus is standing fast,
and he won't seek you out or ask you against your will.)

Each line is end-stopped, containing a complete sense unit, and each ends with a slow, emphatic cadence in which sound and meaning come together – – – : *obdūrā, obdūrat, invītam* ("stand fast," "is standing fast," "against your will"). We find *obdūrā* again as the last word of the poem, again in the final position: *at tū, Catulle, dēstinātus obdūrā* ("but you, Catullus, keep your mind made up, stand fast," 8.19).

Galliambic

Catullus' most astonishing meter is the galliambic, the meter of poem 63—and of 63 alone, since no other complete Latin poem in galliambics survives.[14] The meter takes its name from the Galli (or Gallae), the castrated priests of the Phrygian goddess Cybele; its rushing rhythms represent their frenzied rites. Catullus uses it to tell the story of young Attis, who castrates himself in a moment of religious enthusiasm, leads his followers in an ecstatic dance, wakens to regret his decision, and is ultimately enslaved by the goddess. The details of the meter are complex.[15] Here it is enough to point out that the typical line consists of sixteen mostly short syllables with a strong word break (diaeresis) in the center of the line and that most lines end with a run of four short syllables before a final long. Two short syllables (∪ ∪) are often replaced by one long (−) and vice versa. The meter produces an effect of confusion and frenzy appropriate to the crazed priests of the goddess. It would have sounded nearly as strange to Roman ears as it does to ours with its unusual number of short syllables, its loose light rhythm at the end of the line, and the relentless beat brought about by its nearly invariable strongly sounded break in the middle of the line. These lines from Attis' encouragement of his comrades should convey some impression of the wonderful noise that Catullus makes with this meter. The mid-line word break is marked with ||.

> Phrygi(am) ad domum Cybēbēs, || Phyrygi(a) ad nemora deae,
> ubi cymbalum sonat vox, || ubi tympana reboant,
> tibicēn ubi canit Phryx || curvō grave calamō,
> ubi capita Maenadēs vī || iaciunt[16] hederigerae,
> ubi sacra sanct(a) acūtīs | ululātibus agitant,
> ubi suēvit illa dīvae || volitāre vaga cohors,
> quō nōs decet citātīs || celerāre tripudiīs. (63.20–6)

(To the Phrygian home of Cybebe, to the Phrygian groves of the
   goddess,
where the voice of the cymbals sounds, where the drums boom back,
where the Phrygian fluteplayer sounds a low note with his curved reed,
where the ivy-crowned Maenads violently toss their heads,
where they celebrate their holy rites with shrill shrieks,
where the wandering tribe of the goddess likes to fly,
there we should hurry on swift pounding feet.)

This is a meter that demands to be read aloud, and it is hard to stop once one has started to get a sense of the beat. The most striking feature is the word break. It divides each line in half, strongly closing the first segment with two long syllables (– –), the only regularly occurring pair of long syllables found in the meter. The metrical emphasis (sometimes called the *ictus*) falls on the first of these long syllables, but the natural word accent may or may not. When it does not, there is a clash between meter and pronunciation, between ictus and accent, and the resulting sound can be strange and exciting. Such a clash occurs in the second line above in the words *sonat vox*. The natural word accents fall on the first syllable of *sónat* and on the monosyllable *vóx*, but the metrical emphasis is not on either one, but instead on the *second* syllable of *sonat*. The same thing happens in the next two lines with *cánit Phryx* and *Maenádēs vī*. Anyone who reads the poem aloud will come upon many exotic sound combinations. My favorite is that in line 22: *tibicēn ubi canit Phryx* (the clash of metrical stress and word accent in combination with the strange-sounding word *Phryx* is harsh and exotic—it hardly sounds like Latin at all). The strong word break can also create echoes of sound and sense between the two parts of the line, as in the first verse above, where *Phrygi(am) ad domum Cybēbēs* ("to the Phrygian home of Cybebe") is echoed by *Phyrygi(a) ad nemora deae* ("to the Phrygian groves of the goddess"). In this meter frenzied speed is everything—hence the plethora of short syllables and the long runs of them at line end. But since the meter allows substitution of a long syllable for two shorts, it can also slow down dramatically, as it does in Attis' anguished words of regret when he comes to his senses:

/ / /   / /   / /   /
– – ᴜ – ᴜ – –   – –   ᴜ – ᴜ–
iam iam dolet quod ēgī, | | iam iamque paenitet. (63.73)

(Now, now I rue what I have done, now, now I regret it.)

Dactylic Hexameter

Catullus uses dactylic hexameter in two poems: 62 and 64, the one a wedding song or epithalamium, the other his long epyllion on the wedding of Peleus and Thetis.[17] This meter is counted in metrical units called feet. The line contains six feet; each of the first four may be either a dactyl (– ∪ ∪) or a spondee (– –), its metrical equivalent. The fifth foot is usually a dactyl and the sixth is always a spondee. The verse may be represented thus (the vertical line | shows the division between feet):

$$- \cup \cup |- \cup \cup |- \cup \cup |- \cup \cup |- \cup \cup |- -.$$
$$----------$$

Here are the first three lines of poem 64:

$$-\overset{/}{\cup\cup}\,|- \quad \overset{/}{-}\,| \;- \quad -\,|\overset{/}{--} \quad |\overset{/}{-}\cup\cup|\overset{/}{-}\;-$$
Pēliacō quondam prognātae vertice pīnūs

$$--\,|\;-\;\overset{/}{\cup}\cup\,|- \quad -\,|\overset{/}{-}-|\overset{/}{-}\cup\cup|\overset{/}{-}\;-$$
dīcuntur liquidās Neptūnī nāsse per undās

$$-\cup\cup|- \quad \overset{/}{-}|\;-\;-\;|\overset{/}{-}\;-\;|\overset{/}{--}$$
Phāsidos ad fluctūs et fīnēs Aeētaeōs. (64.1–3)

(Once upon a time pines born on Pelion's peak
are said to have floated through the clear waves of Neptune
to the streams of Phasis and the territory of Aeëtes.)

Since Latin has a large number of long syllables, Catullus' hexameter tends to have a high proportion of spondees. He often has a spondee in the fifth foot, a favorite neoteric mannerism that he uses especially at the end of a passage or to mark high emotion. The third line above not only has a fifth-foot spondee, but is made up almost entirely of spondees; only the first foot is a dactyl.

The hexameter is a wonderfully complex and subtle instrument for verbal music. Its basis, of course, is the line of six feet, with one line following another in succession. Each line has a fundamental rhythm of six beats, with the metrical pulse or ictus falling on the first long syllable of each foot. But that pulse or ictus need not coincide with the word accent. When the accent and ictus do not coincide, the clash sets up a counterpoint, so that we feel two rhythms at once: one inherent in the quantitative meter, and the other in the stress accents of the words. In the first line above, for example, we can mark the first long syllable of each foot (the site of the metrical ictus) by * or ˣ, with * representing a coincidence of ictus and accent and ˣ showing a clash.

$$^\text{x}\cup\cup|^\text{x} \ - \ |^\text{x} \ \ -| \ ^* -| \ ^* \cup\cup| \ ^* -$$
Pēliacō quondam prognātae vertice pīnūs

The ictus and accent clash in the first three feet, coincide in the last three. In other verses the clash may be more or less extensive. Ictus and accent almost always coincide in the last two feet—a practice that keeps our ear from losing the metrical rhythm. It is important to appreciate and understand these rhythmical complexities of the hexameter, but just as with the other meters, correct pronunciation is the key to reading it aloud. The best approach is to observe vowel and syllabic quantities and word accent, and "to let the ... metre make itself felt as an undercurrent."[18]

The hexameter line is characterized by regular internal pauses dividing it into segments. The segments often coincide with sense units or sound patterns or both; they provide the phrasing of the poetry—another counterpoint to the line-after-line succession of dactyls and spondees. Almost every hexameter line has a word break (caesura) within the third foot, usually after the first long syllable. It may also have a break between feet (diaeresis) between the fourth and fifth foot. Each of the three lines above has both a third-foot caesura and a diaeresis after the fourth foot. We can show the divisions thus:

Pēliacō quondam	prognātae	vertice pīnūs
dīcuntur liquidās	Neptūnī	nāsse per undās
Phāsidos ad fluctūs	et fīnēs	Aeētaeōs.

The segments show striking alliteration. In the first line: *Pēliacō, prognātae, pīnūs*. In the second, *Neptūnī, nāsse*. In the third *fluctūs, fīnēs*. Once we think in terms of segments and phrasing, we can also notice striking sound patterns or rhymes, especially in the segments created by the caesura. There is a rhyme in the second line (-*ās* in *liquidās* and *undās*, and an even more interesting one between the first and third line (-*ūs* in *pīnūs* at the end of line 1 rhyming with -*us* in *fluctūs* at the end of the first segment in line 3). Each of the middle segments (*prognātae, Neptūnī, et fīnēs*) has three long syllables (– – –), a pattern so common in poem 64 that Ross has observed, "This rhythm says 'Catullus' just as unmistakably, and as audibly, as the opening chords of the Fifth Symphony say 'Beethoven.'"[19]

We can see (and hear) another nice example of phrasing in Ariadne's lament after Theseus has abandoned her on a desert island.

$$- \cup \cup\ |- \quad \cup\cup|- \qquad -|- \quad - \ | \ - \quad \cup\cup| \ - \ -$$
nulla fugae ratio,　　nulla[20] spēs: omnia mūta,
omnia sunt dēsert(a), ostentant　　omnia lētum. (64.186–7)

(There is no means of escape, no hope. Everything is silent, everything is desolate, everything shows forth death.)

The lines display an artful pattern of anaphora—first of "no" in the first and second segments of the first line (*nulla, nulla*) and then of "everything" (*omnia*), which heads the last segment of 186 and the first and last of 187. The second line is formally divided into three segments by its caesura and diaeresis, as our spacing demonstrates, but if we read it with attention to meaning, we will find only two phrases or sense units. We will hear it thus: *omnia sunt dēsert(a), ostentant omnia lētum*. And since the elision in *dēsert(a)* blurs the caesura, we must make only a very short pause before *ostentant*, as if we were just catching our breath before the final and most powerful statement: "everything shows forth death."

Elegiac Couplet

Elegiac couplet is the meter of Catullus' fifty-one elegies and epigrams (poems 65–116), more poems than he wrote in any other meter. The first line of the couplet is dactylic hexameter; the second the so-called pentameter, which consists of two segments divided by an obligatory word break (diaeresis). Each segment contains two and one-half dactylic feet, so that the line is considered to have a total of five feet, hence the name pentameter. In the first half of the pentameter dactyls and spondees are interchangeable; dactyls are obligatory in the second. The couplet may be represented thus (a single vertical line | shows the division between feet; in the pentameter a double vertical line | | represents diaeresis):

dactylic hexameter: $-\cup\cup|-\cup\cup|-\cup\cup|-\cup\cup|-\cup\cup|--$.
pentameter: 　　　　$-\cup\cup|-\cup\cup|-||-\cup\cup|-\cup\cup|-$.

Elegiacs produce a characteristic effect: the hexameter moves forward (sometimes rapidly) and the pentameter slows down, retarded by its diaeresis and the single long syllable at line end. The couplet can also be seen as rising and falling. A generation after Catullus, Ovid remarked of his own elegiacs:

> sex mihi surgat opus numerīs, in quīnque resīdat. (*Amores* 1.1.27)
> (Let my work rise up in six feet, sink back in five.)[21]

Here are the first two couplets from poem 72 (the whole epigram is translated and discussed in chapter 2). The spacing indicates the principal segments or phrases created by caesura and diaeresis.

```
  – –| –   – | –        –| –   – |– U  U|– –
  Dīcēbās quondam       sōlum tē nōsse Catullum,
    – UU| –   –|  – ||      – U U|– U  U|–
    Lesbia, nec prae mē     velle tenēre Iovem.
  ––|– –   | –        – | –      – | – U U|– –
  Dīlexī tum tē         nōn tant(um) ut vulgus amīcam,
    –  U U| –   –|–  ||    –U U| –   U U|–
    sed pater ut gnātōs     dīligit et generōs.    (72 1–4)
```

(Once upon a time you used to say that you knew Catullus alone, Lesbia, and that you did not wish to hold even Jupiter in preference to me. I cherished you then not as an ordinary man cherishes a mistress, but as a father cherishes his sons and sons-in-law.)

Perhaps the first thing one hears in this passage is the hammering series of five long syllables in the first segment of each couplet: *dīcēbās quondam*, *dīlexī tum tē*. In fact, the two couplets are metrically identical, each containing exactly the same series of longs and shorts. This is an angry poem, and the exactly repeated rhythm pounds its message home. The rhythmic pattern is modulated in the second half of the epigram (lines 5–8), but the first segment of line 5 repeats the five-stroke beat of the first two couplets: *nunc tē cognōvī* ("now I know you"). As often in elegiacs, each couplet contains a complete thought. The segments respond to each other in an almost symmetrical way, and essential words are artfully disposed at the beginnings and ends of lines. In the first couplet: "you said," "Catullus," "Lesbia," "Jupiter." In the second, "I loved," "mistress," "father," "sons-in-law." The two couplets are aurally linked not only by their identical rhythm, but also by the assonance of *ē*, which is especially prominent in the monosyllabic pronouns *tē* ("you"), *mē* ("me"), *tē*, and in the rhyme, *mē / tē*, at the ends of the first segments of lines 2 and 3. The two segments of line 4 end in the rhyming cognates *gnātōs* ("sons") and *generōs* ("sons in law").

Words

Catullus uses a rich and diverse vocabulary, some of which he seems to have coined himself.[22] His varied language takes us across social classes and literary genres, letting us hear the accents of polite and not so polite Roman society. His poems do not speak the way real people spoke (they are poems, after all), but they draw on real speech of several registers, as well as on a wide range of literary language from several traditions and time periods. His educated contemporaries might have blended some of these registers in their own speech in the same way that people today often use jargon or slang or foreign words in conversation. But they would not have used all of them. As native speakers they would have been able to hear and appreciate the artifice of Catullus' poetic language, picking up sudden shifts of register and noticing his audacious neologisms.

The poems use diction from several sources: the language of social performance, diminutives, vulgarisms (including slang and obscenities), poetic compounds, Grecisms, archaisms, the language of aristocratic friendship, and "prosaic" or neutral vocabulary. Words from all these categories appear in all three parts of the collection (polymetrics, long poems, epigrams), but not with equal frequency. The language of social performance is most frequent in the polymetrics, while that of aristocratic friendship is most frequent in the epigrams. Obscenity is common in the polymetrics and epigrams, rare in the long poems. Diminutives appear in the polymetrics and long poems, much less often in the epigrams. The sharpest distinction in usage is between the polymetrics and long poems on the one hand and the epigrams on the other. The epigrams are different stylistically from the other parts of the collection: more austere and less playful linguistically, although at least equally obscene.

The Polymetrics

The polymetrics are written in a lively, natural-sounding idiom spiced with diminutives, the language of social performance, and vulgarisms. Diminutives were a standard part of the Latin vocabulary, formed by adding regular suffixes like *-ulus/ -olus*, *-culus*, *-ellus/ -illus* to the stems of nouns and adjectives. Thus *liber* ("book"), *libellus* ("little book," 1.1), *mollis* ("soft"), *molliculus* ("a little soft," 16.4, 8). Diminutives suggest smallness of size, but also of value or degree, and they can also express pity, affection, or disdain; sometimes they suggest delicacy (Juventius is *flosculus . . . Iuventiōrum*, "tender flower of the Iuventii," 24.1). We glanced at social performance in chapter 3, defining it as "the behavior praised or blamed by the devotees of *urbanitas*."[23] Its lexicon includes many of the words we associate most with Catullus—such words as *lepidus* ("charming"), *venustus* ("attractive"), (*bellus*, "nice"), *facētus* ("witty"), *ēlegans* ("tasteful") and their opposites—but it was also in more general use in elite society, where performance was everything.[24] Vulgarisms include not only obscenities, but slang, oaths, neologisms, and other lexical and grammatical features of everyday low class speech.[25]

Catullus made diminutives a signature feature of his poetry. Many were already available in literary and colloquial language, and he coined many more. He uses an impressive run of both old and made-up diminutives in these lines from his attack on Caesar and Mamurra in poem 57. The diminutives are shown in boldface. The meter is hendecasyllabic.

> morbōsī pariter, **gemell(ī)** utrīque,
> ūn(ō) in **lecticul(ō) ērudītul(ī)** ambō,
> nōn hīc qu(am) ille magis vorax adulter,
> rīvālēs soci(ī) et **puellulārum**. (57.6–9)
> (Equally diseased, a pair of **little twins**,
> both **little scholars** in one **little study couch**,[26]
> not one adulterer more greedy than the other,
> rivals sharing in **little girls**, too.)

In the previous section I noted that Catullus often places striking phrases after the word break in his hendecasyllables. These verses are a nice case in point. Verses 6, 8, and 9 all have a word break after the sixth syllable; the phases after the break are *gemell(ī) utrīque* ("a pair of little twins"), *vorax adulter* ("greedy adulterer"), and *puellulārum* ("little girls"). In line 7 he slides over the break with an elision (*lecticul(ō) ērudītulī*), one of three in the verse; the successive elisions cram "the little scholars" (*ērudītulī*) even more tightly into their "one little study couch." The word *ērudītulī* seems to be a Catullan coinage.

Poem 6 provides a fine example of concentrated use of performance terms and vulgarisms (and of a possible diminutive). Performance terms are shown in boldface. The meter is hendecasyllabic.

> Flāvī, dēliciās tuās Catullō,   1
> ni sint **illepid(ae)** atqu(e) **inēlegantēs**,

vellēs dīcere nec tacēre possēs.
Vērum nescioquid febrīculōsī
scortī dīligis: hoc pudet fatērī.   5
Nam tē nōn viduās iacēre noctēs
nēquīquam tacitum cubīle clāmat
sertīs ac Syriō fragrans olīvō,
pulvīnusque peraequ(e) et hīc et ille
attrītus, tremulīque quassa lectī   10
argūtāti(ō) inambulātiōque.
Nam nil stupra valet, nihil, tacēre.
Cūr? nōn tam later(a) effutūta pandās,
nī tū quid faciās **ineptiārum**.
Quārē, quidquid habēs bonī malīque,   15
dīc nōbīs. Volo t(ē) ac tuōs amōrēs
ad caelum **lepidō** vocāre versū.

(Flavius, you would want to tell Catullus about your sweetheart and you wouldn't be able to keep quiet if she wasn't **without charm and taste**. The truth is that you're in love with some fever-ridden whore. You are ashamed to admit it. For you aren't spending your nights alone. Your bed may be silent, but it shouts, smelling of garlands and Syrian olive, and so do this pillow and that one dented equally and the shaken creaking and back-and-forth motion of the rickety bedstead. For it is of no use (none!) to keep quiet about your debauchery. Why? You wouldn't be sprawling such fucked-out limbs if you weren't doing something **stupid**. So tell us what you've got, good and bad. I want to call you and your darling to the sky in **charming** verse.)

In this poem everyone is judged on performance: Flavius' girlfriend, deemed sight unseen to be "without charm and taste"; Flavius, shown by his appearance to have been doing "something stupid"; and Catullus himself, with his promise to celebrate the pair "in charming verse." But no one actually performs. The girl is described in her absence, Flavius says not a word, and Catullus' "charming verse" is not yet written, or so he implies (this is an important point, and we will come back to it). The word *tacēre* ("to keep quiet") is used three times: twice of Flavius (*tacēre*, 3 and 12) and once of the bed (*tacitum*, 7), which still manages to shout (*clāmat*, 7) about his activities. The only *actual* noise in the poem is "the shaken creaking and back-and-forth motion of the rickety bedstead":

tremulīque quassa lectī
argūtāti(ō) inambulātiōque. (6.10–11)

The word *argūtātiō* ("creaking") seems to be a Catullan coinage. It is elided with *inambulātiōque* to produce an unbroken rocking and rolling succession of syllables (*argūtāti- inambulātiōque*) in a suggestive onomatopoetic line (11) that Tracy considered perhaps "the most remarkable hendecasyllable ever written."[27] The word *tremulī* in line 10, which I have translated "rickety," sounds like a diminutive (compare *ērudītulī*, "little scholars," in poem 57 above).[28] The poem is shocking in its use of coarse and obscene language; the shock value is increased by its position in the collection. It is the first poem to use such language, and it is positioned between the two kiss poems to Lesbia, which are completely different in tone. Catullus claims that Flavius' girl must be a "fever-ridden whore" (*febrīculōsī / scortī*, 4–5). Neither word is obscene, but *febrīculōsus* is a vulgarism found in comedy and *scortum* is ugly (Catullus uses it nowhere else).[29] The word *effutūta* ("fucked-out," 13) is, of course, highly obscene. It is also a Catullan coinage, one of several such coinages in the polymetrics (compare *diffutūta*, 29.13; *confutuēre*, 37.5; *dēfutūta*, 41.1; *futūtiōnēs*, 32.8). Catullus ends the poem with a wish to celebrate Flavius' affair "in charming verse," but in fact he has already done so. As Wiseman observes, "poem 6 is the fulfilment of its own promise."[30] We might add that poem 6 is also a concrete demonstration of "charming verse" (*lepidō versū*). With its focus on performance, play on silence and speech, description of the "shouting bed," notable neologism and sound pattern in line 11, and shocking obscene coinage in 13, it spells out what Catullus had in mind when he promised "a charming new little book" (*lepidum novum libellum*) in poem 1. Now we know what *lepidus* means.

The Long Poems

The long poems (61–68) are not homogeneous in meter or style, and their subjects are diverse (although they all have a preoccupation with marriage). But except for poem 67 they share some striking vocabulary, particularly Grecisms, diminutives, and compounds formed in the Greek manner. Often such words are used in the same verse or in close proximity to each other.

Greek names and Greek case endings are particularly common in poems 63, 64, 65, 66, and 68. Each of these poems is Greek in some way, whether in using an Alexandrian meter such as galliambic (63) or an Alexandrian genre such as the epyllion (64), in translating an

Alexandrian poem (66), in alluding to Greek poetry (64, 65) or in treating stories from Greek myth (64, 68). Each is conspicuously neoteric: learned, allusive, constructed with minute attention to sound, word patterning, and metrical effects. The opening lines of poem 64 contain several striking Grecisms. We looked at these verses in the discussion of the dactylic hexameter. Here they are again. The Grecisms are shown in boldface.

> **Pēliacō** quondam prognātae vertice pīnūs
> dīcuntur liquidās Neptūnī nāsse per undās
> **Phāsidos** ad fluctūs et fīnēs **Aeētaeōs**. (64.1–3)
> (Once upon a time pines born on **Pelion's** peak
> are said to have floated through the clear waves of Neptune
> to the streams of **Phasis** and the territory of **Aeëtes**.)

The verses plunge us—elliptically and allusively—into the tale of the Argonauts and their voyage to capture the golden fleece. They sailed in the Argo, which was made of pine timbers from Mt. Pelion, to the kingdom of the cruel king Aeëtes near the river Phasis on the Black Sea. The words *Pēliacō* and *Aeētaeōs* are both adjectival forms of proper names ("pertaining to Pelion" and "Aeëtean"), which somehow feel more learned and less real than the names themselves. As Sheets puts it, "these are not so much places as ideas of place."[31] *Phasidos* ("of Phasis") is a Greek genitive. Poem 68 contains a verse that is completely Greek in its language and almost too neoteric in its learning. The verse is a pentameter (the second line of an elegiac couplet).

> audit falsiparens Amphitryōniadēs (68.112).
> (the son falsely ascribed to Amphitryon is said [to have])

The reference is to Hercules, son of Zeus. (Zeus had disguised himself as Amphitryon to lie with Amphitryon's wife.) *Amphitryōniadēs* ("son of Amphitryon") is a Greek patronymic that completely occupies the second half of the verse. Catullus modifies it with a Greek-sounding poetic compound of his own manufacture: *falsiparens* ("of false parentage").[32] He uses *audit* (literally "hears") in imitation of the Greek verb *akouein* ("hear"), which often means "hear it said of oneself," or "be said (to)." Greek vocabulary, myth, word formation, and usage—all are represented (and in only three words at that) in this extraordinary verse.

Diminutives are as frequent in the long poems as in the polymetrics. Catullus often shows them off with elegant word order or by putting them with poetic compounds or Grecisms. There is even a striking example in poem 67, which otherwise has little diction in common with the other long poems. Here it is. The diminutive is shown in boldface. The spacing indicates the principal segments or phrases created by caesura and diaeresis.

> languidior tenerā   cui pendens   **sīcula** bēta. (67.21)
> (his **little dagger** hanging droopier than a soft beet)

The *sīcula* ("little dagger") is the penis of an impotent old man. Catullus has coined the diminutive from *sīca* ("dagger"). The middle segment, *cui pendens*, has the three long syllables (– – –) that Ross identified as a characteristically Catullan rhythm (the same cadence appears in the other hexameter verses discussed in this paragraph). The sense of the line is coarse, but its words are arranged with neoteric care.[33] If we overlook *cui* ("his"), the verse contains two adjective-noun pairs arrayed in an interlocking order around a verb form. The order is: adjective a (*languidior*, "droopier"), adjective b (*tenerā*, "soft"), verb (the participle *pendens*, "hanging"), noun A (*sīcula*, "little dagger"), noun B (*bētā*, "beet"). A verse with its words arranged in this way constitutes a Golden Line, a form that Dryden memorably described as: "that verse which they call Golden, of two substantives and two adjectives with a verb betwixt to keep the peace."[34] This stylish arrangement was particularly favored by the neoterics, and Catullus uses it often, particularly in poem 64. It appears in a verse with two diminutives in the description of the Parcae or Fates at the wedding of Peleus and Thetis. The Parcae are spinning the thread of the future of the unborn Achilles; flecks of wool cling to their lips as they smooth the thread with their teeth. The diminutives are shown in boldface. The meter is dactylic hexameter. The spacing indicates the principal segments created by caesura and diaeresis.

> lāneaqu(e) **āridulīs**   haerēbant   morsa **labellīs** (64.316)
> (and bits of wool stuck to their poor dry old lips.)

The order is adjective a (*lānea*, "of wool"), adjective b (*āridulīs*, "poor dry"), verb (*haerēbant*, "stuck"), noun A (*morsa*, "bits"), noun B (*labellīs*, "old lips"). In poem 67 Catullus used a diminutive to express size; here diminutives express pathos. The word *labellīs* is fairly common, but *āridulīs* is not: in classical Latin it occurs only here and in Catullus' fellow neoteric Cinna.[35] In poem 65 Catullus uses a pathetic diminutive and elegant word order in this couplet on his brother's death (the diminutive is shown in boldface). The spacing indicates the principal segments created by caesura and diaeresis in the two lines.

> namque meī nūper   Lēthae(ō) in   gurgite fratris
>   **pallidulum** mānāns   alluit unda pedem. (65.5–6)
> (For just now in the Lethean stream the running water has washed over my brother's **poor pale** foot.)

Lēthaeō ("Lethean") in the hexameter is an adjectival form of a Greek proper name. The five words in the pentameter are arranged in another favorite neoteric pattern. In this arrangement the verb is still placed in the center, and the two adjective-noun pairs that frame it are placed in concentric order (ab verb BA): adjective a (*pallidulum*, ("poor pale"), adjective b (*mānāns*, "running"), verb (*alluit*, "has washed"), noun B (*unda*, "water"), noun A (*pedem*, "foot"). Catullus makes a different use of diminutive and word order in the galliambics of poem 63. The diminutive is shown in boldface. The mid-line word break is marked with ‖.

> rapidae ducem sequuntur ‖ Gallae properipedem.
> itaqu(e), ut domum Cybēbēs ‖ tetigēre **lassulae** (63.34–5)
> (The swift Gallae follow their fleet-foot leader.
> And so when they reach the house of Cybebe **all worn out**)

The diminutive coinage *lassulae* tells us not that the Gallae were "a little weary," but that they were utterly exhausted. The word also contributes metrically to the sense of exhaustion. A galliambic verse typically ends with a rush of short syllables, but the metrical shape of *lassulae* (– ∪ –) slows everything down. At the end of the previous line we find another coinage that presents a sharp contrast with *lassulae* in both sense and rhythm, the compound *properipedem* ("fleet-foot"), which has five short syllables in succession. *Cybēbēs* ("of Cybebe") in the second line is a Greek name with a Greek genitive ending.

The Epigrams

The epigrams use a vocabulary less notable for what it contains (terms of aristocratic friendship, obscenities and vulgarisms, and ordinary, neutral language) than for the conspicuous kinds of words it uses sparingly or not at all: diminutives, Grecisms, and performance language. The resulting diction feels very different from that of the polymetrics and long poems: unadorned and spare but correspondingly powerful, whether it is used for love poetry, mourning, or invective.

The most characteristic feature of the language of the epigrams is its ordinariness or neutrality—words that are not metaphorical, or Greekish, or obscene, or part of a special lexicon like that of performance or aristocratic friendship, but rather the basic substance (the nuts and bolts, we could say) of good literary and spoken Latin. Some scholars call such language "prosaic," but both since it is not confined to prose and because the English word *prosaic* wrongly suggests something banal or pedestrian, it is more accurate simply to call it neutral or ordinary.[36] In poem 85 Catullus deploys this neutral language to powerful effect.[37] We looked at this famous epigram in chapter 2. Here it is again.

Ōd(ī) et amō. quār(ē) id faciam, fortasse requīris.
    nescio, sed fierī senti(ō) et excrucior. (85)
(I hate and I love. Perhaps you ask why I do this. I do not know, but I feel it happening and I am in torment.)

There is nothing fancy here—just simple words of a kind that one might find in any passage of classical poetry or prose. Part of the force comes from the fact that 7 of the 14 words in the epigram are finite verbs (6 of them in the first person, a fact that keeps our attention on the actions and feelings of the speaker), but the rest is achieved by a distillation of feelings and form. The feelings are hatred and love, an inability to explain the paradox, and the pain that results from it. The form is that of the epigram reduced to one of its essential shapes: a question (why?) and an answer, which in this case is no answer at all but a restatement of anguish. (Ezra Pound brilliantly caught the idea with his translation of *nescio*, "I do not know," as "It beats me."[38]) The sounds of this poem are as understated as the vocabulary, but as always with Catullus, it is important to listen to the elisions. The elision in the second verse (*senti(ō) et*) produces a sound effect with *excrucior* that makes the poem end with a sob: *senti- et excrucior*.

At least half of Catullus' 48 epigrams are invectives, and most are obscene in language or implication or both. Poem 74 is one of several epigrams directed against Gellius (the others are 80, 88, 89, 90, 91, 116).

> Gellius audierat patru(um) obiurgāre solēre   1
>   si quis dēliciās dīceret aut faceret.
> hoc n(ē) ips(ī) accideret, patruī perdepsuit ipsam
>   uxōr(em) et patruum reddidit Harpocratēn.
> quod voluit fēcit: nam quamvīs irrumet ipsum   5
>   nunc patruum, verbum non faciet patruus.

(Gellius had heard that his uncle liked to scold if anyone talked about or indulged in love affairs. So that this wouldn't happen to him, he thoroughly banged his uncle's own wife and turned his uncle into Harpocrates. He accomplished his wish. For however much he stuffs the uncle himself now, the uncle won't make a sound.)

The epigram is a carefully constructed obscene joke exploiting the fact that the Egyptian god Harpocrates was a watchword for silence since he was represented with a finger to his mouth. In the first couplet we learn of the uncle's tendency to scold. In the second Gellius takes action, banging his uncle's wife and turning the uncle into Harpocrates. The epigram could have stopped there, with the uncle seemingly stricken to silence by the shame of being cuckolded. But there is more to come. In the third couplet Catullus delivers the punch line, letting us see just how Gellius made his uncle Harpocrates: it isn't outrage but oral rape that keeps him quiet. The word *irrumet* ("stuffs") in line 5 is a common obscenity. Catullus has apparently coined *perdepsuit* ("thoroughly banged") in line 3; it is a compound of the intensive prefix *per* and *depso* ("knead"), a word considered offensive but not actually obscene.[39] He emphasizes it with the sound pattern of the line; the sound *ps* is heard three times: *ips(ī) . . . perdepsuit ipsam*.

The language of aristocratic friendship appears much more often in the epigrams than in any other part of the collection. This is the language that Roman (male) aristocrats used almost as a technical vocabulary to describe the morality of their social relations with each other, whether in politics, with kinsmen, in simple friendship, or even in financial transactions.[40] It includes words like *foedus* ("compact"), *fides* ("fidelity," "loyalty"), *officium* ("duty," "service"), *bene velle* ("to wish well," "to feel good will toward"), *pietas* ("dutifulness," "sense of obligation"), and *pius* ("feeling a sense of obligation"). As we saw in chapter 3, Catullus uses it to describe the relationship he wants to have with Lesbia, trying to move their affair from the purely erotic into a realm of serious reciprocity and commitment. Although his wishes are in vain, the attempt is one of the most original and moving aspects of his poetry. But he also uses the vocabulary in other contexts. In poem 110 he charges Aufillena with what amounts to breach of contract (*fraudand(ō) officiīs*, "cheating on her obligations," 110.7) for not performing sexually as she promised. In 102 he allies himself with those whose (*fidēs animī*, "loyalty of spirit, 102.2) makes them worthy confidants. In 73 he complains of ingratitude from a former friend and tells himself to "stop imagining that anyone can made to feel a sense of obligation" (*dēsine . . . / . . . aliquem fierī posse putāre pium*, 73.2). There is something poignant in Catullus' use of this solemn language, perhaps because he characterizes himself as virtually the only adherent to the values it represents. If it is to be efficacious and meaningful, a language of social commitment must speak to a like-minded community, but no such community exists in Catullus' poetry.

Conclusion

Sound, rhythm, language, and something to say. In this chapter I have tried to bring these elements of poetry together to suggest the extent and intricacy of Catullus' art—how he gives voice to his ideas and lets us hear them, and how those ideas gain in interest and meaning by the ways in which they are expressed. In a recent book on Yeats, Helen Vendler makes a comment that is as true of the ancient poet as of the modern one. She says: "In poetry, as in all the arts, the 'gazing heart' remains the center, but it doubles its might by its own proper means: diction, prosody, structural evolution, a sense of perfected shape."[41] In considering sounds and words and particular rhythmical effects we have thought about some of Vendler's "proper means"—the building blocks, we could say, of Catullus' poetry. In studying his meters we have begun to explore the rest, his poems' "structural evolution" and "sense of perfected shape." We will continue our exploration in the next chapter, on the architecture of the poems.

Notes

1   See, esp., Allen, *Vox Latina: The Pronunciation of Classical Latin*. Helpful accounts may also be found in Moreland and Fleischer, *Latin: An Intensive Course*, 1–4, and Wheelock, *Wheelock's Latin*, xxxix–xliv, and online at http://www.wheelockslatin.com (which includes recordings of the pronunciation).

2. But four important details should be noted.
    1. If the consonant pair consists of a mute (*b, p, d, t, g, c*) + liquid (*l, m, n, r*), syllable division may occur before or between them. A word like *patris*, for example, may be divided into *pa-tris* or *pat-ris*. Thus, its first syllable may be open (*pa-*) or closed (*pat-*).
    2. *qu* counts as a single consonant.
    3. *x* (= *cs*) counts as a double consonant.
    4. *h* does not count as a consonant at all.
3. The translation is Goold's (*Catullus*, 37).
4. For an excellent account, see Rosenmeyer, Ostwald, and Halporn, *The Meters of Greek and Latin Poetry*. See also Quinn, *Catullus*, xxxiii–iv; Goold, *Catullus*, 19–27.
5. The translation is from Godwin, *Catullus. The Shorter Poems*, 27.
6. See chapter 3, p. 53.
7. See chapter 6, pp. 140–3; chapter 8, pp. 213–14.
8. *-um* is elided before the vowel in the next line.
9. In 29 one verse (line 20) begins not with an iamb but a spondee (– –). It is probably corrupt.
10. The translation in English iambic pentameter is by Richard Burton, *The Carmina of Caius Valerius Catullus*, 54.
11. Suetonius (*Divus Iulius* 49, 51) reports the libelous verses chanted against Caesar by the soldiers in his Gallic triumph (46 B.C.); these were not in iambics, but in another highly memorable rhythm called "versus quadratus, "four-square verse." Similar popular songs (perhaps including poem 29) probably made the rounds earlier.
12. There are three instances in the choliambics where a long syllable is resolved into two shorts: 22.19 in the second foot, 37.5 in the first foot, 59.3 in the third foot.
13. The *i* in *iam* is consonantal; pronounce *yam*.
14. A few lines survive from Varro's *Menippean Satires* (see Quinn, *Catullus*, 285) and from Vergil's patron Maecenas (Courtney, *The Fragmentary Latin Poets*, 279–80).
15. See Rosenmeyer, Ostwald, and Halporn, *The Meters of Greek and Latin Poetry*, 93; Thomson, *Catullus*, 375–7.
16. The first *i* in *iaciunt* is consonantal; pronounce *yaciunt*.
17. For an excellent account of the hexameter, see Ross, *Virgil's Aeneid: A Reader's Guide*, 143–52.
18. Wilkinson, *Golden Latin Artistry*, 94. See also Ross, *Virgil's Aeneid*, 143–4.
19. Ross, *Virgil's Aeneid*, 151. The pattern occurs 12 times in 64.1–21.
20. The *a* in *nulla* is short, but the syllable is long because it closed by the two consonants beginning the next word.
21. Coleridge's famous imitation of the couplet builds on Ovid's description:

> In the hexameter rises the fountain's silvery column;
>   In the pentameter aye falling in melody back.

The verses are translated from Schiller:

> Im Hexameter steigt des Springquells silberne Säule,
>   Im Pentameter drauf, fällt sie melodisch herab.

22 Ross, *Style and Tradition in Catullus*, 17–112; Sheets, "Elements of Style in Catullus."
23 See chapter 3, pp. 54.
24 Ross, *Style and Tradition in Catullus*, 104–12; Krostenko, *Cicero, Catullus, and the Language of Social Performance*; Krostenko, "Elite Republican Social Discourse."
25 Sheets, "Elements of Style in Catullus," 194–7.
26 Frank Copley's jokey translation of verses 6 and 7 captures the effect: "two little twins with the same disease / same sweet little school for their Ph.D.'s." Quoted by Quinn, *Catullus*, 257.
27 Tracy, "*Argutatiinambulatioque* (Catullus 6,11)," 235.
28 The point is hard to decide; see Ross, *Style and Tradition in Catullus*, 23 n. 29.
29 But he does use the softer diminutive *scortillum* (10.2). See chapter 3, p. 52.
30 Wiseman, *Catullus and His World*, 141 n. 40.
31 Sheets, "Elements of Style in Catullus," 209.
32 Callimachus uses *pseudopatōr* ("false father," *Hymn* 6.98).
33 For neoteric word order, see Ross, *Style and Tradition in Catullus*, 132–7.
34 John Dryden, preface to *Sylvae*, quoted from Wilkinson, *Golden Latin Artistry*, 215.
35 *levis in aridulo malvae descripta libello* (Cinna, fragment 11.3, Courtney), "written on a dry little piece of bark [*libello*] of smooth mallow." Cinna's and Catullus' phrases (*aridulo . . . libello* and *aridulis . . . labellis*) are similar enough to suggest that one poet was probably imitating the other.
36 Adams and Mayer, "Introduction," *Aspects of the Language of Latin Poetry*, 4.
37 Coleman describes 85 as "the most remarkable case in Latin of a sequence of prosaic words combining to create a powerful poetic effect" ("Poetic Diction, Poetic Discourse and the Poetic Register," 55).
38 Pound, *The Translations of Ezra Pound*, 408; reprinted in Gaisser, ed., *Catullus in English*, 167.
39 Adams, *The Latin Sexual Vocabulary*, 153–4.
40 Ross, *Style and Tradition in Catullus*, 80–95; Lyne, *The Latin Love Poets from Catullus to Horace*, 23–42; Newman, *Roman Catullus and the Modification of the Alexandrian Sensibility*, 318–42; Wiseman, *Catullus and His World*, 101–7.
41 Vendler, *Our Secret Discipline. Yeats and Lyric Form*, xv.

5
Poetic Architecture

> Here is a vebal contraption. How does it work?
> W. H. Auden (*The Dyer's Hand*)

In the last chapter we looked at some of the formal elements of Catullus' art, becoming acquainted with his meters and studying what I called the building blocks of his poetry: his sounds, words, and rhythmical effects. We admired the building blocks individually in the completed structures of verses and poems, just as we might look at a separate stone or cornice or column on a building, trying to understand its contribution to the artistry of the whole. Now we must stand back a few paces and look at the buildings themselves. My purpose is to consider the poems from an architectural point of view: to discern their shapes, to see how they are put together, and above all to appreciate the ways in which poetic structure and poetic meaning are intertwined.

Catullus' poetic architecture operates on several levels, from the word order of individual verses, to the articulation of ideas within a poem, to the linking of poems across the collection by shared language and themes. Several examples of Catullan word order were treated in chapter 4. The connections between poems are often discussed in terms of their physical arrangement in our present collection, an idea that works best for certain clusters of poems like the opening sequence discussed in chapter 2. But since it cannot be demonstrated that the ordering of the poems, although ancient, was designed by Catullus himself (even though some portions of it may have been), I have preferred to look at the structure of the collection in another way, not as a system dependent on physical arrangement but more abstractly, as a web held together by threads of repeated words and ideas that reach out to each other in a dynamic and changing pattern. This intangible pattern comes to life not so much through actual arrangement on the page as through connections and linkages made in the mind of the reader. Some of these linkages have been explored in chapters 2 and 3.

This chapter treats structure at the level of the individual poem, where it can be apprehended in a more concrete way. Poems have links to other poems, but each is also a distinct and separate entity. Within a given poem we may perceive floating threads of association forming different patterns in different lights, but there are also components that we can get our hands on: ideas, words, lines, and blocks of lines that we know the poet has arranged himself. These tangible components will be our focus. In what follows I will first survey some of the techniques that Catullus uses to put them together and then look closely at the architecture of several poems or parts of poems: 7, 46, 64.60–70, 101, and 68.

Ordering Techniques

Catullus has many ways to articulate his ideas and shape them into poetry.[1] His ordering systems can be classified according to different principles, but I find it most useful to think in terms of method. Catullus structures his poems by four principal methods: by repetition, by using blocks of text, by presenting a sequence of temporal or spatial movements, and by deploying the question-and-answer template (defined below). He uses most of these techniques across the collection, often combining them in a single passage or poem in complex patterns that elude diagrams and mechanical analysis. Sound patterns are an essential element in every technique; they crisscross all the poems, reinforcing and cementing their structures. All of Catullus' ordering methods are very ancient, some going back as far as the orally composed and aurally received poetry of Homer, where they helped both the oral poet and his audience to keep their place in a complex narrative. Catullus, unlike Homer, wrote his poems down; he did not need oral mnemonic devices. But his various techniques would still have indicated structures and sense units for his audience, many of whom were listening to his poetry rather than reading it silently. Even the silent readers would have perceived such structural cues as they did Catullus' other sound effects, not only visually, but also aurally, with their well trained inner poetic ear.

Repetition, whether of ideas, words, phrases, or whole verses, is one of the most striking features of Catullus' style. He uses it constantly, and in various ways, to structure and unify his poems. He often frames a poem or a passage with repeated language or ideas in a technique called ring composition. He frames poems 16, 36, 52, and 57 with identical verses. In the case of poem 16, as we saw in chapter 3, the enclosing ring includes repeated ideas as well as repeated language; the thought at the end (verses 12–14) matches that at the beginning (1–4). (The poem is translated and discussed in chapter 3.) In poem 8 the framing verses are not identical, but the poet emphasizes their similarity by using similar sound patterns. (The poem is translated and discussed in chapter 3.)

> Miser Catulle, desinas ineptire (8.1)
> at tu, Catulle, destinatus obdura (8.18)

The vocative *Catulle* occurs at the same point in each line; the next words, *desinas* and *destinatus*, are very similar in sound. The last line ("But you, Catullus, keep your mind made up, stand fast") neatly rounds off Catullus' irresolute monologue and brings us back to its starting point: "Unhappy Catullus, stop being foolish." Structure and sense are nicely matched: Catullus, we could say, is going around in circles. The poet frames other poems with multiple concentric rings of repeated thought and language that encircle a high point or emotional nucleus. Examples of this technique include poem 99 (translated and discussed in chapter 3), poem 17,[2] and poem 68 (discussed below).

Catullus also uses ring composition to enclose sections within a poem. In poem 13 he issues a dinner invitation to Fabullus. The first section (lines 1–8) is constructed with a double concentric ring:

> Cenabis bene, mi Fabulle, apud me   1
> paucis, si tibi di favent, diebus,
> si tecum attuleris bonam atque magnam
> cenam, non sine candida puella
> et vino et sale et omnibus cachinnis.   5
> Haec si, inquam, attuleris, venuste noster,
> cenabis bene—nam tui Catulli
> plenus sacculus est aranearum. (13.1–8)

(You'll dine well, dear Fabullus, at my house in a few days if the gods smile on you, if you bring with you a good big dinner, along with a pretty girl and wine and wit and all kinds of funny stories. If you bring these things, I say, my charming friend, you'll dine well; for the purse of your Catullus is full of cobwebs.)

The external ring (1, 7–8) is signaled by the verses beginning *cenabis bene* ("you'll dine well") and reinforced by the assonance of *mi Fabulle* (1) and *tui Catulli* (7). The inner ring is formed by the repetition of *si . . . attuleris* ("if you bring," 3 and 6). In the center is Fabullus' all-important contribution (lines 4–5): the food, girl, wit, and laughter.

Repetitions may also be used in a linear fashion, to introduce or conclude a series of passages within a poem. Whereas ring composition frames or encloses passages, linear composition articulates them or connects them in parallel. This method lends itself to balancing ideas or passages against each other. Catullus draws on it very neatly in poem 46 (discussed below). He often uses it in epigrams.[3] In poem 86, for example, he contrasts the beauty of Quintia and Lesbia:

>   Quintia formosa est . . . ("Quintia is fair")   86.1
>   Lesbia formosa est . . . ("Lesbia is fair")   86.5

Quintia gets four verses, Lesbia only two. But that's all she needs. Her charms, unlike Quintia's, do not need to be itemized: she has every charm a woman could possibly have. Poem 78 is an attack on Gallus. Each couplet begins with his name, and the opening phrases are metrically identical:

>   Gallus habet fratres . . . ("Gallus has brothers," 78.1)
>   Gallus homo est bellus . . . ("Gallus is a pretty man," 78.3)
>   Gallus homo est stultus . . . ("Gallus is a fool," 78.5)

Catullus sometimes repeats whole verses as refrains marking the ends of stanzas, as in the wedding songs of poems 61, 62, and 64.323–381, but he also uses repeated verses to mark off other blocks of text. In poem 42 he commands a girl to return his writing tablets, dividing his verbal assault into three progressively shorter acts with a repeated chant:

>   "moecha putida, redde codicillos,
>   redde, putida moecha, codicillos!" (42.11–12, 19–20)
>   ("filthy slut, give back the tablets,
>   give back the tablets, filthy slut!")

The optimistic and aggressive first act (1–10) concludes with the first appearance of the chant; the discouraged but determined second act (13–18) ends with the second. In the third act (21–3) Catullus at last acknowledges defeat, capitulating in the final line (24) with a tactfully rephrased address that neatly rounds off the poem: *pudica et proba, redde codicillos* ("chaste and virtuous [lady], give back my tablets").

But repetition is not always easily defined as enclosing or linear, and scholars sometimes disagree about the patterns produced by it. Poem 8 is a notorious case in point.[4] It is framed by a ring, as I noted above. It also has at least one internal ring, the nearly identical verses enclosing Catullus' recollection of past happiness (8.4–7):

fulsere quondam candidi tibi soles	(8.3)
(once the sunny days shone bright for you.)	
fulsere vere candidi tibi soles	(8.8)
(truly the sunny days shone bright for you.)	

But a glance at the full text of the poem reveals many other repeated words and phrases that are much harder to classify.[5] In cases like these it is vain to insist on rigid patterns. The poem has unity and shape (even, as Vendler says of Yeats, "a sense of perfected shape"), and we can discern some of its internal patterning in addition to what I have already mentioned.[6] For, the rest, its repeated words and phrases are placed in an interlocking and reflecting system that baffles diagrams. Quinn's pithy comment well describes it: "Note the mosaic pattern of repetitions."[7]

Catullus also constructs poems with blocks of text. The blocks may be delineated by repeated lines and phrases, but they are important in their own right. Catullus likes to use them as discrete and substantial entities. The blocks are usually but not always roughly equal in length; they tend to balance or contrast with each other; and they show various patterns of internal structure. Although they can be assembled in different ways, they often present a narrative. The blocks in poem 42, as we have just seen, present a little drama in three acts. The Attis poem, 63, alternates blocks of narrative and speech that take Attis from his arrival in Phrygia to his ultimate enslavement by Cybele.

Blocks appear as stanzas in the wedding songs, where they present chronological sequences. The 47 five-line stanzas of poem 61 make us present at the wedding of Manlius Torquatus and his bride, from the invocation and praise of the marriage god, through the nocturnal procession conveying the bride to her new home, to her arrival, to good wishes for the wedding night and hopes that their union will produce a little Torquatus. The stanzas in the wedding song of the Fates in poem 64 are prophetic, beginning with Peleus' wedding night, celebrating the birth and career of his son Achilles, and ending with the sacrifice of Polyxena at Achilles' tomb. Poem 62 is presented in the form of a singing contest between the youths arguing in favor of marriage and the unmarried girls arguing against it. The stanzas make us witnesses to the event, from the beginning of the contest to the inevitable verdict (the girls lose). The young men and girls sing in turn, matching each other line for line in each exchange. Here are the fourth and fifth stanzas.[8] Both choruses address Hesperus, the evening star whose rising signals the start of the wedding procession. The girls speak first.

>   Hespere, quis caelo fertur crudelior ignis? 20
>   qui natam possis complexu avellere matris,
>   complexu matris retinentem avellere natam,
>   et iuveni ardenti castam donare puellam.
>   Quid faciunt hostes capta crudelius urbe?
>   Hymen o Hymenaee, Hymen ades o Hymenaee! 25
>
>   Hespere, quis caelo lucet iucundior ignis?
>   qui desponsa tua firmes conubia flamma,
>   quae pepigere viri, pepigerunt ante parentes,
>   nec iunxere prius quam se tuus extulit ardor.
>   Quid datur a divis felici optatius hora? 30
>   Hymen o Hymenaee, Hymen ades o Hymenaee!
>   (62.20–31)
>
> (Hesperus, what crueler fire rides through the sky?
> For you can tear a daughter from a mother's embrace,
> from a mother's embrace tear a clinging daughter,
> and give the chaste girl to a burning youth.
> What crueler act do enemies commit on capturing a city?
> O Hymen Hymenaeus! O Hymen Hymenaeus, come!
>
> Hesperus, what kinder fire gleams in the sky?
> For with your flame you confirm the marriage contracts,
> which husbands struck, which fathers struck beforehand,
> but did not seal before your fiery light rose on high.
> What gift more longed for is given by the gods than this
>   happy hour?
> O Hymen Hymenaeus! O Hymen Hymenaeus, come!)

The exact structural, verbal, and thematic correspondence between the two stanzas is obvious. Striking features include the contrasting descriptions of Hesperus and the gendered perspectives of the two groups. The descriptions, perfectly matching each other, frame each stanza before the refrain: the girls' lament, "what crueler fire"/ "what crueler act" (62.20,

24), is matched by the young men's praise, "what kinder fire"/ "what gift more longed for" (62.26, 30). The girls emphasize the relation of mother and daughter, the youths the male business of marriage contracts agreed on by fathers and prospective husbands.

The blocks in poem 45 function like those in 62. This poem, on the extravagant and mutual passion of Septimius and Acme, is also an exchange of song. It is divided into three blocks by a refrain. In the first, Septimius declares undying love for Acme; in the second, Acme replies. The refrain closing each passage is a sneeze of good omen by Love (Amor):

> hoc ut dixit, ut ante Amor, sinistra,
> dextra sternuit approbationem.[9] (45.8–9, 17–18)
> (The second he/she said this, Love sneezed blessing ahead, to the left,
>   to the right!)

The competing claims of Septimius and Acme, like the stanzas in 62, are matched to each other in length, structure, and content. But this contest differs from that in 62 in that both singers win. The speaker congratulates the lovers in the third block.

> Nunc ab auspicio bono profecti
> mutuis animis amant amantur.   20
> Unam Septimius misellus Acmen
> mavult quam Syrias Britanniasque:
> uno in Septimio fidelis Acme
> facit delicias libidinesque.
> Quis ullos homines beatiores   25
> vidit, quis Venerem auspicatiorem?
>   (45.19–26)

(Now setting out from this auspicious omen, they love and are loved with mutual affection. Love-sick Septimius prefers Acme alone to any Syria or Britain. In Septimius alone faithful Acme takes delights and pleasures. Who has seen any happier mortals, who a more auspicious Venus?)

This final passage has an elegant symmetrical structure. It is encircled by a two-line ring celebrating the lovers' happiness. The repetition *auspicio / auspicatiorem* both emphasizes the ring structure and points to the theme of the refrain, the good omen of Love's sneezes. The sound pattern of alternating *a*'s and *m*'s in line 20 underlines the lovers' reciprocal devotion: *mutuis animis amant amantur* ("they love and are loved with mutual affection"). The ring encloses two very short parallel sections introduced with similar verses (21, 23):

>   unam Septimius misellus Acmen   (21)
>   uno in Septimio fidelis Acme   (23)

The first section recalls the terms in which Septimius declared his love for Acme (2–7), the second the terms of Acme's declaration of love for Septimius (13–16).

Catullus also uses sequencing as a structural technique, shaping a passage or poem by moving through a succession of temporal or spatial movements. Poem 4 employs both spatial and temporal sequencing. In this poem Catullus points out his yacht (*phaselus*) and reports the story it tells of its history and accomplishments. "That yacht you see, my friends, says it was the fastest of ships," he begins (*Phaselus ille, quem videtis, hospites, / ait fuisse navium celerrimus* (4.1–2). The yacht (with Catullus reporting its words) goes on to cite witnesses of its speed in a geographical catalogue that moves ever eastward from the Adriatic to the Cyclades and Rhodes, on to the Propontis and Black Sea, and finally to its origins as a tree on Mt. Cytorus (4.3–12). At this farthest point, the yacht's narrative changes course. In the second part of the poem (13–24) it returns to Italy, but now the journey is temporal as well as spatial as the yacht tells of standing on Cytorus' heights (as a tree), dipping its oars in the sea for the first time, carrying its master, and at last coming home to a final safe haven, "all the way to this clear lake" (*hunc ad usque limpidum lacum*, 24). The poem ends with a three-line epilogue, now in the voice of Catullus alone:

>   sed haec prius fuere: nunc recondita
>   senet quiete seque dedicat tibi,
>   gemelle Castor et gemelle Castoris.   (4.25–7)

(But these things are past. Now it grows old in secluded retirement and dedicates itself to you, Castor twin and twin of Castor.)

These closing lines are rich in chronological markers. The words *sed haec prius fuere* (4.25) firmly place the yacht's adventures in the past; and *fuere*, in the perfect tense, has the sense of something finished forever that the perfect often connotes. Only a few lines earlier we heard the yacht tell of its transformation from leafy forest and its first voyage; now it is old (*senet*, 26). The poem comes to a quiet close with the elegantly phrased dedication to Castor and Pollux, patrons of seafaring.

Catullus' longest poem, 64, the epyllion interweaving the stories of Peleus and Thetis and Theseus and Ariadne, has the complex structure of a labyrinth. Its first two sections are minutely structured, but follow an overall spatial sequencing. The first section (1–30), which tells of the meeting of Peleus and the sea nymph Thetis, begins on Mt. Pelion in Thessaly, whose pine trees supplied the timbers of *Argo*, and moves out to sea, closing with a line on Thetis' grandparents, Tethys "and Ocean, who encircles the whole world with sea" (*Oceanusque, mari totum qui amplectitur orbem*, 30).[10] The second (31–49), introducing the wedding of Peleus and Thetis, moves from sea to land. It opens in Thessaly and turns steadily inward—from the countryside (31–42), into the house of Peleus with its deeply receding chambers "as far back as the rich palace extended" (*quacumque opulenta recessit / regia*, 43–4), and finally to "the inmost part" (*sedibus in mediis*, 48), where Catullus has placed the marriage bed of the goddess with its embroidered coverlet showing the story of Theseus and Ariadne. The description of Ariadne on the coverlet (64.60–70, discussed below) is also constructed with spatial sequencing.

The final structural technique in this survey of Catullan architectural methods is the question-and-answer template, in which a poem is built around a direct or implied question and its answer. Catullus uses this device at the very beginning of our collection. "To whom shall I give my charming new little book?" he asks in the first line of poem 1, and then proceeds to tell us—and more important, to tell us *why*: "To you, Cornelius. For you used to think my trifles were something" (1.3–4). Catullus uses an implied question in 57:

> Pulcre convenit improbis cinaedis,
> Mamurrae pathicoque Caesarique. (57.1–2)

(They make a pretty pair, the shameless queers, pathic Mamurra and Caesar.)

The question, as often with this technique, is implied in a provocative statement that calls for an explanation: "Why are they a pretty pair?" The explanation follows: they are two indelible blots of vice alike in every respect (verses 6–9 are quoted and translated in chapter 4, p. 89). In this poem the question-and-answer template is combined with ring composition, for the last line exactly repeats the first. As a result, 57 reads like a logical demonstration (statement, proof, re-statement), just as in the old geometry books, where the solution to the proof always concluded "Q.E.D.," that is, *quod erat demonstrandum* ("the point which was to be proved"). Here the Q.E.D. is *pulcre convenit improbis cinaedis* ("they make a pretty pair, the shameless queers").

I have taken these examples of the question-and-answer model from the polymetrics, but it is more common in the epigrams. The format is particularly well suited to the balanced structure inherent in the elegiac couplet, as well as to the kind of bipartite epigram that turns on an introduction or "set up" followed by a paradoxical or invective conclusion. Such poems constitute a substantial portion—but only a portion—of Catullus' epigrams.[11] The most famous example of the question-and-answer format is the epigram we have seen so often, poem 85 (*Odi et amo*, "I hate and I love"), where the question ("Perhaps you ask why I do this") receives a reply rather than an answer: "I do not know, but I feel it happening and I am in torment" (*Nescio, sed fieri sentio et excrucior*). Several other epigrams constructed in this format are clearly in the invective mode. Sometimes the questions are oblique or indirect. In poems 69 and 80 the indirect questions are followed by an indirect explanation, a scurrilous rumor that Catullus takes as the truth. In poem 69 he tells Rufus not to be surprised that no woman wants to have him: people say he stinks. In 80 he asks Gellius why his lips are so white. People say that he is a fellator; *that* must be the explanation.

> sic certe est: clamant Victoris rupta miselli
>   ilia, et emulso labra notata sero. (80.7–8)

(That's it, for sure. Poor Victor's ruptured groin shouts it, *and* the milked sperm-stains around your lips.)[12]

In poem 97 the question is a choice, and the answer a decision.

> Non, ita me di ament, quicquam referre putavi
>   utrumne os an culum olfacerem Aemilio.
> nilo mundius hoc, nihiloque immundior ille est
>   verum etiam culus mundior et melior;
> nam sine dentibus est.   (97.1–5)

(I didn't think—god help me!—that it made any difference whether I sniffed Aemilius' mouth or his asshole. This one is no cleaner, that one no filthier, but in fact his ass is cleaner and better: it doesn't have teeth.)

The answer has the sting or witty point often associated with epigram, a bite characteristic of Martial, but fairly uncommon in Catullus. It could easily end the epigram, as such stings so often do. But we are not yet halfway through the poem; the sting is only a gateway to an ever more obscene and outrageous description of Aemilius' mouth and dubious charms, which finally ends only in line 12.[13] Poems 79 and 89 share a structural pattern, opening with similar language and identical meter and syntax. Here are the first words of 79:

> Lesbius est pulcer; quid ni? (79.1)
> (Lesbius is pretty. Why not?)

And of 89:

> Gellius est tenuis; quid ni? (89.1)
> (Gellius is thin. Why not?)

In each case the explanation that follows is an allegation of incest: of Lesbius with his sister Lesbia, of Gellius with every woman (and man) in his extended family.[14]

Sometimes in the epigrams as in the polymetrics, the question is implied by a statement requiring an explanation. Poem 92 is a good example.

> Lesbia mi dicit semper male nec tacet umquam
>   de me: Lesbia me dispeream nisi amat.
> Quo signo? Quia sunt totidem mea: deprecor illam
>   assidue, verum dispeream nisi amo. (92)
> (Lesbia always maligns me and never shuts up about me. Damned if Lesbia
> doesn't love me. On what evidence? Because my actions are just the same.
> I constantly disparage her, but damned if I don't love her.)

The implied question is a paradox: for Catullus Lesbia's verbal abuse is proof of her love. The explanation? Catullus, who knows he loves Lesbia ("damned if I don't love her"), acts in just the same way. The two couplets are closely parallel: question is balanced by answer, Lesbia's words by Catullus' words, Catullus' interpretation of Lesbia's feelings by his understanding of his own. The impression that in Catullus' mind the two lovers are mirror images of each other is increased by repeated language: the end of the first couplet is almost exactly repeated in the end of the second:

dispeream nisi amat (damned if she doesn't love)
dispeream nisi amo (damned if I don't love).

Each of the building techniques discussed above (repetition, composition by blocks, sequencing, the question-and-answering template) is flexible, variable, and capable of combination with one or more of the others. Our survey has indicated some of the complexity and richness of Catullus' structural artistry, but now it is time for a closer look. In the following sections we will examine the architecture of several poems or parts of poems, both to see how they are put together and to understand the ways in which structure and poetic meaning intersect.

How Many Kisses? (Poem 7)

Poem 7 is Catullus' second kiss poem to Lesbia (5 is the first).[15]

> Quaeris quot mihi basiationes
> tuae, Lesbia, sint satis superque.
> Quam magnus numerus Libyssae harenae
> lasarpiciferis iacet Cyrenis
> oraclum Iovis inter aestuosi   5
> et Batti veteris sacrum sepulcrum,
> aut quam sidera multa, cum tacet nox,
> furtivos hominum vident amores:
> tam te basia multa basiare
> vesano satis et super Catullo est,   10
> quae nec pernumerare curiosi
> possint nec mala fascinare lingua.

(You ask, Lesbia, how many of your kissings are enough for me and more than enough. As great a quantity of Libyan sand lies in silphium-rich Cyrene between the oracle of sweltering Jupiter and the sacred tomb of old Battus, or as many stars, when night is still, see the stolen loves of mortals. To kiss you that many kisses is enough and more than enough for crazy Catullus—kisses that the curious cannot count up nor evil tongue bewitch.)

The structure of this famous poem seems simple enough: a question (how many kisses?) and answer (as many as the sands of the desert and stars of the sky), with the answer enclosed by a ring of corresponding line pairs (1–2 and 9–10):

> You ask, Lesbia, how many of your kissings (*basiationes*) are enough for me and more than enough.
>
> To kiss you that many kisses (*basia*) is enough and more than enough for crazy Catullus.

But Catullus' art is not that simple. The two segments of the ring, although verbally and thematically close, are not identical. The slippage between them brings the lovers' exchange to life and suggests that Catullus is quoting (or rather pretending to quote) Lesbia's words back to her both in the reported question and in his own reply. The word for kisses is different in the two segments, giving the impression that *basiationes* (1) is Lesbia's term, *basia* (9) Catullus'. The contrast would have the effect memorialized in the old Gershwin line "You like tomayto, and I like tomahto." But both kiss words were introduced to literary Latin by Catullus. Before Catullus *basia* was a word only of the spoken language; perhaps, as Ross suggests, it had become a favorite with Catullus' set.[16] *Basiationes* is a Catullan neologism, striking in itself and the more so in the opening line of the poem, where it almost ostentatiously fills the last six syllables of the verse.[17] The arch coinage presents Lesbia as playing with what was already an essentially private language. We can perhaps also hear Lesbia's voice in the second part of the ring in the phrase "crazy Catullus" (*vesano . . . Catullo*, 10), which replaces the simple "me" (*mihi*) of line 1. Her question might have been something like: "Crazy Catullus, how many *basiationes* are enough for you anyway?"

The ring encloses the two comparisons Catullus gives as his answer. Both are as old as the hills—or at least as old as the book of *Genesis*, as Fordyce notes in his commentary.[18] But Catullus treats them in a new way. His innumerable sands are located very precisely, in far-away Libyan Cyrene (the home of Callimachus) between the tomb of Battus (Callimachus' supposed ancestor)[19] and the oracle of "sweltering Jupiter" at the famous temple of Jupiter Ammon. Jupiter is sweltering not only because of the desert heat, but because he is notoriously hot and passionate by nature. The two comparisons, allusively evoking the neoterics' favorite poetic model on the one hand and hinting at the sexual peccadilloes of Jupiter on the other, place Catullus' kiss-counting in a remote landscape somewhere between Callimachean learning and Jovian eroticism, but also between the poles of human limitation (the tomb of the mortal Battus) and divine immortality and omniscience (Jupiter's oracle). Catullus has less to say about the stars of the second comparison, only that they are numerous and that they see "stolen loves" in the still of the night. Although he does not say so, we are probably to assume that they are also remote, eternal, and unconcerned with the human affairs they see—including the "stolen loves" of Catullus and Lesbia.

Poem 7 *could* end at line 10, with the second segment of the ring that encloses the comparisons: "To kiss you that many kisses is enough and more than enough for crazy Catullus." The poem would have a clear and tidy symmetrical structure, and lines 9 and 10 neatly sum up Catullus' answer with a satisfactory air of finality. But of course the poem does not end here. The lines are an example of what is called false closure, an apparent ending that is only a stopping place before a change of direction and the real ending of a work.[20] In 7 the real ending presents yet another way of describing the infinity of kisses that will satisfy Catullus. They must be enough to foil the counting of busybodies or the spells of wicked tongues (11–12). This stipulation brings the tally back to earth, from remote sands and stars to the immediate social world of the lovers. It also sends us back to poem 7's companion piece, poem 5, the first kiss poem, which opens with references to gossiping old men and closes with the idea of foiling the evil eye.

> Vivamus mea Lesbia, atque amemus,   1
> rumoresque senum severiorum
> omnes unius aestimemus assis!
> . . .
> . . . cum milia multa fecerimus,   10
> conturbabimus illa, ne sciamus,
> aut ne quis malus invidere possit
> cum tantum sciat esse basiorum. (5.1–3, 10–13)

(Let us live, my Lesbia, and let us love, and value at one penny all the gossip of strict old men! . . . when we have made many thousands [of kisses], we will mix them up, so that we won't know and no evil man can give us the evil eye when he knows the total of our kisses.)

Now Spring (Poem 46)

In poem 46 Catullus is ready to leave Bithynia at the arrival of spring.[21] He's on his way home, but plans to do some sightseeing on the way. Although he does not say so, he expects his readers to know that he has been serving in Memmius' entourage and that spring heralds the sailing season.

> Iam ver egelidos refert tepores, 1
> iam caeli furor aequinoctialis
> iucundis Zephyri silescit auris.
> Linquantur Phrygii, Catulle, campi
> Nicaeaeque ager uber aestuosae: 5
> ad claras Asiae volemus urbes.
> Iam mens praetrepidans avet vagari,
> iam laeti studio pedes vigescunt.
> O dulces comitum valete coetus,
> longe quos simul a domo profectos 10
> diversae varie viae reportant.

(Now spring is bringing back warm weather, now the rage of the equinoctial sky grows quiet with the west wind's pleasant breezes. Let the plains of Phrygia be left behind, Catullus, and the rich farmland of sweltering Nicaea. Let us fly to the famous cities of Asia. Now the mind, trembling with anticipation, is eager to be off, now feet quicken happy with eagerness. O farewell, dear bands of companions, who set off together on a long journey from home and are brought back in different ways by different paths.)

Catullus uses linear repetition as the structuring device for this elegant little poem. It falls into two sections (1–6 and 7–11), each introduced by two verses beginning with *iam* ("now"). The repetitions are further emphasized by sound patterning, for each pair of lines begins in a similar way: the first *iam* is followed by a monosyllable in long or short *e* (*iam vēr*, 1 / *iam mens*, 7), the second by a disyllable whose vowels are *ae* and long *i* (*iam caelī*, 2, *iam laetī*, 8). But the line pairs are not identical in content. The first announces warm weather and the soft spring breezes; the second shows the effect of the first on the young men in Bithynia: anticipatory eagerness and, quite literally, a spring in their step: "feet quicken with eagerness." (As Elder says, "Even their feet grow green with spring."[22]) The change accompanies a shift or broadening in focus between the two sections. In the first Catullus addresses himself and looks forward to his departure: "let the plains of Phrygia be left behind, Catullus. . . . Let us fly to the famous cities of Asia." In the second, he addresses his friends ("dear bands of companions"), observing that although they came out together, they will all find different ways back.

In chapter 4 I strongly advocated reading Catullus aloud, preferably over and over, to try to hear his verbal music and consider its relation to the structure and content of his poems. Poem 46 will amply repay such effort, for it is full of repeated sounds and sound patterning. Two sounds in particular run through the poem: *ae* and *v* (consonantal *u*, pronounced like English *w*). I want to pay special attention to *v*. It appears first in line 1, in the operative word *ver* ("spring") and again at the end of the first section, in *volemus* ("let us fly") in line 6. But it is everywhere in the second section, occurring seven times in five lines, and always in strong and energetic words: *avet* ("is eager"), *vagari* ("to be off"), *vigescunt* ("quicken"), *valete* ("farewell"), and piling up in a run of three words in the last line, *diversae varie viae* ("different paths in different ways"). It is as if the sound of spring (*ver*) were blowing through the poem, first stirring Catullus to think of travel, then creating a kind of springtime of the mind in the whole group of friends, and at last blowing them home by different routes with its gentle gusts.

Looking at Ariadne looking at Theseus (Poem 64.60–70)

The long centerpiece of poem 64 is a description of the coverlet on the marriage bed of Peleus and Thetis. Its embroidered pictures tell the story of Theseus and Ariadne, beginning with Ariadne on the shore, deserted by Theseus and watching as he sails away. She is described in the excerpt below.

>   quem procul ex alga maestis Minois ocellis   60
>   saxea ut effigies bacchantis, prospicit, eheu,
>   prospicit et magnis curarum fluctuat undis,
>   non flavo retinens subtilem vertice mitram,
>   non contecta levi velatum pectus amictu,
>   non tereti strophio lactentis vincta papillas,   65
>   omnia quae toto delapsa e corpore passim
>   ipsius ante pedes fluctus salis alludebant.
>   Sed neque tum mitrae neque tum fluitantis amictus
>   illa vicem curans toto ex te pectore, Theseu,
>   toto animo, tota pendebat perdita mente.   70

(And from the water's edge with sorrowful eyes Minos' daughter [Ariadne], like the stone likeness of a bacchante, watches him in the distance, alas, watches; and she is tossed by great waves of emotion, not keeping the fine-woven net on her golden head, not covering her bosom [*pectus*] with the light garment that had concealed it, not binding her milky breasts with their rounded band. All these garments had slipped here and there from her whole body, and the salt waves played with them before her feet. But not caring then about her net, nor then about her floating garment, lost, she hung upon you, Theseus, with her whole heart [*pectore*], her whole soul, her whole mind.)

Catullus has used spatial sequencing to shape the passage. After three verses showing the figure of Ariadne on the shore, as frantic as a bacchante and as frozen as a statue of one (60–2), he moves in for a close-up with two descriptions, one of her naked form (63–7), the other of her emotional state (68–70). The ancient rules of rhetoric directed that descriptions of persons should begin at the head and move down to the feet. Catullus follows (and plays with) this rule in both descriptions. In the first he moves from head to chest to breasts, all bare of their accustomed clothing, which appears at the end, swirling in the water by her feet. In the second he starts at the top again, this time referring only to the clothing: the net for her hair and the garment that had covered her bosom. Formally this second description continues to her feet (or at least to the water around her feet), since her garment is "floating" (*fluitantis*). But it really stops with her chest, the seat of emotions and feelings.[23] The word *pectus* in 64 (*pectore* in 69) has both physical and emotional meanings, as my translation indicates ("bosom" at 64, "heart" at 69). Catullus has played on this double meaning in his two descriptions, showing Ariadne stripped naked both physically and emotionally by the shock of Theseus' desertion. He emphasizes the connection and the totality of her experience by insistently repeating the word *toto* ("whole"): in the first description Ariadne's clothes have slipped off her "whole body" (*toto ... corpore*, 66)); in the second she is fixed on Theseus "with her whole heart (*toto ... pectore*, 69), her whole soul (*toto animo*, 70), her whole mind (*tota ... mente*, 70)." The sense of heightened emotion in 69–70 is increased by the repetition of *toto* at the head of each phrase in the rhetorical figure called anaphora. Catullus also points up the parallels between the two descriptions by structuring both with anaphora. In the first he uses *non* ("not") at the beginning of three successive lines (63–5): "not keeping," "not covering," "not binding." In the second he uses another negative in the repeated phrase *neque tum* ("and not then," 68): "not caring then about her net, nor then about her floating garment."

Poem 64 is considered Catullus' neoteric masterpiece, and when we look at this passage we can see why, for it brilliantly exemplifies the principles and interests of neoteric poetics. Its fine-patterned structuring demonstrates the meticulous craftsmanship and attention to detail dear to Catullus and his friends. It belongs to a poem in their favorite genre, the epyllion or miniature epic, and treats the typical theme of the genre, a mythological heroine in distress. Within its small compass (only 11 lines) it gives a full account of her powerful sufferings, moving from we might call a distant view (Ariadne frozen in place like a statue) to a physical description of her unclothed body, and finally into her heart, full of nothing but Theseus.

Each of these three short movements employs a favorite neoteric device for suggesting heightened emotion. In the opening Catullus uses the rhetorical figure called epanalepsis, in which an important word near the end of one verse is repeated a word or so later in the beginning of another: "like the stone likeness of a bacchante, she watches, alas, watches" (*prospicit, eheu, / prospicit*, 61–2). The repetition fixes our attention on Ariadne and the source of her grief—watching Theseus as he sails away. We should also observe that the repetition links our passage to the coverlet description as a whole, the principal portion of which is framed by Ariadne's watching (note the repeated participle *prospectans*, "looking out"):

> namque fluentisono prospectans litore Diae,
> Thesea cedentem celeri cum classe tuetur
> indomitos in corde gerens Ariadna furores. (64.53–5)
>
> quae tum prospectans cedentem maesta carinam
> multiplices animo volvebat saucia curas. (64. 249–50)

(For looking out from the wave-sounding shore of Dia, Ariadne sees Theseus departing with his swift ship, holding unconquerable passion in her heart.)
And looking out in grief then at the departing ship, wounded in her heart, she was turning over manifold cares.)[24]

Catullus secures another emotional effect in the last line of the physical description of Ariadne, which he brings to a close with four long syllables: *alludebant* ("played with"). The usual ending for a verse of dactylic hexameter (the meter of poem 64) is a dactyl followed by a spondee in the rhythm long short short, long long (expressed $- \cup \cup | - -$).[25] Replacing the dactyl with a spondee at this point in the verse is a neoteric mannerism that Catullus likes to use to signal the end of a passage or to mark high emotion. Here he does both, slowing down the rhythm at the end of the description and holding our gaze for a moment on Ariadne's discarded clothing and the waters at her feet.

At the end of the whole passage Catullus turns from his third-person narration to address Theseus: "Lost, she hung upon you, Theseus, with her whole heart, her whole soul, her whole mind." This sudden direct address of a character is called apostrophe ("turning aside"), and it is another favorite rhetorical figure of the neoteric poets and the Augustan poets who succeeded them. Like epanalepsis and the spondaic ending, it gets the reader's attention, fixing it not only on what is happening, but on the emotional effect of what is happening. Apostrophe functions, we might say, as a kind of emotional zoom lens, which the poet uses both to empathize with a character and to invoke the sympathy of the reader.[26] Ordinarily it directs our sympathy to the person addressed, but here it works differently. Theseus is addressed not to direct sympathy to him, but to increase sympathy for Ariadne. The apostrophe reinforces the fact that it is Theseus who is the cause of her grief.

An Offering to the Dead (Poem 101)

In poem 101 Catullus bids farewell to his brother, who has died far from home—in Troy, as he tells us in the laments for his brother's death in poems 65 and 68b.[27] Catullus has come to his burial site to perform the funeral rites.

> Multas per gentes et multa per aequora vectus   1
>   advenio has miseras, frater, ad inferias,
> ut te postremo donarem munere mortis
>   et mutam nequiquam alloquerer cinerem,
> quandoquidem fortuna mihi tete abstulit ipsum,   5
>   heu miser indigne frater adempte mihi.
> Nunc tamen interea haec, prisco quae more parentum
>   tradita sunt tristi munere ad inferias,
> accipe, fraterno multum manantia fletu,
>   atque in perpetuum, frater, ave atque vale.   10

(Having traveled through many nations and through many seas, I arrive, brother, for these sad funeral rites, to present you with the final tribute of death and speak in vain to the silent ashes, since fortune has taken you yourself away from me—alas, poor brother, unjustly taken away from me. But now, at any rate, take these gifts that have been handed down by the ancient custom of our fathers as the grim tribute for the funeral rites. Take them, dripping with a brother's tears, and forever, brother, hail and farewell.)

Poem 101 is an epigram in a more literal way than Catullus' other epigrams, for it is presented as something that might be inscribed on stone. An epigram was originally an inscription, "written on" or carved into a monument. Many real funeral inscriptions (some in elegiac couplets like poem 101) survive from antiquity, and there are many more epigrams of a purely literary nature that were composed to imitate them. Catullus' poem belongs in this latter group. Its traditional pedigree, which would have been obvious to an ancient reader, is part of its powerful emotional effect.

The poem lacks obvious structural markers like those noted elsewhere in this chapter, but it is put together with great art. It has a basic structure of two sections: a statement (1–6) and a request (7–10). In the first Catullus tells his brother that he has come to pay his funeral tribute; in the second he asks him to receive the funeral gifts and says farewell. Coexisting with and complementing this bipartite division is a tripartite structure whose segments are delineated by indications of time (present, past, future) and by verbal repetition (the word *frater*, "brother," uttered at regular intervals). The result is a kind of counterpoint or layering of the two ordering systems. The whole complex structure is drawn together by sound patterns, particularly the incessant repetition of initial *m*, which appears in nearly every line of the poem.[28]

The first section (1–6) begins in the present, moves progressively back into the past, and ends again in the present. Catullus, having traveled far to get there, announces his presence at the tomb: *advenio*. (I have translated *advenio* as "I arrive," but one could also say, "I come," or even "I am here.") He then moves back into the past, explaining what has brought him to this moment: first the need to perform the funeral rites[29] and then the more remote event, the reason for that need, the death itself. The internal chronology of the section depends only on the tenses of its verbs and the logical sequence of events; there are no temporal markers like "next" or "formerly." The section closes with a cry of lament: *heu miser indigne frater adempte mihi* ("alas, poor brother, unjustly taken away from me," 6). The verse returns us to the present moment of grief, and the word *frater* echoes Catullus' first call to his brother in line 2.

The temporal movement is more complex in the second section (7–10). The time shifts from present to past and back again in lines 7–9, and finally to an endless future in 10. The second section begins where the first one ended: in the present. Its opening word is *nunc* ("now," 7), the first temporal marker in the poem. But things soon become more complicated, as we can see if we look again at lines 7–9. (I have slightly revised the translation given above in order to follow the Latin word order as closely as possible.)

> Nunc tamen interea haec, prisco quae more parentum
>   tradita sunt tristi munere ad inferias,
> accipe, fraterno multum manantia fletu. (101.7–9)

(But now, at any rate, these gifts that have been handed down by the ancient custom of our fathers as the grim tribute at the funeral rites, take them, dripping with a brother's tears.)

The three verses open and close in the present: "But now, at any rate, these gifts ... take, dripping with a brother's tears." In between Catullus reverts to the past—not the recent past of his brother's death as before, but the remote past of sacred tradition ("[the gifts] that have been handed down by the ancient custom of our fathers as the grim tribute at the funeral rites"). The gifts are the focus of all three lines; the structure presents them as belonging to both past and present, handed down in a continuum of grief. The last line of the section looks into the future: *atque in perpetuum, frater, ave atque vale* ("and forever, brother, hail and farewell," 10).

This line also repeats the word *frater*, which has appeared twice before. It has been used at four-line intervals, almost like a refrain, and always in the same place in the line (beginning the second half of the pentameter).[30] The three verses in which it appears encapsulate the thought of the poem:

> advenio has miseras, frater, ad inferias (2)
> (I arrive, brother, at these sad funeral rites.)
>
> heu miser indigne frater adempte mihi. (6)
> (Alas, poor brother, unjustly taken away from me.)
>
> atque in perpetuum, frater, ave atque vale. (10)
> (And forever, brother, hail and farewell.)

The repetition of *frater* is striking in itself, but it also evokes a particular aspect of Roman funerary ritual, the *conclamatio*, in which the name of the dead person was called out three times by the closest relatives. In its last appearance *frater* is combined with the ritual formula *ave atque vale* ("hail and farewell") spoken at the end of a funeral and often found in grave inscriptions—an important detail that reminds us that in form at least the epigram *is* a grave inscription. But the importance of funeral ritual in the structure of the poem does not end here. Catullus says in 101 that he has come to perform the funeral rites (*inferiae*), but we should note that the epigram itself is a performance of the rites. They are announced in the first section, and actually carried out in the second. The *inferiae* consisted of two parts: the presentation of funeral offerings (*munus*) and the last words spoken to the dead. All three elements appear in both sections of the epigram: *inferiae* (in the phrase *ad inferias*) at 2 and 8, the *munus* (which I have translated "tribute") at 3 and 8, and the last words at 4 and 10 (in 4 Catullus has come "to speak in vain to the silent ashes," and in line 10 he does so—*ave atque vale*).

Chinese Boxes: Poem 68b

Poem 68 is printed in various ways in modern editions, sometimes in a single block as 68, sometimes divided by a break between verses 40 and 41, and sometimes as two separate poems, 68a and 68b, with continuous line numbering so that 68b begins at verse 41.[31] Like most modern scholars, I consider this division into two poems to be correct. Poem 68b is the subject of our discussion.

In 68b Catullus thanks his friend Allius for letting him use his house for an erotic rendezvous. The woman is unnamed, but as in so many other poems we have seen, she can only be Lesbia. Catullus compares her arrival at the house to Laodamia's arrival as a bride at the house of Protesilaus, discusses Protesilaus' departure for the Trojan War, and grieves for the recent death of his brother in Troy. He goes on to discuss Laodamia's love and loss and his own acceptance of his mistress' infidelity and concludes with thanks to Allius. The poem is structured in a complex pattern often referred to as a Chinese box, with several concentric rings enclosing a central panel. This central panel is the emotional heart of the poem: Catullus' lament for the death of his brother. The surrounding rings are variously counted and defined, and scholars disagree on details.[32] These difficulties arise both because of corruptions and lacunae in the text and from Catullus' complex technique, which resists both simple diagrams and efforts to discover exact line-by-line symmetry of parts. The rings are not always marked off from each other by clearly demarcated boundaries; instead, they are so closely connected that they sometimes merge into each other like the colors in a rainbow. But the main lines are clear. Most scholars would say that the central panel is encircled by at least four rings that we could label (beginning with the outermost ring) Allius, Catullus and Lesbia, Laodamia, and Troy. I treat the poem as containing five rings, dividing the Catullus and Lesbia ring into two.

In the discussion that follows we will begin with the outermost ring (on Allius) and work toward the center.

The Allius ring (41–50 and 149–60) is signaled by both verbal and thematic repetition in the opening couplets, which emphasize both Allius' service (*officiis*) and Catullus' determination to memorialize it. The ring opens thus:

> Non possum reticere, deae, qua me Allius in re
>   iuverit aut quantis iuverit officiis,
> ne fugiens saeclis obliviscentibus aetas
>   illius hoc caeca nocte tegat studium. (68.41–4)

(I cannot leave unsaid, goddesses [i.e., Muses], in what matter Allius helped me or with what great services he helped me, lest fleeing time with its forgetting ages cover over with blind night this kindness of his.)

It is picked up with these verses:

> hoc tibi, quod potui, confectum carmine munus
>   pro multis, Alli, redditur officiis,
> ne vestrum scabra tangat robigine nomen
>   haec atque illa dies atque alia atque alia. (68.149–52)

(This gift composed of song (the best I could) is returned to you, Allius, for your many services, lest this day and the next and the days after that coat your name with scaly rust.)

Poetry is an important theme in both passages, as the Muses in line 41 and the "gift composed of song" in 149 attest. But the essential idea is friendship and the reciprocity it demands. The word *officiis* ("services"), which appears in the same position at the end of the first couplet of each ring (42 and 150), makes the point, invoking the obligations of aristocratic friendship so important to elite Roman men.[33] Allius helped Catullus with great services and Catullus is repaying his services in the only way he can ("the best I could") with a gift of poetry that will bring immortality to his friend. But it is also important to remember the exact nature of Allius' service: it consisted in providing Catullus with a trysting place to meet another man's wife. This is an important point to which we will return presently.

The ring devoted to Catullus (51–69 and 135–48) is thematically and verbally less balanced than that devoted to Allius. The first part treats Catullus' remembrance of his burning and shipwrecked passion and Allius' gift of his house for a rendezvous, the second his acceptance of

Lesbia's infidelity and his acknowledgement that their affair is adulterous.

The Lesbia ring (70–6 and 131–4) is very brief, and its edges blur into the Catullus ring on one side and the Laodamia ring on the other—perhaps appropriately, since its whole content is quite literally liminal. We can call it: "Lesbia on the threshold." Here is the first part of the ring.

>   quo mea se molli candida diva pede   70
>   intulit et trito fulgentem in limine plantam
>   innixa arguta constituit solea,
>   coniugis ut quondam flagrans advenit amore
>   Protesilaeam Laodamia domum
>   inceptam frustra, nondum cum sanguine sacro   75
>   hostia caelestis pacificasset eros. (68–70–6)

(There [to Allius' house] my radiant goddess brought herself with soft step and set her gleaming foot on the well-worn threshold, stepping on it with her squeaky sandal, just as once Laodamia, flaming with love of her husband, arrived at the house of Protesilaus—a house begun in vain since a sacrificial victim had not yet pacified the lords of heaven with sacred blood.)

And the second.

>   aut nihil aut paulo cui tum concedere digna
>   lux mea se nostrum contulit in gremium,
>   quam circumcursans hinc illinc saepe Cupido
>   fulgebat crocina candidus in tunica. (68.131–4)

(Deserving to yield to her [i.e., Laodamia] either not at all or only a little, my light of love brought herself into my embrace, and Cupid, often flitting around her on this side and that, gleamed, radiant in his saffron tunic.)

The two passages are linked to each other by verbal repetition. The verb *contulit* ("brought") in 132 echoes *intulit* ("brought") in 71, and words of brightness and shining appear in both segments (note *candida*, 70 / *candidus*, 134; *fulgentem*, 71 / *fulgebat* 134). We know that the woman on the threshold is Lesbia, but Catullus has deliberately not given her name. In the first passage she is a "radiant goddess," in the second "my light of love," accompanied, like Venus herself, by a radiant Cupid. The final link between the two parts of the ring is the Laodamia simile, introduced in the first part and rounded off in the second. The step of

Catullus' radiant goddess on Allius' threshold is like the arrival of the mythological heroine Laodamia, coming as a bride to the house of her husband Protesilaus.[34] The comparison makes the woman's arrival like that of a bride (although we know it is not), and it also hints at the ill-omened nature of Catullus' affair since the house of Protesilaus and Laodamia was "begun in vain" (75).

The two parts of the Laodamia ring (77–86 and 105–30) are of very different lengths, to the distress of scholars in search of exact or even approximate proportional correspondence.[35] The first section is devoted to the intensity of Laodamia's passion and the fact that Protesilaus was destined to die at Troy. In the second, much longer passage Catullus turns aside from the narrative to addresses Laodamia directly in an apostrophe: "By this fate then, beautiful Laodamia, the marriage dearer than life and soul was snatched from you" (105–7). He mentions Laodamia's loss and goes on to describe the depth and complex nature of her passion with three strange similes.[36] Her love was deeper than the pit dug by Hercules to drain the plain of Pheneus; her husband was dearer to her than a late-born child to an aged grandfather; she was more passionate than a dove or a promiscuous woman. In their strangeness and intensity the similes correspond to the similes of burning, tears, and shipwreck describing Catullus' passion in the first part of the Catullus ring (51–69). The correspondence is thematic rather than symmetrical, cutting across the ring structure to connect Catullus and Laodamia—another important point that will concern us presently.

The Troy ring (87–90 and 101–4) is so closely intertwined with the central panel on Catullus' brother that we must consider the whole passage (87–104) together. (The spacing below indicates the places generally identified as separation points.)

>   Nam tum Helenae raptu primores Argivorum
>   coeperat ad sese Troia ciere viros,
>   Troia (nefas!) commune sepulcrum Asiae Europaeque,
>   Troia virum et virtutum omnium acerba cinis,   90
>
>   quae nunc et nostro letum miserabile fratri
>   attulit. Ei misero frater adempte mihi,
>   ei misero fratri iucundum lumen ademptum,
>   tecum una tota est nostra sepulta domus;
>   omnia tecum una perierunt gaudia nostra,   95
>   quae tuus in vita dulcis alebat amor.
>   Quem nunc tam longe non inter nota sepulcra
>   nec prope cognatos compositum cineres,

> sed Troia obscena, Troia infelice sepultum
>   detinet extremo terra aliena solo.   100
>
> Ad quam tum properans fertur ⟨lecta⟩ undique pubes
>   Graeca penetralis deseruisse focos,
> ne Paris abducta gavisus libera moecha
>   otia pacato degeret in thalamo.   (68.87–104)

(For then because of Helen's abduction Troy had begun to rouse against itself the leaders of the Argives—Troy (unspeakable!), the common grave of Asia and Europe, Troy the bitter ash of all men and courage,

which now has brought wretched death to my brother, too. Alas, brother, taken away from me, wretched! alas, the glad light of life taken away from the wretched brother! Our whole house is buried with you; with you have perished all our joys that your dear love fostered in life. And now so far away—not among well-known graves nor laid to rest near the ashes of your kin, but buried in obscene Troy, in barren Troy—a foreign land holds you, in far distant ground.

To this [Troy] then hastening, the Greek youth, mustered from every direction, are said to have abandoned their inmost hearths in order that Paris might not enjoy his stolen paramour and spend undisturbed leisure in a bedroom free from war.)

The edges of ring and panel overlap both structurally and syntactically. Lines 89–90 in the first part of the Troy ring not only belong to the same sentence as the opening of the lament for Catullus' brother, but also resonate verbally and thematically with its final couplet (99–100). The insistent repetition of Troy ("Troy—unspeakable!" / "in obscene Troy, in barren Troy") and the idea of its being a burying ground encircle the central lament. The second part of the Troy ring (101–4) is closely linked to the first. Indeed, as several scholars have pointed out, the link is so close that the central panel could be removed without leaving a gap in the sense. This second segment makes a harsh judgment on the conduct of Paris and Helen: *moecha* (103), which I have translated as "paramour," means "adulteress." The judgment inevitably reflects on Catullus and his "radiant goddess"—not so different, we might think, from Paris and his "stolen paramour."

    Catullus' lament for his brother (91–100), which I have called the emotional heart of the elegy, is one of four similar expressions of grief in our collection.[37] It falls into three parts, each focusing on a different aspect of Catullus' distress. Like the second segment of the Laodamia ring, the section moves from third-person narration to direct address or apostrophe, emphasizing the emotional connection between poet and character. The first part of the lament (91–3) is a cry of pain drawing together the death, the brother, and Catullus—but especially the brother and Catullus. Some form of the word *frater* ("brother") appears in all three lines. The death is *miserabile* ("wretched"); both Catullus and his brother are called *misero* ("wretched").[38] Lines 92–3 are closely linked by the repeated words *ei*, *misero*, *frater*, and *ademptum* ("alas," "wretched," brother," "taken away"). The second part (94–6) treats the brother's death as a metaphorical burial: "Our whole house is buried with you; with you have perished all our joys." The third (97–100) turns to the brother's actual burial in Troy, in a foreign land so far away; the thought takes us back to the opening segment of the Troy ring and the curse on Troy, "the common grave of Asia and Europe."

The complex concentric structure of poem 68 is a fascinating technical tour de force, but it is more than that. It plots the importance and inter-relationships of Catullus' themes in 68 and ultimately expresses their meaning. The concentric rings map the three orders of emotional attachment that matter to Catullus, with their degree of importance increasing as we move to the center: on the outside, friendship (Allius), next, erotic love (the radiant goddess), and finally, at the emotional apex, familial love (the brother).

The structure also maps—we might almost say diagrams—a change in the way that Catullus speaks of his affair. Since the ring structure lends itself to balance and symmetry—to doubling back on itself—rather than to forward movement or narrative, it might seem that that there is no action in the poem. As Feeney puts it: "What actually *happens* in 68? A man provides a house—a woman arrives—the rest is analogy and reflection, nested within the expression of thanks to Allius."[39] But this is not quite right. Something does happen: the woman crosses the threshold. In the first part of the Lesbia ring the woman arrives: "She brought herself there" (*quo . . . / intulit*, 71). In the second she brings herself into Catullus' embrace (*nostrum contulit in gremium*, 132). One moment she is resting her foot on the doorsill. The next, she is in Catullus' arms. We do not see her step across. Instead, Catullus diverts our attention with the passages devoted to Laodamia and Troy and the all-important central panel. The effect is that the events in these sections seem to be taking place—or perhaps going through Catullus' mind—*as* the woman crosses the threshold. Once she is on the other side, Catullus looks at both her and their affair with a pragmatic realism we do not see earlier in 68 or elsewhere in his poetry. He realistically accepts her promiscuity:

> quae tamen etsi uno non est contenta Catullo,
> > rara verecundae furta feremus erae,
>
> ne nimium simus stultorum more molesti. (68.135–7)

(Even though she is not content with Catullus alone, still I will put up with the occasional lapses of my discreet mistress, so as not to be troublesome as stupid men are.)

And for the first time he explicitly spells out the adulterous nature of their affair:

> nec tamen illa mihi dextra deducta paterna
> > fragrantem Assyrio venit odore domum,
>
> sed furtiva dedit media[40] munuscula nocte
> > ipsius ex ipso dempta viri gremio. (68.143–6)

(And she did not come, escorted on her father's right arm, to my house fragrant with eastern perfume, but in the middle of the night gave me stolen joys taken from the very embrace of her husband himself.)

Catullus does not say what has turned his radiant goddess into another man's wife or replaced the bridelike picture of the woman on the threshold with the admission that she did not come to his house on her father's arm in a wedding procession but stealthily gave him the sexual favors that belonged to her husband. Perhaps it was her action in stepping across the doorsill of their trysting place, or perhaps it was what went through Catullus' mind as he saw her crossing: Laodamia's blighted marriage, the death of his brother, and the causes of the Trojan war (adultery and the need to punish it).

Underlying all the themes arrayed in Catullus' complex structure is the idea of marriage and the family, symbolized by the *domus* (house), which appears in almost every ring: the house of Allius, which is also a kind of play house or pseudo-house for Catullus and the woman (68, 156), the "house begun in vain" of Protesilaus and Laodamia (74), the buried house of Catullus and his brother (94), the deserted hearths of the Greeks (102), and the non-existent house to which the woman never comes as a bride (144). But not all the important parallels in this elegy are laid out in corresponding rings. A moment ago I mentioned that a parallel between Laodamia and Catullus cuts across the ring structure, in that the Laodamia similes of 107–30 correspond in their strangeness and intensity to the similes for Catullus in 51–69. Since the similes occur in different rings (the second part of the Laodamia ring and the first part of the Catullus ring), we can say that the correspondence is somehow off-center, pulling the symmetrical fabric of the poem askew. The structural irregularity is matched by a twist in sense. Formally, and in terms of the ring structure and threshold comparison, Laodamia is a model for the woman. In terms of emotion, however, she is a model for Catullus: it is Catullus, not the woman, who corresponds to Laodamia in grief and passion.

Conclusion

Catullus is a master of poetic architecture. Like all the best architects, he controls a range of building techniques, using and combining them in shapes that express, enhance, and, above all, *create* meaning. His structures are carefully put together—solidly built, we might say—but their designs, even when they seem most obvious, avoid the obvious, for he knows how to add the unexpected detail or suggest a surprising parallel that alters our perception of the shape of the whole. In poem 7 he tells Lesbia how many kisses he wants, framing his answer with corresponding verses; but the ring composition is an example of false closure, a stopping place before Catullus rephrases his answer and changes the direction of the poem to link it with poem 5. In poem 46 he uses linear repetition and sound patterns in an asymmetric two-part structure. In poem 64.60–70 he uses spatial sequencing and follows the rules for description of persons prescribed by ancient rhetoric to describe the desolate Ariadne; but he does so *twice*, in order to depict both the outer and the inner conditions of his heroine and the relation between them. In poem 101 he uses a complex and subtle structure that combines a bipartite division into two sections of unequal length with a three-fold pattern of time and verbal repetition. The resulting contrapuntal arrangement articulates and ties together the poem's several themes—loss, ancestral tradition, funerary ritual, time, and distance—in an almost three-dimensional array. In poem 68b he uses complex ring composition to frame an emotional center (a lament for his brother), but avoids perfect symmetry on both the structural and thematic level. The corresponding parts of the concentric rings are of unequal lengths, and Laodamia, the mythological heroine formally compared to Lesbia, is in fact more like Catullus.

In the last two chapters we have been looking at the formal means by which Catullus secures his poetic effects: sound, language, meter, and structure. These are tangible elements that we can see and hear and use as entrance points into the thought and feeling of the poetry. For the most part I have been discussing these elements as neutral building blocks, perhaps culturally conditioned like the funeral lament or stemming from rhetorical tradition like the way to describe a person, but not conditioned or given meaning by their use in earlier literature. But the elements in Catullus' poetry are not neutral counters given meaning only by his use of them. They come into his hands layered with the usage and meaning imparted by generations of earlier poets, both Greek and Latin. This aspect of Catullus' poetry will be the subject of the next chapter, on intertextuality.

Notes

1 The best general discussion I know is Wiseman, "Structural Patterns in Catullus," in *Cinna the Poet*, 59–76. For an enlightening history of structural interpretations, see Schmiel, "The Structure of Catullus 8: A History of Interpretation." The commentaries of both Thomson and Quinn touch on the structure of individual poems.
2 Wiseman, "Structural Patterns in Catullus," 63–4.
3 In addition to the following, examples include poems 87 (translated and discussed in chapter 3, p. 58) and 95 (translated and discussed in chapter 1, pp. 16–17).
4 For four very different analyses, see Wiseman, "Structural Patterns in Catullus," 62; Quinn, *Catullus*, 115; Schmiel, "The Structure of Catullus 8"; Fowler, "First Thoughts on Closure," 99–101.
5 For the Latin text, see p. 56. The role of verse 11, for example, is particularly difficult. Does it end the first section of the poem (1–11) as I have suggested or begin the second (11–19), forming a ring with line 19?
6 E.g., the fine pattern shaping the barrage of questions in 15–18. The pattern begins with *quae tibi manet vita* ("what life awaits you?") in the second half of 15 and continues with an alternation of different cases of the interrogative pronoun. Pronouns beginning *qu* are placed at the beginning of each line, those beginning with *cu* at the start of each line half: *quis / cui* (16), *quem / cuius* (17), *quem / cui* (18).
7 Quinn, *Catullus*, 115
8 Close correspondence also appears in stanzas 8 and 9 (verses 39–58). But some aspects of the poem's structure are unclear, as portions of the sixth and seventh stanzas are lost.
9 The text of lines 8 and 17 is disputed. Most editors read *hoc ut dixit, Amor sinistra ut ante*. I have used Gratwick's text and translation ("Those Sneezes: Catullus 45.8–9, 17–18," 235–6).

10 The details of the structure of the section are more complex. To give just one example, Catullus uses the mention of Mt. Pelion and its pines in line 1 and a reference to the ship's construction with pines by Athena (8–10) to frame an oblique summary of the *Argo*'s voyage to capture the Golden Fleece (2–7).

11 The model (set-up, conclusion) was formulated by Lessing in the eighteenth century as normative for epigram. (His terms were *Erwartung* and *Aufschluss*, "expectation" and "conclusion.") It works best for Martial (Lessing's main epigrammatic model), much less well for Greek epigram and most of Catullus. See Watson, "Epigram"; Sullivan, *Martial: The Unexpected Classic*, 221–4; Smith, *Poetic Closure*, 196–203.

12 The translation is Green's (*The Poetry of Catullus*, 189).

13 For a good discussion, see Skinner, *Catullus in Verona*, 118–19.

14 It has been suggested that Catullus uses similar structures and allegations in 79 and 89 to link Lesbius (Clodius) and Gellius. Tatum, "Friendship, Politics, and Literature in Catullus," 499; Skinner, *Catullus in Verona*, 90–1.

15 For discussions of poem 7, see Commager, "Notes on Some Poems of Catullus," 84–6; Segal, "Catullus 5 and 7: A Study in Complementaries"; Janan, *When the Lamp is Shattered*, 58–62.

16 Ross, *Style and Tradition in Catullus*, 105–6.

17 For Catullus' coinages to fill this place in the hendecasyllable line, see chapter 4, p. 78.

18 Fordyce, *Catullus*, on 7.3. The comparisons appear together at *Genesis* 22.17.

19 Battus was the legendary founder of the town of Cyrene. Callimachus calls himself "Battiades" (son or descendant of Battus) in *Epigram* 21, and Catullus refers to him as *Battiades* at 65.16 and 116.2.

20 For examples and discussion, see Smith, *Poetic Closure*, 67–9; Fowler, "First Thoughts on Closure," 98–101.

21 The structure and sound patterns in 46 are discussed by Elder, "Notes on Some Conscious and Subconscious Elements in Catullus' Poetry," 103–4, 120–1.

22 Elder, "Notes on Some Conscious and Subconscious Elements in Catullus' Poetry," 120.

23 See the entry for *pectus* in *Oxford Latin Dictionary*. Both *animus* and *mens* are generally located in the chest.

24 It is a small sign of Catullus' intricate art that the sense of these two passages is not quite identical. In the first she sees Theseus departing, in the second the ship. Why? Because so much has happened in the meantime that Theseus has moved too far away for her to see him; she can see only the ship.

25 For the dactylic hexameter, see chapter 4, pp. 84–6.

26 Apostrophe appears again in 64 in the description of the arrival of Bacchus (he has come to carry off Ariadne): "Iacchus [Bacchus] was rushing—seeking you Ariadne, and on fire with your love" (... *volitabat Iacchus /* ... */te quaerens, Ariadna, tuoque incensus amore*, 64.251–3). It is also used in poem 68, discussed below. But the most famous instance might be Virgil's apostrophe to Dido in the *Aeneid* as he tells how she watched Aeneas and his men getting ready to leave Carthage: "What feelings did you have then, Dido, as you saw such things, what groans did you utter?" (*quis tibi tum Dido, cernenti talia sensus, quosve dabas gemitus* ... *Aeneid* 4.409–9).

27 For excellent discussions of 101, see Biondi, "Poem 101"; Feldherr, "*Non inter nota sepulcra*: Catullus 101 and Roman Funerary Ritual."

28 The force of the repeated sounds becomes evident if one reads the poem aloud. For more on the sound patterns, see Biondi, "Poem 101," 181, 185–6.

29 The purpose in the purpose clause of lines 3–4 precedes Catullus' arrival. As the secondary tenses of the subjunctives (*donarem* and *alloquerer*) indicate, the actions in the clause "depend psychologically on *vectus* ['having traveled']." Biondi, "Poem 101," 182.

30 For the division of the pentameter, see chapter 4, pp. 86–7.

31 Mynors in the Oxford Classical Text prints 68 as a single poem but shows a break between verses 40 and 41. Thomson prints it as two poems, 68a and 68b. For the rationale for separating 68a and 68b, see Wiseman, "Catullus, 'Poem 68,'" in *Cinna the Poet*, esp. 76–90; Thomson, *Catullus*, 472–4.

32 See, e.g., Wiseman, "Structural Patterns in Catullus," 70–6; Bright, "*Confectum Carmine Munus*: Catullus 68"; Courtney, "Three Poems of Catullus," 95–7.

33 For the ideals and vocabulary of aristocratic friendship, see chapter 3, p. 58; chapter 4, pp. 96–7.

34 The three-word pentameter *Protesilaeam Laodamia domum* (74) is as elegantly Greekish as 68.112, discussed in chapter 4, p. 92. *Protesilaeam* is an adjectival form of a proper noun ("pertaining to Protesilaus"); it takes up the first half of the line (– ∪ ∪ – – –). The three words (Protesilaus', Laodamia, home) convey the essence of the situation; and their order puts Laodamia literally *inside* the house of Protesilaus.

35 For three different suggestions of ways to restore symmetry, see Wiseman, "Structural Patterns in Catullus," 72–6; Bright, "*Confectum Carmine Munus*"; Courtney, "Three Poems of Catullus," 95–7.

36 For more on the similes, see Feeney, "'Shall I compare thee?' Catullus 68B and the Limits of Analogy." The Hercules simile is brilliantly explained by Tuplin, "Catullus 68," 131–6.

37 The lament is the subject of poem 101, considered above. It is imbedded in a longer elegy at 65.5–14 (see chapter 6, pp. 144–5) and 68a.15–26; in both poems Catullus refuses a friend's request for poetry on the grounds of his grief. Verses 68a.20–4 are nearly identical to 68b.92–6; scholars have used the similarity both to deny and to defend the idea that 68 is a single poem.

38 But since line 93 contains no possessive pronoun ("my" or "your"), *misero fratri* might also refer to Catullus, called wretched since he has lost his brother ("the light of his life," as we might say).

39 Feeney, "'Shall I compare thee?'," 35 (reprinted in Gaisser, ed., *Catullus*, 433).

40 The reading transmitted by our oldest manuscripts is *mira* ("marvelous"), which is generally agreed to be wrong. I follow Thomson in printing *media*; Goold prints *muta* ("silent").

6

Songs for Mixed Voices: Allusions, Intertexts, and Translations

---

> What counts as an intertext and what one does with it depends on the reader.
> Don Fowler ("On the Shoulders of Giants")

In previous chapters we have noted that Catullus' poems reach out and refer to each other, so that ideas and phrases from one resonate in another, bringing their context with them.[1] These echoes invite the reader to supplement the sense of one poem with that of another, activating latent possibilities for meaning. The collection is a dynamic ensemble or system whose parts interact with each other; as the perspective of the reader changes, the themes of the poems fall into different patterns like the shifting images of a kaleidoscope (an analogy I used in chapter 2). If any single poem had survived without the rest, it could certainly be intelligible and interesting in its own right; but however interesting it might be, it would be diminished, shorn of the associations that give it depth and nuance in the collection. In effect, it would be a different poem. To take a single example, if we had only poem 3, it would still appear as a charming and pathetic lament on the death of the sparrow that had belonged to Catullus' girl (*meae puellae*), and we could still argue about whether to read it as a *double entendre*; but it would lack the emotional resonance it has as a part of the collection. We would not feel the affective force of the phrase *meae puellae* (a force gained from its appearance in other poems), and we would know nothing of Catullus' great love affair since the poem contains no mention of Lesbia—"that Lesbia, whom Catullus loved above all, more than himself and everyone dear to him" (58.2–3).

But although the collection is a system, it is not a closed system. Catullus' poems resonate not only with each other, but also with previous poetry, both Greek and Roman. Although much of this poetry is lost and we cannot pick up or interpret its echoes, we can still identify many links between Catullus' poems and what has survived. Identifying traces or citations of one poet or poem in another is a longstanding preoccupation of classicists, and any commentary on an ancient author is full of lists of what are variously called parallels, echoes, borrowings, imitations, or allusions. But trying to interpret such traces—that is, trying to see what meaning they bring to the work in which they are found—is an activity that has blossomed only in the last generation or so. There is a growing bibliography of important theoretical discussion on such questions as what constitutes an interpretable echo of one poem in another and whether textual citation and the ideas it suggests can be considered intentional on the part of the author or whether such echoes must be seen as an an inescapable property of language and texts.[2] Modern scholars generally agree that textual citation contributes meaning, invoking the tenets of reader response criticism to maintain that the contributed meaning is activated by the reader in the process of reading. A reader who does not recognize the citation will not find it meaningful or try to interpret it; and different readers will not necessarily agree on either the importance or the meaning of a given citation. As Fowler points out: "Intertextuality . . . is ultimately located in reading practice, not in a textual system . . . what counts as an intertext and what one does with it depends on the reader."[3] The test of an interpretation's validity is whether it makes sense in the context of a particular poem and whether it is convincing to others in the contemporary interpretative community.[4]

The subject of this chapter is the presence of earlier texts in Catullus and the ways in which their words and voices mingle with and ultimately become his own, adding depth and meaning to the poems in which they appear. In discussing these textual traces I will use the terms allusion and intertext interchangeably, along with such words as reference, imitation, citation, and echo. Our concern in every case will be to interpret the effect of such textual traces, not to recover the intention of the poet, for we do not have access to the mind of Catullus any more than to his emotional biography. We will look both at the translations (poems 51 and 66) and at several poems containing smaller intertexts (70, 65, 64, and 101).

Signposts of Allusion (Poems 70 and 101)

Poem 70 is a good place to begin, for it has intertextual resonance with poetry both inside and outside the system of the collection. This epigram both reaches out to other poems in Catullus and contains additional intertexts of two different kinds: it patterns itself on an epigram of Callimachus, clearly signposting the allusion;[5] and it alludes to an old adage or commonplace. The poem was discussed in chapter 2, but it will be useful to look at it again, this time paying closer attention to its intertexts.

We will start with Catullus and Callimachus. (Catullus' signposts of allusion and their counterparts in Callimachus are shown in boldface.)

First Catullus:

> Nulli se **dicit** mulier mea nubere malle
>   quam mihi, non si se Iuppiter ipse petat.
> **Dicit**: sed mulier cupido quod dicit amanti,
>   in vento et rapida scribere oportet aqua. (70)

(My woman **says** that she would rather marry no one than me, not if Jupiter himself should ask her. She **says**, but what a woman says to an eager lover should be written on the wind and rushing water.)

Now Callimachus:

> Kallignotos **swore** to Ionis that he would never love
>   anyone, male or female, more than her.
> He **swore**, but it's true, what they say: the vows
>   of lovers never reach the ears of the gods.
> Now he burns for a boy, and the poor girl
>   (as they also say) is out in the cold.
>   (Callimachus, *Epigram* 11, Nisetich translation)

The poems are in the same meter (elegiac couplets) and have a similar theme: the unreliability of a lover's promises. But Catullus' allusion is signalled—guaranteed, in fact—by a stylistic marker: the positioning and repetition of "says" (*dicit*) in lines 1 and 3, which imitates the positioning and repetition of "swore" in lines 1 and 3 of Callimachus.[6] The echo is emphatic in line 3, where the verb in each poem appears at the beginning of the verse, followed by a strong pause and the word "but." Callimachus' epigram has 6 verses, Catullus' only four, but the allusion is so strongly signposted that the force of his omitted final couplet is still felt. Catullus' four lines strongly imply that the woman (surely Lesbia) will be untrue to her words; the shadow presence of Callimachus' ending spells it out.[7]

But Catullus' epigram also differs from Callimachus' in several important respects. Catullus' is in the present tense and personal; Callimachus' impersonal and in the past. The most important difference from the standpoint of intertextuality, however, is in the sex of its characters: Catullus has reversed the sexes of betrayed and betrayer, casting himself in the role of the girl Ionis, and the woman in that of the man Kallignotos. Such cross-casting is a frequent feature in his poetry. Female characters are often his emotional counterparts, both in similes (as in the case of Laodamia in poem 68, as we noted in chapter 5) and in other intertexts, as we shall see presently. The woman of poem 70, on the other hand, appears almost double-gendered, and with the worst aspects of both. As Kallignotos she has the unattractive role of the careless masculine betrayer. But she is also tarred with the faithlessness proverbially (and misogynistically) deemed characteristic of women. Catullus' statement in the second couplet ("what a woman says to an eager lover should be written on the wind and rushing water") has various parallels in ancient literature. The closest one I know is a fragment of Sophocles: "I write the oath of a woman on the water."[8] But the allusion is probably general, to the proverbial conception rather than to a particular passage.

The intertexts in poem 70 suggest interesting complexities below the smooth surface of the epigram. The Callimachean intertext tells us what will happen next and inverts the gender roles of Catullus and Lesbia, striking a chord that resonates with ideas in several other poems in the collection. It is worth lingering for a moment over the implications of this last point. We have frequently noted the ways in which poems reach out to other poems in the collection (or system, as I have called it). Now it seems that references to texts outside the system can set in motion additional reverberations within it, strengthening its internal links. The second intertext, the imbedded proverb on the unreliability of women's words, functions as proverbs generally do: as a nugget of unassailable ancient wisdom. In this poem, as we have seen, Catullus makes Lesbia anonymous, calling her only *mea mulier* (my woman); the proverb too deprives her of individuality, placing her in the category, "woman," and imputing to her the fickleness it has defined as characteristic of her race.

Poem 101, like poem 70, was discussed earlier (for the full text and translation, see chapter 5). Like poem 70, it too contains a clear signpost of allusion to a Greek model, this time to the opening of Homer's *Odyssey*, as Conte has pointed out.[9] Here are the opening verses of both (the words in Catullus marking the allusion are shown in boldface).

First Catullus:

> **Multas** per gentes et **multa** per aequora vectus
>   advenio has miseras, frater, ad inferias,
> ut te postremo donarem munere mortis
>   et mutam nequiquam alloquerer cinerem. (101.1–4)

(Having traveled through **many** nations and through **many** seas, I arrive, brother, for these sad funeral rites, to present you with the final tribute of death and speak in vain to the silent ashes.)

Now Homer:

> Tell me, Muse, of the man of **many** ways, who was driven on
> **many** journeys,[10] after he had sacked Troy's sacred citadel.
> **Many** were they whose cities he saw, whose minds he learned of,
> many the pains he suffered in his spirit on the wide sea,
> struggling for his own life and the homecoming of his companions.
> Even so he could not save his companions, hard though
> he strove to; they were destroyed by their own wild recklessness.
>   (Homer, *Odyssey* 1.1–7, Lattimore translation, slightly modified)

The principal marker is Catullus' *multa* ("many"), which echoes Homer's insistence on the multiplicity of Odysseus's nature and experience. Homer calls Odysseus "the man of many ways" (*polutropon*), and he uses the word *polla* or *pollōn* ("many") three times in the first four lines: "driven on *many* journeys"; "*many* were they whose cities he saw"; "*many* the pains." Catullus evokes the wanderings of Odysseus for his own long and varied journey to his brother's tomb, but before we try to see how the allusion functions in 101, we must turn to a later appearance of it, at a significant moment in Vergil's *Aeneid*.[11] Aeneas, another wanderer, has come to the underworld to consult with the shade of his dead father Anchises. Anchises greets him thus:

> Quas ego te terras et quanta per aequora vectum
> accipio! quantis iactatum, nate, periclis!
>   (*Aeneid* 6.692–3)

(I receive you, my son, having traveled through what lands and over how many seas, tossed about by how many dangers!)[12]

Vergil, as Conte notes, is remembering both Homer and Catullus. The repeated exclamatory pronouns, *quas* (what!), *quanta* (how many!), *quantis* (how many!), recall Catullus' and Homer's repetition of *multa/polla*. Vergil's *quanta per aequora vectum* ("having traveled through how many seas") closely echoes Catullus' *multa per aequora vectus* ("having traveled through many seas"). The phrase *quantis iactatum . . . periclis* ("tossed about by how many dangers") is in the spirit of Homer's "was driven on many journeys."[13]

The allusion to the *Odyssey* in poem 101 is more open-ended than that to Callimachus in poem 70, leaving the reader to consider how to interpret it and in what ways Catullus is like (or unlike) Odysseus. But the passage in the *Aeneid* gives us an important insight from one early interpreter. Vergil, arguably the most gifted reader in antiquity, treats it as a reference to Odysseus' journey to the underworld in book 11 of the *Odyssey* and specifically to his meeting there with his mother.[14] Aeneas meets and communicates with his father in the underworld, just as Odysseus had spoken with his mother. But Catullus, despite his own Odyssean journey, lacks the power of an epic hero: he cannot bridge the gap between life and death to reach his kinsman. He can only come to his brother's tomb, present his funeral gifts, and "speak in vain to the silent ashes." The idea of a partially failed journey is also present in the intertext: Odysseus in his wanderings struggled to save his companions as well as himself but was unable to do so (*Odyssey* 1.5–7).

Like the intertext in poem 70, that in 101 also strengthens the epigram's ties with other poems in the collection. The allusion to the *Odyssey* evokes the idea of Troy, not mentioned in the epigram, and subtly reminds us that the brother died there, drawing the poem and its themes more closely to poems 65 and especially to 68a and 68b, where the connections linking Troy, the brother, and death are more fully developed.

Translations and Cover Letters: Poems 50, 51, 65, and 66

Translation can be seen as intertextuality taken to its upper limit, for it brings the whole of the imitated text—not just a part of it or an allusion to it—into the new poem. But poetic translations are not just duplicates of their models put into a different code. Catullus' translations in particular are new works of art in their own right, poems not just *brought across* (translated) from Greek to Latin, but *brought into*—we might better say transplanted—into the system of his own poetic collection, where they take on connections and meanings not present in their originals. In this section we will consider poems 51 and 66, the one translated from Sappho, the other from Callimachus. Each is a gift to a friend, and each is preceded in the collection by a poem that acts a cover letter, a role that is clearly stated in the case of 65, only implied in that of 50.

Playing with Poetry (Poems 50 and 51)

Poem 50 is a verse letter in which Catullus reminds Calvus of the fun they had had writing verses the previous day :

> Yesterday, Licinius, having nothing to do,
> we fooled around a lot on my tablets
> since we had agreed to be frivolous,
> each of us writing little verses
> played now in one meter, now in another,
> going back and forth in jest over the wine. (50.1–6)[15]

Afterwards, Catullus maintains, he was too excited to eat or sleep, anxious to see daybreak so that he could enjoy Calvus' company again. Finally exhausted, he composed a poem for him:

> hoc, iucunde, tibi poema feci,
> ex quo perspiceres meum dolorem.
> Nunc audax cave sis, precesque nostras,
> oramus, cave despuas, ocelle,
> ne poenas Nemesis reposcat a te.
> Est vemens dea; laedere hanc caveto. (50.16–21)
> (I made this poem for you, dear friend,
> so that you could see my distress.
> Now don't be rash, and I beg you,
> don't scorn my prayers, my precious,
> lest Nemesis take vengeance on you.
> She's a powerful goddess. Take care not to offend her.)

"I made this poem . . . so that you could see my distress." The words seem to describe poem 50, which clearly enumerates the symptoms of Catullus' "distress" (*dolorem*, 17) in its central verses (7–15): restlessness, loss of appetite, excitement, and exhaustion. The language has a strong erotic cast, as critics have noted.[16] But "this poem" (*hoc poema*) can also refer to what follows: poem 51, his translation from Sappho, which also describes the physical symptoms of emotional turmoil. On this reading, poem 50 is an invitation to Calvus to continue their poetic game, and the two poems provide the opening for a renewed exchange of verse.[17] But the readings are not mutually exclusive. The phrase, "I made this poem," reads both ways; its doubleness is part of the poetic play that will continue in poem 51.

Poem 51 is a translation of fragment 31 of Sappho. Here is Catullus:

> Ille mi par esse deo videtur,
> ille, si fas est, superare divos,
> qui sedens adversus identidem te
>   spectat et audit
>
> dulce ridentem, misero quod omnis   5
> eripit sensus mihi: nam simul te,
> Lesbia, aspexi, nihil est super mi
>   . . .[18]
>
> lingua sed torpet, tenuis sub artus
> flamma demanat, sonitu suopte   10
> tintinant aures, gemina teguntur
>   lumina nocte.
>
> Otium, Catulle, tibi molestum est;
> otio exsultas nimiumque gestis;
> otium et reges prius et beatas   15
>   perdidit urbes.
>
> (That man seems to me to be a god.
> He, if it is allowed, seems to surpass the gods,
> who sitting opposite you, again and again
> Watches and hears you
>
> laughing sweetly—a thing which robs me,
> poor wretch, of all my senses.[19] For the moment
> I catch sight of you, Lesbia, I have none left
> . . .
>
> But my tongue is numb, a thin flame
> runs under my limbs, my ears ring
> with their own noise, my eyes are
> covered by twin night.[20]
>
> Idleness, Catullus, is your problem;
> In idleness you are excited and restless.
> Idleness before now has ruined
> kings and rich cities.)

Catullus' poem is very close to its model.[21] Both poems are in Sappho's characteristic meter, the Sapphic strophe, which Catullus uses only here and in poem 11. Both Sappho and Catullus present themselves as observing a man and a woman together—a godlike man next to a laughing woman. The man is godlike both because he is in the woman's presence and because he can withstand it (and in Catullus' version, withstand it "again and again"—*identidem*).[22] The poet, on the other hand, is thrown by one glimpse of her into a faint, or into what the ancient critic Longinus in his discussion of Sappho called "delirious passion."[23] Perhaps the observing poet is jealous; most modern critics have said so. But I believe that his principal theme is admiration, of the woman's charm on the one hand, and of the man's apparent self possession on the other.

Yet the two poems are not identical. Catullus' poem differs from Sappho's in ways large and small. Here we can consider only some of the major differences. Catullus describes the situation and his symptoms in three stanzas (lines 1–12), Sappho in four. Catullus' last stanza (13–16), generally called "the *otium* stanza," has no counterpart in Sappho.[24] Catullus names names: the woman is called Lesbia (7), the observer Catullus (13). The woman in Sappho is anonymous, and Sappho does not mention her own name. Catullus' poem is a lyric in the modern sense of the term, on a theme personal (or ostensibly personal) to the poet, and intended for private performance and reading, while Sappho's is a public lyric, composed for oral performance at a communal event.[25] Sappho's poem speaks to a public occasion; Catullus' resonates with other poems in his collection. Perhaps most important, the sex of the observer is different in the two poems. In translating Sappho, Catullus has ascribed to himself the symptoms of "delirious passion" expressed by a woman. He is presenting his emotional life in female terms, employing the same kind of cross-casting or reversal of sex roles that we observed in poems 68 and 70. We will return to the matter of cross-casting presently, for it is an important thread linking 51 with 11, Catullus' other poem in sapphics. First, however, we must see how poem 51 fits into the poetry game with Calvus.

At the beginning of poem 50 Catullus describes the play:

> each of us writing little verses
> played now in one meter, now in another,
> going back and forth in jest over the wine. (50.4–6)

The game sounds a lot like the kind of poetry contests we saw in the last chapter in the discussion of poems 62 and 45.[26] One player introduces a theme, and the other must respond, building on it and trying to top it. Catullus and Calvus also challenged each other by setting their themes in different meters (*modo hoc modo illoc*, 50.5). At the beginning of this discussion I suggested taking 50 as an invitation to continue the game. If we read poems 50 and 51 together, we might even speculate that Catullus is proposing a variation on it: introducing a theme (the physical symptoms of emotional excitement) in 50, and transposing it in 51 not only into a different meter, but also into a different voice and key. In 50 the meter is hendecasyllabic, the voice that of the Catullan persona, the key friendship, with its physical symptoms of excitement expressed in erotic or near-erotic terms. In 51 the meter is sapphic strophe, the voice Sappho's ventriloquized by that of the Catullan persona, and the key erotic passion. How might Calvus respond? Perhaps with another translation, in still another meter; perhaps with a new theme played out in two different versions in the manner of poems 50 and 51.

A reading of the poems along these lines also suggests ways to look at two details in 51: the mention of the name Lesbia in 51.7 and the *otium* stanza at the end. Lesbia, of course, is Catullus' beloved, and the name is a metrically equivalent pseudonym for Clodia. But Lesbia also means "woman of Lesbos," i. e., Sappho. Catullus has given his darling a name with poetic associations, complimenting her elegance as well as her wit and literary taste.[27] The name has a double association (Clodia and Sappho), particularly in 51, but even here readers tend to privilege the meaning "Catullus' beloved" over the meaning "Greek poet." Yet here especially the name Lesbia has both meanings. We should acknowledge its doubleness just as we acknowledged the doubleness of *hoc poema* in 50. Lesbia in 51 is Catullus' usual Lesbia, to be sure, but she is also Sappho, and Catullus' sensations on seeing her are both erotic and poetic at the same time, just like his sensations in poem 50. In poem 51 Catullus is dazzled by Lesbia—that is, by *both* Sappho and Clodia.

The *otium* stanza is one of the great controversies in Catullus, and critics remain divided about whether it belongs to poem 51. Discomfort with it arises from the facts that it has no counterpart in Sappho and no obvious connection to the rest of Catullus' translation. Its defenders make various arguments, the most important in terms of the present discussion being that the stanza picks up the theme of *otium* ("leisure," "lack of useful activity") from the beginning of poem 50: "Yesterday, Licinius, having nothing to do" (*hesterno, Licini, die otiosi*, 50.1). The idea of having nothing to do, of playing around with time on one's hands, brackets the two poems, opening the one and closing the other. To put it another way, we can say that the poetic contest of poems 50 and 51 is set—appropriately—in a frame of leisure.

Poems 51 and 50, translation and cover poem, are closely connected expressions of the delight in playing with poetic form that Catullus shared with his friend. But 51 is related in a different way to poem 11. These two poems, linked by meter, have often been taken to represent the beginning and ending of the affair with Lesbia: the one, so goes the thinking, Catullus' shy approach by way of a translation indirectly expressing his feelings, the other a harsh and contemptuous dismissal.[28] The connection between them is marked linguistically; both use the word *identidem* ("again and again," 51.3, 11.19), which appears in Catullus only in these poems. The poems are also linked by their use of Sappho and the device of cross-casting. In poem 11 Catullus sends a message to his girl (*meae puellae*, 11.15) by way of Furius and Aurelius.

> cum suis vivat valeatque moechis,
> quos simul complexa tenet trecentos,
> nullum amans vere, sed identidem omnium
>   ilia rumpens;
>
> nec meum respectet, ut ante, amorem,
> qui illius culpa cecidit velut prati
> ultimi flos, praetereunte postquam
>   tactus aratro est.   (11.17–24)
> (Let her live and flourish with her lovers,
> whom she holds three hundred at once in her embrace,
> loving no one truly, but again and again busting
> the balls of all.
> And she should not count, as before, on my love,
> which has fallen by her fault like a flower
> on the edge of a meadow after it has been touched
> by a plow going by.)

Catullus' comparison of his love to a broken flower resonates with two different pictures in earlier poetry: Homer's comparison of a young dying warrior to a poppy drooping in the rain (*Iliad* 8.308–10) and the image of a bride's virginity as a flower to be plucked or destroyed, which appears in Sappho.[29] The passage in Sappho is a fragment, probably from an epithalamium.[30] Only two verses are preserved:

> like the hyacinth in the mountains that the shepherd men
> trample with their feet, and on the ground the purple flower . . .
> (Sappho, fragment 105c, Jenkyns translation)

The Sappho intertext feminizes Catullus' love (it is like the lost virginity of the bride) and places him in the female emotional role that he plays in poems 68, 70, and 51. But Catullus' image is masculine as well, for we must not forget Homer's dying youth, cut down in his prime. The unnamed girl (surely Lesbia) is in the masculine role, playing the plow to Catullus' flower. But she is also female—excessively so, as we see in the preceding stanza, where her voracious female sexuality takes over and destroys the virility of her many lovers. Both characters, then, are double-gendered. Catullus is a victim in both genders, like both the dying young warrior and the young bride with her innocence destroyed. Lesbia is destructive in both: cast both as a man who deflowers a bride and as a rapacious woman who unmans her lovers.

Haec expressa tibi carmina Battiadae (Poems 65 and 66)

Poem 65, like 50, accompanies a translation sent to a friend. The friend is Quintus Hortensius Hortalus, a prominent orator a generation older than Catullus; and the translation is from Callimachus' *Lock of Berenice*.[31] It is the first poem in the collection in elegiac couplets and the first to mention the death of Catullus' brother, a theme confined to the elegies and epigrams.

The elegy is Catullus' reponse to Hortalus' request for a poem. It takes the form of a single long sentence of 24 verses structured in three sections: a concessive clause (although grief calls me away from the Muses, 1–4), an explanatory digression (for my brother has died at Troy and I will always lament his death, 5–14), and a main clause (nevertheless I will send you this translation of Callimachus, 15–24). This simple structure is the armature of an elegant and extremely complex poem, a cover letter to be sure, but one with intertextual references that resonate with themes both in 66 and elsewhere in the collection. These intertexts are contained in similes. Given Catullus' predilection for feminine emotional models, it can be no accident that the characters in both similes are female. The first simile appears in Catullus' lament for his brother:

> numquam ego te, vita frater amabilior,
> aspiciam posthac? At certe semper amabo,

>   semper maesta tua carmina morte canam,
>   qualia sub densis ramorum concinit umbris
>   Daulias, absumpti fata gemens Ityli.   (65.10–14)
>   (Shall I never see you hereafter, brother
>   dearer than life? But certainly I will always love you,
>   always sing songs made sad by your death,
>   like the ones the Daulian sings under the dense shade of the branches,
>   lamenting the fate of lost Itylus.)

The Daulian woman (wife of Tereus, king of Daulia) slew her son Itylus, was transformed into a nightingale, and thereafter perpetually sang of her grief.[32] Catullus is echoing a passage from book 19 of the *Odyssey* in which Penelope speaks to the disguised Odysseus. She says that she is torn by the competing claims of husband and son, for if she continues to wait for Odysseus' return, she risks letting the suitors squander her son's inheritance. When she tries to sleep, her thoughts race back and forth:

>   As when Pandareos' daughter, the greenwood nightingale,
>   perching in the deep of the forest foliage sings out
>   her lovely song, when springtime has just begun; she, varying
>   the manifold strains of her voice, pours out the melody, mourning
>   Itylos, son of the lord Zethos, her own beloved
>   child, whom she once killed with the bronze when the madness was on her;
>   so my mind is divided and starts one way, then another.
>   (*Odyssey* 19.518–24, Lattimore translation)

Catullus' allusion is clearly marked by his near translation of the second line in Homer (compare his "under the dense shade of the branches" with Homer's "in the deep of the forest foliage"). Catullus and Homer's Penelope use the nightingale simile a little differently: his initial point of comparison is the sadness of his song, hers the rapid movement of her thoughts. But basic to both is the idea of grief and the endless mourning for a dead kinsman. The Homeric intertext also contains two ideas that seem not to be in Catullus' poem, at least for now: the responsibility of the nightingale for Itylus' death, and the dilemma of divided loyalties. The thought that Catullus might feel some responsibility for the loss of his brother is never mentioned or even hinted at in 65 (or in 68 or 101), but the nightingale simile lets it at least slide under the surface of our reading: there are several versions of the myth, but in all of them the nightingale kills her son.

The idea of divided loyalties, latent in the section on the brother's death, comes to life in the second intertext, which dominates the last section of the poem.

> sed tamen in tantis maeroribus, Hortale, mitto
>   haec expressa tibi carmina Battiadae,
> ne tua dicta vagis nequiquam credita ventis
>   effluxisse meo forte putes animo,
> ut missum sponsi furtivo munere malum
>   procurrit casto virginis e gremio,
> quod miserae oblitae molli sub veste locatum,
>   dum adventu matris prosilit, excutitur,
> atque illud prono praeceps agitur decursu,
>   huic manat tristi conscius ore rubor.   (65.15–24)

(But nevertheless in such great grief, Hortalus, I send you these translated verses of Battus' son [Callimachus], lest you think that your words, entrusted in vain to the wandering winds, have slipped from my mind, as the apple sent as a secret gift from her lover rolls out of the chaste lap of a maiden (the poor girl put it under her soft garment and forgot). It is shaken out when she jumps up at her mother's arrival and tumbles down in a rush, and a guilty blush spreads over the unhappy girl's face.)

We are in a curious position with regard to the intertext of Catullus' simile. It is generally agreed that he is alluding to Callimachus' story of Acontius and Cydippe from book 3 of the *Aetia*.[33] That story, which was very famous in antiquity, also includes a fateful apple. (Acontius, in love with Cydippe, presented her with an apple inscribed with the words, "By Artemis, I will marry Acontius." When she read the inscription aloud, she was committed to the vow.) Although much of Callimachus' story is lost and its surviving fragments have little in common with the situation in Catullus, the allusion seems vouched for by circumstantial evidence, both from the fragmentary ancient summary of the missing sections and from treatments of the story of Acontius and Cydippe by later poets. We can be (almost) certain of the presence of Callimachus in the passage, but have no way to interpret it beyond saying that it is an elegant touch to use a Callimachean allusion to lead into a translation from Callimachus (poem 66).

The simile itself is difficult. Does the apple refer to Hortalus' words, which have nearly slipped Catullus' mind, or to the poem that tumbles out as a gift to his friend?[34] I think it is both: the apple tucked up and forgotten is Hortalus' request, but the one that rolls out—the same apple, transformed by poetic alchemy in the middle of the simile—is the gift of poetry.³⁵ Yet the issue at the heart of both the simile and poem 65 as a whole is the same: the dilemma of conflicting claims—a conflict anticipated by Penelope's quandary in the Homeric intertext of the nightingale simile. When the girl hides her lover's gift, she is deceiving her mother; when she shows it (inadvertently), she betrays her lover. Catullus must neglect either brother or friend, for he will fail in his duty by honoring the claims of either.

In poem 66 he solves the dilemma—obliquely and brilliantly—by translating Callimachus' *Lock of Berenice*.³⁶ Callimachus' elegy, which ends book 4 (the last book) of the *Aetia*, at first sight seems an unlikely vehicle for exploring serious themes. It is highly learned court poetry, written to compliment Berenice, the queen (and cousin—the point is important) of Ptolemy III Euergetes, ruler of Alexandria. Berenice, a recent bride when Euergetes set out on a military expedition, vowed a lock of her hair for his safe return. Euergetes came back in triumph, and the lock was duly shorn and dedicated. When it disappeared from the temple where it had been placed, Conon, the court astronomer, discovered it as a cluster of stars in the sky. This whole event, which may have been staged by Euergetes and Berenice as propaganda, is commemorated in Callimachus' poem in a first-person narration by the lock itself. Catullus seems to have translated his model very closely, but it is impossible to be sure since only about a third of Callimachus' elegy survives, and that in very fragmentary form.³⁷ Enough does survive, however, to demonstrate its outline and general themes and to let us consider how a translation of this poem in particular not only responds to the problem set out in 65 but also resonates with themes elsewhere in the collection.

Callimachus' poem is ideally suited to honor the claims of both friendship and fraternal love. Its frivolous character actually enhances its charm as a gift to a friend, and the technical difficulty of rendering Callimachus' recherché language into elegant and equally recherché Latin makes it a neoteric tour de force calculated to appeal to a connoisseur of things Greek (as Hortensius seems to have been).³⁸ The themes of the elegy, on the other hand, are serious, or become so, when it is translated (and transplanted) into the context of Catullus' other poems. In the previous section I suggested that in poem 51 Catullus transposes the theme of 50 from the key of friendship into that of erotic passion. In translating Callimachus in 66 he transposes again, this time putting some of his major themes into a different emotional register. Speaking in the overwrought and arch, but nonetheless pathetic, voice of the severed lock, he transposes serious ideas into a key of frivolous play. But the themes can still be heard even in their playful setting, just as musical motifs in the scherzo of a sonata or symphony can resonate with and reprise those in darker movements. Seen in this light, poem 66 answers Catullus' need to grieve for his brother. It also, as we will see, lets him treat (and reconcile) his favorite themes of erotic and familial love. Not surprisingly, these themes are expressed in a female voice: the grammatical gender of the lock (*coma*) is feminine.[39]

The idea at the heart of 66 is the pain of separation—of the lock from Berenice, of the lock from her fellow locks, and of Berenice from her husband. The lock, speaking from her new place in the heavens, cries out to Berenice:

> invita, o regina, tuo de vertice cessi,
>   invita: adiuro teque tuumque caput. (66.39–40)
> (against my will, O queen, I left your crown,
> against my will. I swear by you and your head.)[40]

We may smile at the lock's swearing by the *head* of Berenice, but her feelings are serious, and the repetition of the emotive word *invita* ("against my will") emphasizes her sincerity.[41] She makes a similar comment some lines later after describing her exalted position as a constellation;

> non his tam laetor rebus, quam me afore semper,
>   afore me a dominae vertice discrucior. (66.75–76)
> (I do not rejoice in these things so much as I am in torment that I will always be away from—be away from—the head of my mistress.)[42]

In a discussion of poem 64 in the last chapter, I pointed out the emotional effect of the rhetorical figure called epanalepsis, in which an important word near the end of one verse is repeated a word or so later in the beginning of another.[43] In 64 Catullus uses the device to stress the pathos of Ariadne's situation; here the lock uses it (a little operatically) of herself: *me afore semper, / afore me a dominae vertice* ("I will always be away from—be away from—the head of my mistress"). The idea of eternal absence, so emphasized here, is not in Callimachus, where the lock says only: "I am grieved that I shall no longer touch that head." A small change, we might think, and so it is. But it is still worth noting, for it is by small changes as well as large ones that a translation of one poem into another becomes a new work of art with its own story to tell. The affective epanalepsis here sends us back to a comparable one in the lament for his brother in 65. There, the repeated word is "always" (*semper*), shown below in boldface.

> Shall I never see you hereafter, brother
> dearer than life? But certainly I will **always** love you,
> **always** sing songs made sad by your death. (65.10–12)

The shorn lock was grieved for by her fellow locks—sister locks, as both poets call them:

> abiunctae paulo ante comae mea fata sorores
>   lugebant . . . (66.51–2)[44]
> (My sister locks were mourning my fate, cut off
> from them a little before . . .)

Why "sister locks"? If we are thinking in terms of poem 65, the phrase reminds us of Catullus, bereft by the loss of his brother, also "cut off a little before." In the context of 66, the phrase emphasizes the lock's kinship with Berenice's other tresses—survivors, we could say, of the fatal severing—but it also ties into the other sibling relation and separation in 66: that of Berenice and Euergetes. The royal pair, actually cousins, were officially described as brother and sister, in conformity with the custom of sibling marriage the Ptolemies had taken over from their Egyptian predecessors.[45] The lock teasingly alludes to the double relationship when she reminds Berenice of her distress at being separated from Euergetes.

> et tu non orbum luxti deserta cubile,
>   sed fratris cari flebile discidium,
> cum penitus maestas exedit cura medullas. (66.21–3)
> (and bereft, you did not mourn your empty bed,
> but the sad separation from your dear brother,
> when grief utterly consumed your sorrowful heart.)[46]

The lock's words are ironic, for she knows that Berenice does not love Euergetes *only* "like a brother." Far from it, for she is concerned here and elsewhere in the poem to emphasize the queen's sexual passion for her husband, which seems to have been an important element of Ptolemaic propaganda.[47] The sibling-conjugal relationship, so foreign to the modern reader, was intended to present the marriage of the royal couple as a complete union, both familial and sexual. It was foreign to Catullus too, but the idea has some points in common with his own idealized picture of an erotic love with the same deep emotional resonance as that between close (male) kin.

Poem 66 is a poem about love and loss, but with a happy ending. The lovers are reunited, and even the lonely lock eternally separated from her mistress has an immortal existence in the heavens and can demand to be honored with sacrifices. (She wants the lavish perfumes exclusive to married women that were denied to her when the queen was still unwed, 89–93.) The poem presents Catullus' deepest themes, but transformed and dreamlike, as in a fantasy: the loss of his brother, the longing for an ideal love based on passion and affection, the pain of loneliness and separation. I have taken the list from the collection as a whole, but the themes of 66 resonate especially with those in poems 63 to 68. In 63 Attis castrates himself, mourns, and is forever changed; in 66 the lock is the severed part, mourns, and is forever changed. In 64 we hear of the marriages of both Peleus and Thetis and Theseus and Ariadne; neither can compete with the romance of Euergetes and Berenice.[48] Poem 67 tells of an adulterous wife; 66 praises chastity, warning women against impure adultery (79–88).[49] In 68 Catullus mourns his brother; Laodamia, a bride as new as Berenice, loses her husband for ever; and Catullus recalls an adulterous, wedding-like assignation with an unnamed woman (undoubtedly Lesbia). In 66 all these unhappy pieces are turned over to present a different aspect. We can even think, if only in passing, of the lock in the sky as answering Catullus' grief in poem 65 (as well as in 68 and 101), for it speaks not as the bereaved one but as the one forever lost—reflecting the kind of pain felt by Catullus himself.

Time after Time (Medea and Ariadne in Poem 64)

Poem 64 is Catullus' masterpiece, a stunning example of what seems to have been the essential neoteric genre, the epyllion.[50] An epyllion (the term is modern) is a miniature epic, a poem in epic meter (dactylic hexameter) in hundreds rather than thousands of verses, and often on an "unepic" theme—not heroic adventure, but unhappy or even criminal love, with emphasis on a heroine and her emotions. Catullus' poem is the only surviving neoteric epyllion, but from both Alexandrian and later Roman examples it is clear that epyllia tended to feature certain formal elements, the most common of which is a story within a story, sometimes narrated by a character, sometimes presented in an ecphrasis (description of a work of art). In poem 64 the frame story is the wedding of Peleus and Thetis, the inner story the ill-fated romance of Theseus and Ariadne, which is woven or embroidered on the coverlet of the marriage bed. The poem is learned (formidably so). It features various and often contradictory voices and perspectives, and it is deeply layered with intertextual echoes and allusions both literary and visual.

In what follows I will consider what I regard as its most important intertext, which is a story rather than a single text. The story is that of Medea, and Catullus alludes to it with echoes from Apollonius Rhodius, Euripides, Callimachus, and Ennius. The story is used in both the frame and the ecphrasis, but it is most prominent in the ecphrasis, where Medea appears as almost an alter ego of Ariadne. Catullus' use of the Medea intertext is enriched and complicated by two central paradoxes in the poem. The first is an irreconcilable chronological contradiction between the frame, where the *Argo* is said to be the first ship, and the ecphrasis, which shows Theseus sailing away in a ship, evidently long before the voyage of the Argonauts. The second paradox is the fact that although the whole story of Theseus and Ariadne is told in the ecphrasis, only two of its scenes are said to be shown on the coverlet.

Catullus' poem begins with the voyage of the Argonauts:

> Peliaco quondam prognatae vertice pinus
> dicuntur liquidas Neptuni nasse per undas
> Phasidos ad fluctus et fines Aeetaeos,
> cum lecti iuvenes, Argivae robora pubis,
> auratam optantes Colchis avertere pellem   5
> ausi sunt vada salsa cita decurrere puppi,
> caerula verrentes abiegnis aequora palmis.
> . . .
> illa rudem cursu prima imbuit Amphitriten.   11
> (Once upon a time pines born on Pelion's peak
> are said to have floated through the clear waves of Neptune
> to the streams of Phasis and the territory of Aeëtes.
> when chosen youths, the oak heart of Argive manhood,
> hoping to carry off the golden fleece from the Colchians,
> dared to run down the salt waves in a swift ship
> sweeping the blue-green sea with oars of fir.
> . . .
> That ship first introduced inexperienced Amphitrite to sailing.)

The work is allusive from the start. Its allusiveness is marked with what has been called a neoteric footnote or an authority formula, the word *dicuntur* ("are said," 2), which announces that the poet is referring to a predecessor or an earlier version of his story. In this case the source is the tragedy of Medea, which also begins with a reference to the building of *Argo* on Mt. Pelion. Catullus is thinking of both Euripides' *Medea* and Ennius' *Medea Exul*, which closely imitated it.[51] In 64.4–5 his use of Ennius' Latin is unmistakable. Here is Ennius:

>   quae nunc nominatur nomine
>   Argo, quia Argivi in ea delecti viri
>   vecti petebant pellem inauratam arietis
>   Colchis
>   (Ennius, *Medea Exul* 211–14)
>   ([the ship] which is now called by the name
>   Argo, because chosen Argive men
>   sailing in it sought the golden fleece of the ram
>   from the Colchians)

Catullus does not explicitly name the ship as Ennius does, but he is close otherwise. His opening clearly suggests that his subject will be the voyage of *Argo*, and his allusions to the tragedies of Euripides and Ennius point us specifically to the part of the story that features Medea. In the next verses he follows the ship on her maiden voyage, and tells how the Nereids (sea nymphs) came up from the depths to marvel at the sight.

It is only in line 19 that Catullus reveals what is apparently his true subject, the marriage of Peleus and Thetis. He makes the revelation in an elegant and arresting set of verses:

>   tum Thetidis Peleus incensus fertur[52] amore,
>   tum Thetis humanos non despexit hymenaeos
>   tum Thetidi pater ipse iugandum Pelea sensit. (64.19–21)
>   (Then for Thetis Peleus is said to have been kindled with love,
>   then Thetis did not disdain marriage to a mortal,
>   then to Thetis the father himself thought Peleus should be joined.)

This is the first time in the poem that we have heard of either Peleus or Thetis, but Peleus was traditionally one of the Argonauts, and Thetis (we realize now) was one of the admiring nymphs. Catullus has surprised us by creating what seems to have been a false expectation about his subject and by creating a dissonance between what is suggested by the allusions (Medea) and what is asserted by the text (Peleus and Thetis). But the expectation is not really false. Rather, we have just witnessed Catullus' first move in a complex creation of narrative and allusion, text and intertext, story and story.

His second move is the manipulation of time—or more precisely, chronology—a trick he uses even more strikingly in the ecphrasis, as we will see presently. In direct conflict with almost universal ancient authority, he has reversed the chronology of the wedding of Peleus and Thetis and the launching of *Argo*; for in other versions, the voyage begins after the wedding and even after the birth of Achilles. In Apollonius Rhodius' epic *Argonautica*, the baby Achilles is brought for Peleus to see as the *Argo* sails.[53] By reversing the order of the two stories Catullus makes one dependent on the other: the voyage of *Argo* is responsible for the romance of Peleus and Thetis. To put it another way, the romance of Peleus and Thetis is presented as an episode within the *Argo* story. Indeed, it has become *the* episode within the *Argo* story, for immediately after the verses in which he mentions Peleus and Thetis (19–21, quoted above), Catullus salutes the Argonauts in an apostrophe that recalls the conclusion of Apollonius' *Argonautica*.

> O nimis optato saeclorum tempore nati
> heroes, salvete, deum genus! O bona matrum
> progenies, salvete! iter ⟨um salvete, bonarum!⟩
> vos ego saepe, meo vos carmine compellabo. (64.22–5)
> (O born in the much hoped-for time of the ages,
> hail, heroes, race of the gods! O noble sons
> of noble mothers, hail! again hail!
> You I will often address, you I will address in my song.)

Here is Apollonius:

> Be gracious, best of men, race of the gods! And may these songs be sweeter for men to sing from year to year. (*Argonautica* 4.1773–5)

This is the final appearance of the Argonauts in poem 64, but we have one last glimpse of Medea at the end of the frame story, for Catullus brings her—by allusion—to the wedding of Peleus and Thetis, whose details recall the wedding of Jason and Medea in Apollonius (*Argonautica* 4.1139–98).[54]

The most striking feature in both weddings is the marriage bed. Medea's was covered with the stolen golden fleece, Thetis' with the tapestry showing the story of Ariadne and Theseus.

> haec vestis priscis hominum variata figuris
> heroum mira virtutes indicat arte.
> Namque fluentisono prospectans litore Diae
> Thesea cedentem celeri cum classe tuetur. (64.50–3)
> (This garment, embellished with the images of men of former times,
> depicts the deeds of heroes with wondrous art.
> For looking out from the wave-resounding shore of Dia,
> [Ariadne] watches Theseus departing with his swift ship.)

His swift ship. This is the major and irreconcilable contradiction at the heart of the poem. Theseus belonged to the distant past in comparison to Peleus and Thetis. This much is confirmed both by Catullus' language ("the images of men of former times," 50) and by the hero's appearance as a well-known figure embroidered on their wedding coverlet. But if it was really the *Argo* that first sailed the sea, as Catullus assured us in the frame story ("that ship first introduced inexperienced Amphitrite to sailing," 11), where did Theseus get his ship? Catullus has deliberately manufactured the difficulty. He has followed Apollonius in reversing the traditional chronology, which placed Theseus and Ariadne after *Argo*, but he has introduced a contradition *not* present in Apollonius by insisting that *Argo* was the first ship.[55] Apollonius had good reason for his innovation: inverting the chronology allowed him to have Jason invoke Ariadne's assistance of Theseus as an example for Medea, naturally omitting the fact that Theseus later deserted her (*Argonautica*, 3.997–1004). Catullus' purposes are more complex. In the frame story he reversed the order of events so that the meeting of Peleus and Thetis became an inset in the story of the Argonauts. Here the result of his manipulation is a chronology that is not merely reversed but impossible. The chronological contradiction, which makes it impossible to give priority either to the story of Medea or to that of Ariadne, in fact will bring them both to mind at once, almost as if they were the *same* story and happening at the same time.

The coverlet displaying the story is strange in its own right. Like other ecphraseis, it has both an external viewer or audience (the reader) and an internal one, the character or characters within the poem seeing and interpreting the object.[56] In 64 the wedding guests are the internal audience: they are the only characters actually said to see the coverlet. But Catullus' description is unusual in almost every other respect, for it omits most of the elements typical of an ecphrasis. We are not told where the coverlet came from, who made it, what connection it has with Peleus and Thetis or what they thought of it (in fact, there is no sign in the poem that they ever saw it), or how we are to imagine it as a physical object.

The last point is particularly striking. In other ecphraseis the reader is frequently and explicitly reminded of the physical aspects of the object being described: of its material, of the positioning of scenes on its surface, of the fact that the figures are of metal, wood, or fabric. In all the 217 verses of this long ecphrasis, however, Catullus makes only three explicit references to the physical object. Two frame the description. The ecphrasis begins:

> haec vestis priscis hominum variata figuris
> heroum mira virtutes indicat arte.   (64.50–1)
> (This garment, embellished with the images of men of former times, depicts the deeds of heroes with wondrous art.)

It ends:

> talibus amplifice vestis decorata figuris
> pulvinar complexa suo velabat amictu. (64.265–6)
> (The garment luxuriously decorated with such images
> enclosed and covered the couch with its drapery.)

The third reference describes the placement of a scene:

> at parte ex alia florens volitabat Iacchus.   (64.251)
> (But on the other side was hastening young Iacchus.)

As a consequence, only two of the many scenes in Ariadne's story are actually described as being on the coverlet: the first, introduced by lines 50–1, of Ariadne standing on the shore watching Theseus sail away (50–70), and the last, the arrival of Bacchus / Iacchus (251–64), introduced by line 251. Only these are available to the wedding guests, the internal audience.[57] These two scenes were probably also well known to Catullus' readers, for they were frequently represented in Roman wall painting. Our existing examples are from Pompeii—that is, much later than Catullus; but there is good reason to believe that the Pompeian images are descended from Alexandrian prototypes and perhaps also from earlier pattern books.[58] Figures 1 and 2 show outline drawings of typical Pompeian representations of the two scenes. The external audience in

Figure 1. Ariadne on the Shore. Reprinted from H. Roux Ainé and M. L. Barré, *Herculaneum et Pompéi. Recueil Général des Peintures, Bronzes, Mosaïques, etc.* (Paris, 1861), vol. 2, pl. 35.

poem 64 (ourselves as readers) sees these familiar scenes, as well as several transitional passages, and three additional episodes: Theseus and Ariadne in Crete, Ariadne's lament, and the death of Theseus' father, Aegeus.

The two scenes available to the wedding guests are both introduced in the familiar descriptive language of ecphrasis. The other scenes are introduced by authority formulas, that is, by expressions used in storytelling. Theseus and Ariadne in Crete and Ariadne's lament are introduced

Figure 2. The Arrival of Bacchus. Reprinted from H. Roux Ainé and M. L. Barré, *Herculaneum et Pompéi. Recueil Général des Peintures, Bronzes, Mosaïques, etc.* (Paris, 1861), vol. 2, pl. 33.

by *perhibent* ("they tell," 76, 124), the death of Aegeus by *ferunt* ("they say," 212). We might suggest, then, that in his ecphrasis Catullus has woven description with narration to present two coverlets in one: the first for the wedding guests to see, embroidered with two famous scenes from the Ariadne myth, the other for us, interwoven and amplified with digressions, explanations, speech, and excursions into past and future—that is with narrative, which changes the meaning of the embroidered pictures.

The coverlet seen by the wedding guests is appropriate in every way to the wedding of Peleus and Thetis, for it shows both Ariadne's plight and the arrival of Bacchus, which seems to imply her rescue and marriage to the god. (The meeting of Ariadne and Bacchus is not spelled out in the description, but the guests would assume a happy ending, since Bacchus is described as "on fire with love" (*incensus amore*, 253) and the marriage is a standard feature of the story.)[59] The coverlet for us as readers is more complicated. It shows, by allusion, a second story not visible on the first; for the story of Medea—first in love, then betrayed, and finally destructive—runs through the narrative episodes as a disturbing counterpoint to that of Ariadne.

Medea makes her first appearance in the flashback to Theseus and Ariadne in Crete. Ariadne falls in love at first sight in a scene (86–98) that powerfully evokes Medea's first sight of Jason in Apollonius (*Argonautica* 3.286–90). The elements are all there: the court of a dangerous king, the arrival of a handsome stranger, and a virginal princess instantly on fire with love. Eros shoots Medea with his arrow in Apollonius. Eros (or rather, Cupid, his Roman counterpart) is to blame in Catullus, too, although less directly. Catullus addresses Cupid at the end of the scene in language recalling the effect of Eros' arrow on Medea. Here is Apollonius: "Medea overflowed in her heart with sweet pain" (*Argonautica* 3.290). Now Catullus:

> sancte puer, curis hominum qui gaudia misces (64.95)
> (divine boy, you who mix joy with sorrow for mortals.)

Medea is invoked, again indirectly, in Theseus' killing of the Minotaur (Ariadne's brother), for the monster's death recalls Jason's killing of Apsyrtus (Medea's brother). The Minotaur is described as "tossing his horns in vain to the empty winds" (*nequiquam vanis iactantem cornua ventis*, 111), while Jason fells Apsyrtus "like a huge bull with mighty horns" (*Argonautica.* 4.468).[60] Catullus does not tell us how we are to picture Ariadne in this scene, or whether she watched her lover kill her brother. Medea turned her eyes away and tried not to see at all (*Argonautica.* 4.465–7). Is Medea in these scenes of love and death a model for Ariadne, or Ariadne for Medea? In the chronology of this poem the question is absurd: all one can say is that they exist together in a loop of time where they have become all but merged and indistinguishable.

Medea appears again in Ariadne's lament (132–201), most of which has been uttered before, by the Medeas of Euripides, Apollonius, and

Ennius. She regrets that Theseus' ship ever came to Crete (171–2) in language that recalls the similar sentiment about the building of *Argo* at the opening of Ennius' *Medea Exul*.[61]

> Iuppiter omnipotens, utinam ne tempore primo
> Gnosia Cecropiae tetigissent litora puppes (64.171–2)
> (All-powerful Jupiter, if only in the beginning
> the Athenian ships had not touched the Cnossian shores.)

Compare Ennius:

> Utinam ne in nemore Pelio securibus
> caesa accidisset abiegna ad terram trabes. (Ennius, *Medea Exul* 208–9)
> (If only the beam of fir had not had not been cut with axes
> and fallen to earth in the Pelian grove.)

The allusion links (or superimposes) the chronologically impossible voyages of Theseus and Jason. Like Medea, Ariadne curses her lover as cruel and faithless (132–48), reminds him of how she helped him (149–51), laments the hopelessness of her situation (152–87), and utters a curse (188–201). The lament, like the scenes of Ariadne's falling in love and the killing of the Minotaur, presents Ariadne as Medea, but also Medea as Ariadne. Jason told the young Medea in Apollonius that she could be as happy as Ariadne, and so she is. Catullus' Ariadne, like the young Medea, fell in love and assisted at the murder of her brother, and we see where her trust has led. Like Medea, Ariadne has left father, mother, and sister to follow her brother's murderer. Now she wants Theseus similarly bereft. "Let him bring the pollution of death on himself and his own!" (*funestet seque suosque*, 64.201), she cries. Her prayer is answered with the death of Aegeus in the next scene. If we wanted to be fanciful, we could say that Ariadne has become mature and deadly like the Medea in Euripides or at the end of the *Argonautica*: like them, she can kill at a distance.[62]

Aegeus, too, of course, is connected with Medea, for in Euripides it is Aegeus who gives her sanctuary in Athens after she has killed her children. But we can also see her, indirectly as always, in Catullus' flashback to Aegeus' farewell to Theseus on his departure for Crete (212–37); for Aegeus' words, "son, just now restored to me at the extremity of my old age," cite the sole surviving fragment from the speech of Aegeus to Theseus in Callimachus' epyllion, *Hecale*.[63] The scene in Callimachus was much better known to sophisticated Roman readers than it is to us. In Callimachus Theseus has arrived unexpectedly from Troezen, has escaped Medea's attempt to poison him, and is now being addressed by Aegeus, his new-found father; presently he will set off to catch the bull of Marathon.

In the chronology of poem 64 Aegeus' speech, like Theseus' whole expedition, is a logical impossibility. In mythological tradition the first meeting of Aegeus and Theseus in Athens occurs *after* Aegeus' marriage to Medea, hence after Medea has killed her children and long after the *Argo* sailed for the golden fleece. So much is consistent with the tradition of the Argo as the first ship that Catullus insists on in the frame story; but it is flatly contradicted by the priority of Theseus' ship and the Ariadne story that he presents in the ecphrasis. By alluding to Callimachus' scene Catullus, with neoteric coyness, once more draws our attention to the contradiction he has manufactured. We are in another loop of time where stories come together. In the last we found Medea in Ariadne railing at her faithless lover, and here too Medea lurks between the lines; for she is present in the intertext, and she is indispensable to the reunion of Aegeus and Theseus. Although she goes unmentioned here, we recognized her only a moment ago in Ariadne's curse, already responsible for a death in Athens.

To sum up. In poem 64 Catullus has combined literary and mythological intertextuality with narrative complexity to create a learned and multi-layered work of great poetic art. His epyllion has not only an inner and outer story, but stories within stories. In the first section of the frame story he has constructed a miniature epyllion, framing the meeting of Peleus and Thetis with the voyage for the Golden Fleece. In the inner story of Theseus and Ariadne he invokes another story, that of Medea—a shadow story called up by allusion. In the concluding section of the frame story (not discussed here) he presents yet another tale, this time in a prophecy delivered by the Fates as a wedding song for Peleus and Thetis: the story of their son Achilles. All these stories are refracted through two paradoxes built into the structure of the poem: the chronological contradiction between the frame and ecphrasis, and the fact that although we are told the whole story of Ariadne and Thetis, only two scenes from it are depicted on the wedding coverlet. The chronological paradox creates an impossible narrative space—what I have called a loop of time—where different stories come together to become the same story, and all times exist at the same time. The paradox of the ecphrasis creates a coverlet that is double woven, or two tapestries in one, displaying two competing visions of the past to its different audiences. Like a hologram, the coverlet changes its meaning and appearance with the perspective of the beholder, revealing now an appropriate parallel to the joyful wedding of Peleus and Thetis, now a disturbing contrast that emphasizes, not Ariadne's rescue and marriage with the god, but human loss, betrayal, and destruction: the story of Medea.

Conclusion

Catullus drew on both Greek and Roman poetry freely and creatively. His work is dense with the themes, words, rhythms, and even whole poems of his predecessors. These intertexts complicate and enhance his poetry in various ways. In poem 70 the Callimachean intertext both spells out what will happen next and casts Catullus in the female role, a part he is also assigned by the intertexts of 51, 11, 65, and 66. In poem 101 the allusion to Homer establishes Catullus as a counterpart of Odysseus and implicitly contrasts his futile journey to his brother's tomb with Odysseus' ability to bridge the barrier between living and dead to speak with his mother's ghost. The intertext in 66 (Callimachus' *Lock of Berenice*) treats several of Catullus' essential themes (love, familial grief, marriage, a female voice) in a frivolous scherzo that resonates with their serious treatment elsewhere in the collection, particularly in poems 63 through 68. In poem 64, the intertext is not a single poem, but a story, that of Medea, allusively evoked by citations of several different works, both Greek and Roman.

Poetry like this certainly entitles Catullus to the epithet *doctus* ("learned"), which was applied to him in both antiquity and the Renaissance. *Doctrina* ("learning") was an essential aspect of neoteric poetry, which was a self-conscious amalgam of the recherché style, themes, and techniques of the Greek Alexandrians (especially Callimachus) with the Roman literary tradition. The neoteric poet had to be fully bilingual and so steeped in the recondite and abstruse literature of his second culture that he could use it easily, not just strewing nuggets of it on the surface, but incorporating it into the deep structure of his work. Such poetry also makes demands on the reader. Catullus' fellow neoterics and the learned connoisseurs of his own and the next generation or two shared his literary interests and cultural background (or most of it), but over time readers and fashions changed. In the next chapter we will consider some of those changes and how they affected the later reception of Catullus.

Notes

1. Chapter 2, pp. 31–6; chapter 3, pp. 57–60.
2. See, esp., Fowler, "On the Shoulders of Giants: Intertextuality and Classical Studies"; Hinds, *Allusion and Intertext*; Conte, *The Rhetoric of Imitation: Genre and Poetic Memory in Virgil and Other Latin Poets*, 23–95; Conte, "Poetic Memory and the Art of Allusion"; Edmunds, *Intertextuality*; Wills, *Repetition in Latin Poetry: Figures of Allusion*, 1–41.
3. Fowler, "On the Shoulders of Giants," 24.
4. Ibid., 20.
5. For markers and signposts of allusion, see Wills, *Repetition in Latin Poetry*, 15–41.
6. The position in line 3 is identical, but slightly altered in line 1, where Callimachus' "swore" (*ōmose*) is the first word and Catullus' corresponding *dicit* the third.
7. For the woman's identity and the implied conclusion, see chapter 2, pp. 32–3.
8. Sophocles, fragment 811 in Snell, ed., *Tragicorum Graecorum Fragmenta*, vol. 4. The wind and water carry the woman's words away in Propertius 2.28.8 and Ovid, *Amores* 2.16.45–6.
9. Conte, "Poetic Memory and the Art of Allusion," 168–75. See also Conte, *The Rhetoric of Imitation*, 32–9.
10. Lattimore has "who was driven far journeys" in lines 1–2. I have changed the translation to show the use of *polla* (many) in the Greek: *hos mala polla / plangthē*.
11. The allusion in Vergil was pointed out by Conte. See "Poetic Memory and the Art of Allusion," 169–71. See also Conte, *The Rhetoric of Imitation*, 33–5.
12. The translation is slightly modified from that in Conte, *The Rhetoric of Imitation*, 35. I have changed Conte's "borne through what lands" to "having traveled through what lands" in order to translate *vectus/vectum* with the same word in both Catullus and Vergil.
13. As Conte says ("Poetic Memory and the Art of Allusion," 171; *The Rhetoric of Imitation*, 34), *iactatum* (tossed about) "recreates the energy of" Homer's *plangthē* ("was buffeted or was driven").
14. See Biondi, "Poem 101," 187–9.
15. The Latin text is quoted in chapter 2, p. 24.
16. See Quinn, ed., *Catullus*, 238–9.
17. For 50 as an invitation to continue the game, see Burgess, "Catullus c. 50: The Exchange of Poetry." For 50 and 51 as a pair, see Wray, *Catullus and the Poetics of Roman Manhood*, 95–9, with earlier bibliography.
18. Line 8 is lost. Various supplements have been proposed. Thomson prints *vocis in ore*, omitted here.

19 I have borrowed from Goold's translation for lines 5 and 6.
20 Catullus' phrase *gemina nocte* is hard to translate comfortably into English. I have translated it literally: "twin night."
21 For the text and translation of Sappho fr. 31, see Page, *Sappho and Alcaeus*, 19–20; Janan, *When the Lamp Is Shattered*, 25–6. Sappho's text is printed in Quinn, ed., *Catullus*, 241–2, and Fordyce ed., *Catullus*, 407. Comparisons of Catullus' text with Sappho's can be found in Quinn, 242–6, and Thomson, ed., *Catullus*, 327–31. For more detailed comparisons, see Wormell, "Catullus as Translator"; Greene, "Re-figuring the Feminine Voice: Catullus Translating Sappho." For discussion, see Miller, "Sappho 31 and Catullus, C. 30: The Dialogism of Lyric," with earlier bibliography.
22 Catullus has added this point; it is not in Sappho.
23 Longinus, *On the Sublime*, 10.1.
24 The end of Sappho's poem is lost, but enough remains of its final stanza to indicate that in the *otium* stanza Catullus is either departing from it entirely or going in a new direction. Her last line (17) begins with a few intelligible words, *alla pan tolmaton, epei*, which Page translates "but all must be endured, since" (*Sappho and Alcaeus*, 20).
25 See Miller, "Sappho 31 and Catullus C. 51."
26 See chapter 5, pp. 104–7. For evidence of such an exchange between Catullus and Calvus, see the discussion of poem 96 in chapter 1, pp. 14–15.
27 Propertius and Tibullus in the next generation did likewise, both naming mistresses after Apollo, god of poetry. Propertius uses Cynthia (from Apollo's birthplace, Mt. Cynthos on Delos), Tibullus Delia (from Delos).
28 But the only evidence for this idea is the two poems themselves. For the tendency to construct a narrative from the poems, see chapter 8, pp. 213–14.
29 Catullus also uses the image in his marriage songs (61.87–90 and 62.39–47). See Edwards, "Apples, Blood, and Flowers: Sapphic Bridal Imagery in Catullus," with earlier bibliography.
30 See Jenkyns, *Three Classical Poets: Sappho, Catullus, and Juvenal*, 45–7.
31 For Hortensius, see Tatum, "Friendship, Politics, and Literature," 489–90. For Callimachus' poem, see below.
32 Catullus is conflating at least two versions of the story (see Quinn, ed., *Catullus*, 353–4; Thomson, ed., *Catullus*, 446). For a good discussion, see Wiseman, *Catullan Questions*, 17–20.
33 Callimachus, fragments 67–75. For a translation, see Nisetich, *The Poems of Callimachus*, 141–50. For discussion, see Hunter, "Callimachean Echoes in Catullus 65"; Skinner, *Catullus in Verona*, 14–18.
34 For the arguments, see Skinner, *Catullus in Verona*, 14–15, with earlier bibliography.

35 There is a similar slippage between simile and referents in 68.51–66; see Feeney, "Shall I Compare Thee . . .?" 37–9.
36 Callimachus, fragment 110. The text is printed in Fordyce ed., *Catullus*, 407–8. For a translation, see Nisetich, *The Poems of Callimachus*, 163–7. For discussion, see Fantuzzi and Hunter, *Tradition and Innovation in Hellenistic Poetry*, 85–8; Gutzwiller, "Callimachus' *Lock of Berenice*: Fantasy, Romance, and Propaganda."
37 Poem 66 has 94 verses; we have only about 30 verses of Callimachus' poem, 21 of which are continuous. For close comparison of Catullus' Latin with Callimachus' Greek, see Wormell, "Catullus as Translator"; Clausen, "Catullus and Callimachus."
38 For Hortensius' interest in Greek culture, see Tatum, "Friendship, Politics, and Literature," 489 n. 46.
39 Callimachus uses the masculine nouns *plokamos* and *bostruchos*, but modern scholars consider his lock not "unambiguously male" (Fantuzzi and Hunter, *Tradition and Innovation in Hellenistic Poetry*, 87 nn. 176–7).
40 Callimachus' line corresponding to l. 39 is lost, but most of the next is preserved: "I swear, by your head and your life" (Nisetich, trans., *The Poems of Callimachus*, 165).
41 Vergil seems to have registered the seriousness of 39, for he used a slightly modified version of it in the poignant words of Aeneas to the shade of Dido in the underworld: *invitus, regina, tuo de litore cessi* ("against my will, queen, I left your shore," *Aeneid* 6.460).
42 The corresponding verses of Callimachus read: "I am not so delighted with all that, as I am grieved / that I shall no longer touch that head" (Nisetich, trans., *The Poems of Callimachus*, 166, slightly modified). I have replaced Nisetich's "never again" with "no longer," which is a more literal translation of Callimachus' *ouketi*.
43 Chapter 5, p. 117.
44 Callimachus has: "My sister tresses / were mourning me, just then cut off" (Nisetich, trans., *The Poems of Callimachus*, 165).
45 Euergetes' father, Ptolemy II, married his full sister Arsinoe II (both were called Philadelphos, "lover of sister/brother"). His grandfather, Ptolemy I, married his half-sister Berenice, grandmother of our Berenice. For a family tree, see Fordyce, ed., *Catullus*, 329.
46 The corresponding verses in Callimachus are lost.
47 See especially Gutzwiller, "Callimachus' *Lock of Berenice*," 365–9.
48 The lock wittily alludes to a third marriage from 64, the projected union of Ariadne and Bacchus (64.251–64), when she mentions Ariadne's transformation into a star (66.59–62).
49 Since these verses have no counterpart in Callimachus, some scholars see them as a Catullan addition. For arguments against the idea, see Thomson, ed., *Catullus*, 460–1; Gutzwiller, "Callimachus' *Lock of Berenice*," 381–2.

50   Important discussions include Bramble, "Structure and Ambiguity in Catullus LXIV"; Thomas, "Catullus and the Polemics of Poetic Reference"; Zetzel, "Catullus and the Poetics of Allusion"; Jenkyns, "Catullus and the Idea of a Masterpiece"; Clare, "Catullus and the *Argonautica* of Apollonius Rhodius"; and DeBrohun, "Catullan Intertextuality: Apollonius and the Allusive Plot of Catullus 64." The interpretation in this section draws predominantly on Gaisser, "Threads in the Labyrinth: Competing Views and Voices in Catullus 64."

51   For details, see Thomas "Catullus and the Polemics of Poetic Reference"; Zetzel, "Catullus and the Poetics of Allusion." See also Konstan, *Catullus' Indictment of Rome*, 67–74.

52   *fertur* ("is said") is another example of the authority formula, used even though (or perhaps to emphasize that) Catullus' version has no authority. See Gaisser, "Threads in the Labyrinth," 584–5 (= Gaisser, ed., *Catullus*, 223–4); DeBrohun, "Catullan Intertextuality," 299.

53   *Argonautica* 1.557–8; see also *Argonautica* 4.790–809.

54   The similarities are spelled out by Zetzel, "Catullus and the Poetics of Allusion," 260 (= Zetzel in Gaisser, ed., *Catullus*, 209).

55   For a detailed discussion, see Weber, "Two Chronological Contradictions in Catullus 64."

56   For the features of ecphrasis, see Gaisser, "Threads in the Labyrinth," 588–91 (= Gaisser, ed., *Catullus*, 228–31), with earlier bibliography.

57   Forsyth, "Catullus 64: Dionysus Reconsidered."

58   Fredrick, "Beyond the Atrium to Ariadne: Erotic Painting and Visual Pleasure in the Roman House"; Gaisser, "Threads in the Labyrinth," 593 n. 49; 606 n. 90 (= Gaisser, ed., *Catullus*, 234 n. 49; 249 n. 90).

59   Whether their assumption would be correct is a different matter. See Wiseman, "Catullus' *Iacchus and Ariadne*."

60   Clausen, "Ariadne's Leave-taking," 220 n. 5.

61   For more on Ariadne and Ennius' Medea, see Zetzel, "Catullus and the Poetics of Allusion," 258–9 (= Zetzel in Gaisser, ed., *Catullus*, 206–8).

62   Euripides' Medea kills Jason's new wife and her father with a poisoned robe. Apollonius' Medea kills the bronze giant Talos with a magic curse (*Argonautica* 4.1654–88).

63   *gnate . . . /reddite in extrema nuper mihi fine senectae* (64.216–17). Cf. Callimachus' "you have come beyond my expectation" (*Hecale*, fr. 8, Hollis). The allusion was pointed out by Weber, "Two Chronological Contradictions in Catullus 64," 265.

7

Receiving Catullus 1: From Antiquity through the Sixteenth Century

---

> *quo licet ingenio vestrum celebrate Catullum,*
> *cuius sub modio clausa papirus erat.*
> Benvenuto Campesani
>
> (With all your talent celebrate your Catullus,
> whose light had been hidden under a bushel.)

In poem 1 Catullus prayed to the Muse that his work would "remain enduring for more than a single age" (1.10). His wish was granted, although just barely, as we will see. Like all works of literature, Catullus' poetry was very much of its place and time even when it was not directly concerned with what we might call current events. It was imbedded in and meaningful in its own cultural context, which included everything from habits of speech and fashions in dress, poetry, and art to social *mores*, political events, and physical surroundings. We can describe such a context in various ways. Thomas Greene called it a *mundus significans*, a signifying universe, which he defined as "a storehouse of signifying capacities potentially available to each member of a given culture."[1] The *mundus* of any literary work is ephemeral and passes away even when the work itself is preserved. The words may remain, but their meaning and context change—subtly or drastically—depending on the degree of alteration in the world they describe. Here is how Greene puts it:

> The signifier is rooted in the activity of a society which alters, but the word in its apparent stability fails to respond sensitively to that alteration. Beneath the apparent constancy of the *verbum* ["word"], the *res* ["actuality"] of experience is sliding into new conformations with the immense complexity of history.[2]

Readers too have their own signifying universes, their own worlds of experience, signs and symbols, from which they approach and interpret the past. Within even a few years the reader's *mundus* diverges from that of the poet and his work, and the difference increases over time.

It is essential to realize that all readings and interpretations are historically contingent, *including our own*. All of us, whether we mean to or not, impose on Catullus (or any other ancient author) the assumptions and values we have absorbed from our own world; inevitably we read Catullus' poetry through the lenses of our own time. And so did all our predecessors, from the Augustan poets to the readers and critics of the twentieth century. This principle of historical contingency has two important corollaries. The first is that no one has an unmediated encounter with the past. Later readers see ancient authors not only through the lens of their own time, but also—in a compound prescription—through the lenses of previous interpreters, who provide the assumptions on which, consciously or unconsciously, their successors form their own views. The second corollary is that not only the interpretation but the survival of classical authors has depended on this continuum of reading, which Charles Martindale calls a "chain of receptions."[3] Martindale's dictum that "meaning is always realized at the point of reception" has become a watchword in studies of interpretation and reading.[4] But its converse is also true: if meaning is not realized, reception does not take place. If at a given point a work is not meaningful to readers in terms of their own world, they will ignore it—or as we might say, they will not receive it. If too many potential points of reception are missed, the work will be lost, simply because no one cares enough about it to produce or acquire copies of the text. This was nearly the fate of Catullus.

This chapter and the next are concerned with the reception of Catullus at several key moments of his history. This chapter treats Catullus' fortunes from antiquity to the end of the sixteenth century. In the next, we will consider his reception in England and America. In both chapters we will pay special attention to the conceptions of Catullus' character and personality formed by later readers and the ways in which those conceptions determined the interpretation of his poetry. Catullus' persona, as I argued in chapter 3, is so vivid, sympathetic, and realistic that readers from antiquity on have been convinced of its absolute sincerity. Persuaded that they know and understand him, that on some level he is just like them, readers have not only identified with Catullus, but identified Catullus with themselves. The mental portraits readers paint of Catullus are self-portraits, and their features change over time, molded as they are not only by the individual personalities but also by the historical circumstances—the signifying universes—of their creators.

Martial's Catullus

Catullus had a profound influence on the next generation of poets: the Augustans Horace, Vergil, Propertius, Tibullus, and Ovid.[5] Each of the Augustans took something different from the neoteric program, now mature and fully integrated into the Latin poetic landscape. Each also took something different from Catullus. Horace, although he conspicuously fails to acknowledge it, built on Catullus' use of Greek meter and borrowed some of his themes. Vergil used parts of poem 64 in the *Fourth Eclogue*, imitated Catullus' neoteric style in the Aristaeus epyllion at the end of the *Fourth Georgic*, and made Ariadne an important component of Dido in *Aeneid* 4.[6] Propertius, Tibullus, and Ovid used Catullus and Lesbia as the model for the love-struck poet and faithless mistress of their elegies. Ovid in the *Metamorphoses* constructed a long series of epyllia and played with Catullan and neoteric narrative technique.

Catullus' popularity continued through the Silver Age (the period from around the death of Augustus in 14 to that of Trajan in 117), but he was now popular in a different world and for different reasons.[7] The hurly-burly of the late Republic, where a Catullus could attack a Caesar with impunity, had given way first to Augustan order and then to the dangers and sycophancy of the Empire. Caesar invited Catullus to dinner, Augustus exiled Ovid, Domitian's reign of terror silenced a generation. The city itself was now greatly changed. It was as violent, dirty, and dangerous as it had been in Catullus' day, but it had become a polyglot metropolis, transformed by the building programs of the Caesars and the arrival of new inhabitants from every corner of the empire. The cultural world, too, had altered. Neoteric poetry, no longer new, had become a cliché. Poets and readers in the Silver Age valued Catullus, but not for his learning, stylistic innovation, and emotional complexity. Instead, they admired his talent for invective, his use of erotic themes (both homosexual and heterosexual), and his obscenity. They liked his short poetry best. To take only a few examples: the elder Pliny and both Senecas mention only the polymetrics; polymetrics or epigrams are the subject of six of Quintilian's seven references to Catullus. There are some favorites: the attack on Caesar and Mamurra in poem 29, the dedication poem (1), the claim that the poet's life is separate from his poetry (16), the kiss poems (5, 7, 48), and the poems on Lesbia's sparrow (2 and 3).

Catullus' most enthusiastic admirers in the Silver Age were Martial (c. 38–c. 101) and the younger Pliny (c. 61–c. 112), two men very different both from each other and from Catullus in social position and attitude. Catullus, living in the relative freedom of the late Republic, was a wealthy young man with excellent connections. He could afford to be in the literary avant-garde, to live for his poetry, and to insult anyone he liked, from Caesar and Pompey to the demagogue Publius Clodius, the brother and lover of his Lesbia. Martial had no such advantages. He came to Rome from Spain around 64 A.D. Lacking both money and social position, he lived on the unreliable generosity of various patrons and occasional gifts from the emperor. He needed to please the rich and famous and to avoid making dangerous enemies. Pliny, by contrast, was a rich man who spent his career in government, holding a series of imperial administrative positions. He is most famous today for his letters, but he also dabbled in poetry for amusement. He claims to have tossed off his verses in an idle hour, "in the carriage, in the bath, at table" (*Epistles* 4.14.2), and apparently there were other amateur versifiers like him, for he says that he followed "the example of many" (*Epistles* 7.4.8) in composing a volume of hendecasyllabic poems.

Unlike Pliny, Martial was no amateur versifier. He was a highly talented professional who made his living with his poems—over 1500 of them, published in 15 books in a twenty-year period at the end of the first century. He claims Catullus as his principal model throughout his poetry, constantly invoking Catullus' name and imitating his themes and turns of phrase. In over 200 poems he uses Catullus' characteristic meter, the hendecasyllable. But Martial's poetry is very different from Catullus', and its Catullan flavor emphasizes its distance and disjunction.[8] His persona is not serious or tormented, but brash, crass and jocular. Catullus ends his first poem with a wish for poetic immortality. Martial's concern in his opening epigram is present popularity. Byron's translation neatly catches its tone.

> He, unto whom thou art so partial,
> O reader! is the well-known Martial,
> The Epigrammatist; while living,
> Give him the fame thou wouldst be giving;
> So shall he hear, and feel, and know it:
> Post-obits rarely reach a poet.
> (Martial 1.1, George Gordon,
> Lord Byron, trans.)

Martial rejects Alexandrian learning and mythology in favor of contemporary home truths and observations, and his poems contain not a hint of Catullan emotion or devotion to a single beloved. Like Catullus, Martial often writes invective, but his epigrams are the product of dangerous times: although often offensive, they are designed to offend no one in particular. The butts of his satire and obscene jests are types; real people receive pleasantries and compliments. Brash and sycophantic or not, Martial is no slavish imitator. He creatively and liberally exploits his model, taking Catullus' poems apart, putting a witty spin on their ideas, and reassembling them in new and surprising combinations. There are many examples of his technique, but his treatments of poems 2, 3, 5, and 16 would be especially important to later readers of Catullus.

Martial's most famous contribution to the reception of Catullus is his obscene interpretation of the sparrow of poems 2 and 3. He plays with the idea in several epigrams, but most notoriously at the end of epigram 11.6, which combines the sparrow of poem 2 with the kisses of poem 5. Addressing his slave boy Dindymos, he says:

> Da nunc basia, sed Catulliana:
> quae si tot fuerint quot ille dixit,
> donabo tibi Passerem Catulli. (Martial 11.6.14–16)
> (Now give kisses, but Catullan-style,
> and if these be as many as he said,
> I will give you the sparrow of Catullus.)

These lines are typical Martial. He has provided a witty conclusion to his own epigram, made a surprising juxtaposition of themes from two different Catullan poems, and all but spelled out a shocking interpretation of Catullus' sparrow as his penis.[9] The idea would both delight and scandalize Renaissance readers, and critics are still debating its validity (although I think that most today would agree with it).[10]

Martial's treatment of poem 16 had a less contentious but perhaps even more important influence on Catullus' reception, especially in the Renaissance. Catullus' poem falls into several parts as shown below (the Latin text is given in chapter 3).

> I'll bugger you and stuff it down your throats,
> queer Aurelius and faggot Furius!
> who think from my verses—because they're
> a little soft—that I'm not quite modest.

For it is right for the true poet to be chaste himself,   5
but not necessary for his verses to be so;

they only have wit and charm
if they are a little soft and not quite modest,
and can stir up sexual excitement—
I don't mean for boys, but for these hairy old men   10
unable to move their stiffened loins.

You, because you have read of many thousands
of kisses, do you think me hardly a man?
I'll bugger you and shove it down your throats.

Poem 16 easily lends itself to Martial's technique of dissecting and reassembling his models. It contains three principal ideas. We can call them "the critic's complaint" (lines 1–4 and 12–14, framing the poem), "the poet's excuse" (a distinction between the poet's verses and his behavior, 5–6), and "the recipe for successful poetry" (lines 7–11). Martial saw that he could use these elements together or separately to state his own poetic program. In epigram 1.35 he uses the critic's complaint (shown in italics below) and the recipe for successful poetry (shown in boldface), but omits the poet's excuse.

> *Versus scribere me parum severos*
> *nec quos praelegat in schola magister,*
> *Corneli, quereris.* **sed hi libelli,**
> **tamquam coniugibus suis mariti,**
> **non possunt sine mentula placere.**   5
> Quid si me iubeas thalassionem
> verbis dicere non thalassionis?
> Quis Floralia vestit et stolatum
> permittit meretricibus pudorem?
> **Lex haec carminibus data est iocosis,**   10
> **ne possint, nisi pruriant, iuvare.**
> Quare deposita severitate
> parcas lusibus et iocis rogamus,
> nec castrare velis meos libellos.
> Gallo turpius est nihil Priapo.   15
>   (Martial 1.35)

(*You complain, Cornelius, that I write verses not quite serious and not of the sort that a schoolmaster might dictate in school;* **but these poems, like husbands with their wives, cannot please without a prick.**[11] What if you were to order me to celebrate the wedding song in words not of the wedding song? Who puts clothes on the Floralia and allows the modesty of the matron's dress to harlots? **This law has been established for playful poems: that they cannot please unless they are aroused**. Therefore, put away your seriousness, I ask, and go easy on my sport and jests—and don't wish to castrate my poems. Nothing is more disgusting than a eunuch Priapus.)

The critic's complaint in Martial recalls that in Catullus, and the final cadence in the first line, "not quite serious" (*parum severos*), echoes Catullus' "not quite modest" (*parum pudicum*, poem 16.4). But the echo also highlights an essential difference between the two complaints. Furius and Aurelius are describing Catullus, whereas Martial's critic Cornelius is referring not to the poet, but to his *verses*. Martial presents the recipe for poetry in two parts: first as an analogy (poems, like husbands, need a prick in order to please, 3–5) and then as a law (*lex*, line 10) that "verses cannot please unless they are aroused" (*ne possint, nisi pruriant, iuvare*). Martial's law recalls the prescription in Catullus—but again with a difference. In Catullus the successful verses must be titillating: they must "stir up sexual excitement" (*quod pruriat incitare*, 16.9) or—as we might render it, "stir up *what feels* sexual excitement" (that is, the penis)—of the boys and men in the next line. In Martial, however, the verses themselves must be aroused.[12]

But what about "the poet's excuse"? By omitting it Martial has also banished everything that goes with it: that is, the personal and affective elements of his model. He makes no attack on his critic and omits all concern with the persona and the poet's relation to the behavior described in his poetry. This poem, we could say, is not about a person or a persona, but about a prick (*mentula*). This point is worth looking at more closely, because Martial took the *mentula*, as he took so much else, from Catullus 16. It's right there in Catullus' first line, not mentioned by name but clearly understood as the instrument involved in the threat: "I'll bugger you and shove it down your throat." But as always with Martial and Catullus, it is the differences that matter. Catullus invokes the *mentula* obliquely, Martial explicitly. In Catullus the *mentula* is personal. It appears both in the frame (1–4, 12–14) and in the central argument. The *mentula* in the frame belongs to the poet, and its use in a sexual attack on his critics will allay their doubts about his masculinity; the *mentula* in the argument belongs to the boys and men to be aroused by titillating poetry (8–11). In Martial the *mentula* is depersonalized and transformed into a symbol of obscenity. It appears first in line 5: "these poems, like husbands with their wives, cannot please without a prick." It appears next—this time obliquely—in line 11: playful poems "cannot do any good unless they are aroused." And at the end: "don't castrate my poems. Nothing is more disgusting than a eunuch Priapus." This final image makes Martial's point and sharply distinguishes his argument from Catullus'. Both arguments are programmatic. Catullus uses the *mentula* as part of the teasing game of hide and seek about poetry and reality that he has created between himself and his readers (see chapter 3). Martial uses it to establish the poet's playful verse as the embodiment of an aroused Priapus.

In epigram 1.35 Martial draws on two of the programmatic elements that he found in Catullus' poem 16. He uses the third, "the poet's excuse," by itself as the conclusion of epigram 1.4: "my page is naughty, my life pure" (*lasciva est nobis pagina, vita proba*). But Catullus is not his immediate model. As we saw in chapter 3, Catullus' language is indirect and ambiguous. He distinguishes between the words and life of the poet in general terms and makes no unequivocal statement about his own life and character:

> For it is right for the true poet to be chaste himself,
> but not necessary for his verses to be so. (16.5–6)

Martial, however, is not interested in subtlety of this kind. In epigram 1.4 he is excusing his racy poems to the dangerous and straitlaced emperor Domitian, and he wants to introduce no doubts or confusion. The context requires a neat antithesis between art and life, and he finds his model in Ovid's unambiguous words to Augustus: "my life is chaste, my Muse playful" (*vita verecunda est, Musa iocosa mea*, *Tristia* 2.354).

The poet's excuse in both Catullus' formulation and the simplified version of Ovid and Martial would become a staple in Catullan imitation, and the process was well on its way a few years after the publication of Martial's first book of epigrams. Pliny draws on both Catullus and Martial in a defense of his own not very racy book of poetry. He says:

> Scimus alioqui huius opusculi illam esse verissimam legem, quam Catullus expressit:
> > nam castum esse decet pium poetam
> > ipsum, versiculos nihil necesse est;
> > qui tum denique habent salem ac leporem,
> > si sunt molliculi ac parum pudici.
>
> (Pliny, *Letters* 4.14.5)

(Anyhow, we know that the soundest law of this little work is Catullus' statement:

> For it is right for the true poet to be chaste himself,
> but not necessary for his verses to be so;
> they only have wit and charm
> if they are a little soft and not quite modest.)

Pliny attributes his excuse to Catullus (quoting four verses rather than two from poem 16), but his use of Martial is guaranteed by the word "law" (*legem*) in his introduction, which he took directly from Martial (epigram 1.4.8).

Catullus had a profound influence on the poets of the Silver Age; but they exercised an equally great influence on Catullus. They turned him into a poet for their own time, changing him from a varied and complicated neoteric into an epigrammatist who looked a lot like Martial: amusing, popular, untroubled by emotional complexity or tiresome Alexandrianism. It was this Catullus, or this *picture* of Catullus, that they transmitted to succeeding generations.

Catullus Goes Underground

It is one of the ironies of literary history that the admiration and imitation of Martial, along with that of Pliny and other lesser poets of the Silver Age, probably contributed to Catullus' virtual eclipse from the end of the second century on. Martial and his contemporaries had no interest in the qualities that modern readers admire in Catullus: his elegant urbanity, his learned Alexandrianism, his passionate emotion, the window he gives us into the world of late republican Rome. Instead, they promoted him as a poet of light verse and epigram, a genre that spoke of and to *their* world in a voice whose accents they could easily recognize. The voice was that of his chief imitator, Martial, who soon found more readers than his model. Why read an old fashioned and sometimes difficult poet like Catullus, when one could so easily enjoy Martial's smooth and racy epigrams? In the second century Aulus Gellius and Apuleius knew some of Catullus' poems; the poet of the *Ciris* and the author of an epitaph for a pet dog knew others.[13] But even then texts were no doubt already becoming scarce, and we can be sure that fewer still were preserved when scribes transferred the works of ancient authors from roll to codex around the fourth century.

After the second century Catullus essentially disappears from view for a thousand years.[14] A few later writers mention his name or quote a verse or phrase at second hand, and there are various scraps of evidence for the transmission of the text; but after the second century we can point to only a tiny handful of people for the next millennium who undoubtedly read Catullus: the scribes who copied his poems. The number might be as small as three or as large as four or five: the scribe (or scribes) who transcribed his poetry from roll to codex in the fourth century, the scribe of a ninth-century anthology containing poem 62, and the scribe of the single manuscript we know of that survived the Middle Ages. Catullus surely had some other readers, but we do not know who they are. No one we can name displays clear and irrefutable knowledge of so much as a single poem.

We know that Catullus made the journey from antiquity to the Renaissance (he arrived, after all) but we do not know how or by what route. It is as if we were tracing a submarine or an underground stream, our evidence a faint blip of sonar or a tell-tale puddle, a mention here, a possible sighting there, a dubious one somewhere else. But at last, around 1300, Catullus washed up on the shores of the Renaissance, with only the poor manuscript he stood up in and a few laudatory testimonia from antiquity. We do not know what his manuscript looked like, for it was copied soon after its discovery and then lost or destroyed; and we do not know who found it, or where. Scholars call this lost manuscript V (for Verona, Catullus' home city). It is the ancestor of all our existing manuscripts.[15]

A contemporary epigram preserved in two of our earliest manuscripts commemorates the discovery and identifies the discoverer, but in the form of a riddle, which no one yet has managed to solve.[16]

> *The Verses of Master Benvenuto Campesani of Vicenza*
> *on the Resurrection of the poet Catullus of Verona*
> An exile, I come to my country from distant lands.
> A fellow-countryman was the cause of my return,
>   that is, one to whom France assigned a name from the reeds
>   and who marks the journey of the passing crowd.
> With all your talent celebrate your Catullus,
>   whose light had been hidden under a bushel.

Only one point in the riddle is clear: someone from Catullus' home city of Verona discovered the manuscript "in distant lands" and brought it back to Verona. Confusion surrounds the rest.

Pontano's Catullus

The discovery of Catullus was greeted with enthusiasm, for he was one of the most celebrated poets of antiquity and he had been lost for a thousand years.[17] The difficulty was that no one knew what to do with him. Scholars copied his manuscripts, but at a very slow rate. (There are only four manuscripts from the first hundred years after his discovery, and only half a dozen more from the next fifty.)[18] They tried to correct the text, collected quotable verses for their anthologies, and included Catullus in lists of obscene poets when they sought either to excuse or to condemn scandalous verse. For the most part, however, they did not imitate or try to interpret his poetry, largely because they could not read it. Catullus' text was notoriously corrupt. Poems were run together; there were metrical problems without number; the point—and often even the subject—of many poems was lost. Furthermore, although the humanists admired the learning of Catullus' poetry (or rather, admired the *idea* that it was learned) they were vague about the details. They knew that the poet was called *doctus Catullus* ("learned Catullus") by other ancient writers, but they had little notion of what his learning entailed. At this period Greek studies were in their merest infancy, and much that we take for granted about Alexandrian literature was unknown. (In fact, two of the texts most important for understanding Catullus' learned Alexandrianism were discovered only in the twentieth century. Both are from the *Aitia* of Callimachus: the prologue, which sets out Callimachus' poetic programme, and the *Lock of Berenice*, which Catullus translated in poem 66.)

Real engagement with Catullus began only after around 1400, with Catullan imitations of very different kinds by two Florentine humanists, Leonardo Bruni (1370?–1444) and Cristoforo Landino (1424–1504). Sometime between 1405 and 1415 Bruni composed an obscene hendecasyllabic pastiche of poems 41–3, which had been transmitted as a single poem in V.[19] A generation later Landino wrote an imitation of poem 11 and composed three variations on poem 8 in a collection he called the *Xandra*.[20] Neither Bruni nor Landino, however, had any influence on later Catullan poetry. Bruni's ugly pastiche sank with hardly a trace, and Landino's imitations, metrically and thematically more like Roman elegy than Catullan lyric, were left behind in what would turn out to be the main focus of Renaissance imitation, the hendecasyllabic poems.

It was Giovanni Gioviano Pontano (c. 1429–1503) who set Catullan poetry on the course it was to follow throughout the Renaissance.[21] Pontano, one of the greatest Renaissance Latin poets, had come to Naples as a young man and become a friend and disciple of the poet Antonio Beccadelli, known as Panormita, who had written a collection of obscene poetry called *Hermaphroditus* in imitation of Martial and the *Priapeia*. Pontano's association with Panormita and his poetry would be decisive, for it showed him that he could use Martial as a way to approach Catullus. The idea is not so strange as it might seem to a modern reader. Catullus had landed in the Renaissance virtually out of nowhere, in a single corrupt manuscript, and with no baggage of late antique or medieval imitation, interpretation, or scholarship. But Martial could supply the lack. Reversing what might seem to us the obvious order, most people in the Renaissance read Martial before they read Catullus. Many manuscripts of Martial were available; he had been studied by Boccaccio in the 1370s, and by nearly every humanist afterwards; and his epigrams were widely imitated.[22] Best of all, his poems both imitated and interpreted Catullus, as we saw in the previous section. Reading Catullus through Martial, Pontano saw a light and racy epigrammatist, witty and often obscene, without emotional complexity, political animus, or Alexandrian complexity. It was this Catullus who would dominate fifteenth-century interpretation.

It is important to point out, however, that the Catullus perceived by Pontano and his successors was not identical with Martial's Catullus. The civilization of Catullus and Martial was gone, and with it the basic cultural assumptions that they had shared both with their ancient readers and with each other. Pontano and the other humanists were Italians, not Romans, and they saw both Martial and Martial's Catullus with Renaissance eyes. Thus, we might think of them as reading Catullus through both Martial's lens and their own—seeing neither a versatile Alexandrian nor a poet of light and racy verse, but rather a new figure, the Renaissance Catullus.

With Martial as his guide, Pontano produced a collection of Catullan poetry within a year of his arrival in Naples (*Pruritus*, 1449).[23] Two other collections followed: *Parthenopaeus sive Amores* (1457) and *Hendecasyllabi sive Baiae*, written throughout the 1490s and completed around 1500 or so. The three collections differed in tone and subject. *Pruritus* was more explicitly obscene than the others and closer to Panormita and the *Priapeia*. *Parthenopaeus* (which incorporates some of the less obscene poems from the *Pruritus*) embarks on a sophisticated literary program.

The *Hendecasyllabi*, erotic poems of Pontano's old age, have moved farthest from explicit imitation of Catullan subjects to an almost elegiac celebration of the enfeebled and fragile, but enduring, Eros of old men.[24]

All three collections are frankly sensual, and all have as their point of departure Catullus' recipe for successful verses, codified into a law by Martial and Pliny: that light poetry is an aphrodisiac whose purpose is to arouse and titillate the reader. Pontano exploits the entire "law" in the formulation of Pliny, which specifies the arousal of both boys and hairy old men: in the program poems of his three collections he applies it to the stages of his own life and those of his friends. The "critic's complaint" and "poet's excuse" play little part, and Pontano makes no attempt to separate himself from his verses.

The *Pruritus* ("Titillation") opens with the following poem:

> *Lectorem Alloquitur*[25]
> Pruritum feret hic novus libellus
> Ad rubri luteum dei sacellum,
> Qui semper puerisque furibusque
> Minatur gladioque mentulaque.
> At tu, si sapias, cave, libelle.
>
> *Address to the Reader*
> This new little book will bring sexual excitement
> to the mud shrine of the ruddy god
> who always threatens boys and thieves
> with his sword and prick.
> But you, little book, if you're smart, watch out!

Pontano's poem is full of programmatic allusions: to Catullus (*hic novus libellus*, in line 1), to the *Priapeia* (the ruddy god is Priapus), and to Martial (whose book often takes on the character of a sexually attractive boy). Its first word, *pruritum* ("sexual excitement" or "titillation"), announces the theme and title of the collection, but also alludes both to Catullus' recipe and to Martial's restatement of it. Here is Catullus:

> et quod pruriat incitare possunt (16.9)
> (and can stir up sexual excitement)

and Martial:

ne possint, nisi pruriant, iuvare (epigram 1.35.11)
(they cannot please unless they are aroused).

The final poem of the *Pruritus* opens in a similar spirit. Here are its first six lines:

> *Leonti Tomacello sodali suo*[26]
> Leon, delitium tui poetae,
> Nostrum dum legis arrige ad libellum
> Cuius nequitiae procaxque lusus
> Possunt herniolam senis voracis
> Samarrae patris irrumationum,
> Vel siquid mage languidum, incitare.
>
> *(To his friend, Leonte Tomacelli)*
> Leonte, darling of your poet,
> as you read, be aroused at our book,
> whose naughtiness and wanton play
> can stir up the ruptured limb
> (and nothing can be more limp than that)
> of deep-throated old Samarra, father of irrumation.)

Leonte Tomacelli was a friend and near contemporary of the young Pontano. Samarra is otherwise unknown, but certainly old. Thus, the poem, which at first sight is not so close to Catullus' poem 16, is in fact a demonstration of its poetic recipe: that light poetry must arouse not just boys but also sexually exhausted old men. The perspective is certainly that of youth (of Pontano and his friend) rather than age (as represented by the disgusting Samarra).

Catullus' poem 16 was also Pontano's starting point in the *Parthenopaeus* a few years later. In the first poem he sends off his book with an admonition: "Go little book, ... as a gift to my charming friend." The friend is Lorenzo Bonincontri, and the book will find him making love to his naked wife, Cecilia. The book will find a resting place in Cecilia's lap, the natural place for Pontano's poetry. Here is how he describes it:

> Legem versiculis dedere nostris
> Aetas et male sobrius magister,
> Ut tantum teneras ament puellas,
> Ut sint virginibus nihil molesti,
> Ut molles, lepidi, leves, iocosi;
> Quos uxor canat in sinu mariti,

> Quos coniux legat in sinu puellae,
> Quos discant pueri, senes et ipsi,
> Siqui sunt pueris ineptiores,
> Et castos fugiunt timentque versus.
> (Pontano, *Parthenopaeus* 1.1.6–15)

> (Youth and the scarcely sober master
> have laid down the law for our little verses:
> that they love only susceptible girls,
> that they be not troublesome to maidens,
> that they be soft, charming, light, playful, the kind of thing
> that a wife croons in the embrace of her husband,
> or a husband reads in the embrace of his bride,
> that boys learn—and old men, too,
> if there are any who are more foolish than boys
> and fear and flee chaste verses.)

The "law" (*legem*) that governs Pontano's verses is the pleasure principle of poem 16 in the familiar codification of Martial, but its purview has been greatly altered and expanded beyond the predominantly homosexual obscenity of Martial (and of Pontano himself in the *Pruritus*) to a sensual heterosexual romanticism that includes even the married love of Bonincontri and Cecilia. Pontano's innovation not only rewrites the old law, but it also—and this is more important—reverses the conventions of ancient erotic poetry, which celebrates illicit love, but never marriage. The love of Lesbia sung by Catullus was outside the conventions of society and at odds with them. Pontano has removed the conflict, and with his intimate depiction of Bonincontri and his wife he announces a new direction for Catullan poetry.

Almost forty years after the *Parthenopaeus*, Pontano embarked on his last and most ambitious Catullan poems, the *Hendecasyllabi*, or *Baiae*, so called after the famous resort on the Bay of Naples where Pontano and his friends, like the ancients before them, sought girls and pleasures.[27] Baiae's revivifying springs provide the setting, but also symbolize the possibility of recovering the lost joys of Eros, for Pontano and most of his addressees are now old men. A strange subject for Catullan poetry, we might think—for Catullus himself died young, and the subjects of his poetry are quintessentially youthful. But poem 16 is still Pontano's subtext, this time as the springboard for an exploration of the power of poetry—specifically, of the *Hendecasyllabi* of his title—to create erotic adventures and to arouse and please old men.

In his three collections Pontano established himself as the modern heir of Catullus. From now on Catullan poetry would speak in the language of Martial, but with the Renaissance voice and accent of Pontano; and subsequent poets would see Catullus in Pontano's terms, which they could imitate or react to or reject, but never ignore.

Pontano's Catullus was often as obscene as Martial's Catullus or Catullus himself, but he was more sensual than either, both stylistically and in content. Pontano wrote most of his imitations in hendecasyllables (other meters predominate only in *Parthenopaeus*); and he created the particular version of the hendecasyllable that was to characterize subsequent Catullan poetry. His hendecasyllables are recognizably Catullan, for they reproduce Catullan tricks of style and achieve a lightness and delicacy generally absent in Martial, but they also exaggerate Catullan features (particularly assonance, diminutives, and the use of internal repetitions or refrains) to create an effect that is unmistakably new—sensuous, lyrical, and sometimes almost hypnotic. The first verses of his poem "To Fannia" from *Parthenopaeus* exemplify his treatment.

> Amabo, mea cara Fanniella,
> Ocellus Veneris decusque Amoris,
> Iube, istaec tibi basiem labella
> Succiplena, tenella, mollicella;
> Amabo, mea vita suaviumque,
> Face istam mihi gratiam petenti. (*Parthenopaeus* 1.11.1–6)
> (Please, my dear Fanniella,
> Apple of Venus' eye, and ornament of Amor,
> Tell me to kiss these sweet lips of yours
> Juicy, delicate, so very soft;
> Please, my life, my kiss,
> Do me this favor, since I ask.)

By reading these lines aloud one can see that they are like Catullus, but more so—with more diminutives, more assonance, more repetition and sound play. Particularly striking is the play on Fannia's name. Pontano turns it into a diminutive, *Fanniella*, playing on the *-ell* sound with *ocellus* in the next word, rhyming it with *labella* ("sweet lips") at the end of line 3 and adding a double rhyme at the end of line 4: *tenella*, *mollicella* ("delicate," "so very soft").

Pontano's sensual erotic poetry, more explicit than anything in Catullus, often lovingly describes physical pleasure. In *Parthenopaeus* 1.5, "Ad pueros de columba" ("To the boys, concerning the dove"), Pontano selects a recipient for his "snow-white dove," evoking both the kiss poems and Lesbia's sparrow. After rejecting the boys of his title as *mali cinaedi* ("wretched catamites"), he decides that the dove wishes to go to his girl (*puella*) instead:

> Huius tu in gremio beata ludes,
> Et circumsiliens manus sinumque
> Interdum aureolas petes papillas. (*Parthenopaeus* 1.5.17–19)
> (You will play happily in her lap,
> and hopping about, you will peck her hands and bosom
> and sometimes her pretty golden breasts.)

He continues:

> Impune hoc facies, volente diva,
> Ut, cum te roseo ore suaviatur
> Rostrum purpureis premens labellis,
> Mellitam rapias iocosa linguam,
> Et tot basia totque basiabis,
> Donec nectarei fluant liquores.
>   (*Parthenopaeus* 1.5.26–31)
> (You will do this without fear, if the goddess wishes:
> when she kisses you with her rosy mouth,
> pressing your beak with purple lips,
> you may playfully snatch her honey-sweet tongue
> and you will give kisses and kisses again,
> until the streams of nectar flow.)

There could hardly be a better example of the Renaissance tendency to read Catullus through Martial. Pontano's poem is a *contaminatio* or blending of poems 2–3[28] and Martial 11.6, which interprets Catullus' sparrow not as a bird but a penis, as we saw in the previous section.

Both Pontano's use of poem 16 as the basis for his poetic program and his obscene treatment of the sparrow became essential elements for later poets writing in the Catullan style. Pontano's successors played endless changes on the ideas of poem 16, but most, unlike Pontano himself, emphasized what I have called "the poet's excuse," some using Martial's formulation, others quoting Catullus. The excuse had its most obvious use as a justification for obscenity, but its real functions were literary. Throughout the Renaissance it identified its user as a Catullan poet and a subscriber to the principles of Catullan poetry established by

Pontano—even if his verses were not lascivious. From the time of Pontano on, poems on kisses and sparrows or doves appeared by the score.[29] Pontano himself wrote nearly a dozen poems on kisses, and other poets wrote books or cycles of kiss poems. Among the most famous of these cycles was the *Basia* ("Kisses") by the brilliant Dutch Neo-Latin poet Johannes Secundus (1511–36), which inspired still more imitations. Often later poets, like Pontano and Martial, combined the sparrow or dove with the kissing theme to speak more or less openly of either homosexual and heterosexual intercourse.

But the sensual Catullus was not to everyone's taste, and neither of the ideas naturalized by Pontano went unchallenged, even in his lifetime. Both the poet's excuse and the obscene sparrow or dove (with or without kisses) came under attack. In the late 1480s the excuse was attacked twice in short succession, first by the Carmelite monk Battista Spagnoli, better known as Mantuan, and then by Pontano's own friend and student, Michele Marullo, who criticized the positions of both Pontano and Mantuan. It is important to note that the use of the poet's excuse changes the terms of the discussion, bringing into play not only what poetry should or should not do, but also what it says about the character of its creator.

Mantuan's work is entitled "A Poem against poets writing unchastely" (*Contra poetas impudice scribentes carmen*)–*Contra poetas*, for short. The poem is a diatribe against not just obscene or sensual poetry, but erotic poetry of any kind. It rejects the Catullan excuse out of hand:

> Vita decet sacros et pagina casta poetas:
>   Castus enim vatum spiritus atque sacer.
> Si proba vita tibi lascivaque pagina, multos
>   Efficis incestos in veneremque trahis.
>   (Mantuan, *Contra poetas* 19–22)
> (A chaste life and a chaste page befit holy poets,
>   for chaste and holy is the inspiration of bards.
> If your life is pure and your page is lascivious,
>   you make many unchaste and draw them into sexual activity.)

Mantuan acknowledges the possibility of a persona whose behavior cannot be equated with that of the poet himself, but he thoroughly disapproves of it: the poet of erotic verses, even if chaste himself, leads others to sin. Two points are noteworthy here. First, Mantuan's account of the poet's excuse conflates Catullus and Martial. He derives the word *castus* and the idea of holy poets from Catullus. Compare the Catullan lines we have seen so many times before:

> nam castum esse decet pium poetam
> ipsum, versiculos nihil necesse est (16.5–6)

But the language in Mantuan's third line comes from Martial, epigram 1.4. Compare Mantuan's *si proba vita tibi lascivaque pagina* ("if your life is pure and your page is lascivious") with Martial's *lasciva est nobis pagina, vita proba* ("my page is naughty; my life pure"). I have had to translate *lasciva* differently in the two poets: "naughty" in Martial, but "lascivious" in Mantuan. And that brings me to the second point: Mantuan may use the same language as Martial and Catullus, but he intends a different meaning. Given the context and what is known about him from other sources, Mantuan cannot possibly have anything as light as "naughty" or "playful" in mind for *lasciva*. Only "lascivious" will do. His use of *castus* is still more interesting. We can translate it as "chaste" as in Catullus, but the meaning is different. For Mantuan chastity is not, as it was for Catullus, a matter of avoiding pathic homosexuality. It is a matter of absolute sexual purity. Elsewhere in the poem he says: "Chaste is the mother of God, chaste the Master of Olympus. The unchaste soul cannot taste the ambrosial feast."[30]

Marullo's poem, on the other hand, is an elaborate refutation of the poetic programs of both Pontano and Mantuan, for he both rejects explicit or obscene verse and insists on his right to write chaste love poetry.[31] He rejects the poet's excuse. For him the "law" is not Martial's contrast between the moral standards of the poet's life and his poetry, but an insistence on their similarity:

> Sic iuvat in tenui legem servare pudori
>   Et quae non facimus dicere facta pudet.
>   (Marullo, *Epigram* 1.62.21–2)
> (so we are pleased to keep the law in delicate modesty
> and ashamed to speak of things we do not do.)

The obscene sparrow also came under attack in the 1480s and '90s, but here the target was a philological discussion rather than Pontano's poetic treatment. The philologist was Angelo Poliziano, who published this interpretation of Catullus in his *Miscellanea* of 1489.

> *In what sense the sparrow of Catullus is to be understood,*
> *and a passage pointed out in Martial.*[32]

That sparrow of Catullus in my opinion allegorically conceals a certain more obscene meaning which I cannot explain with my modesty intact. Martial persuades me to believe this in that epigram of which these are the last verses:

> Give me kisses, but Catullan style.
> And if they be as many as he said,
> I will give you the sparrow of Catullus.

For he would be too inept as a poet (which it is wrong to believe) if he said he would give the sparrow of Catullus, and not the other thing I suspect, to the boy after the kisses. What this is, for the modesty of my pen, I leave to each reader to conjecture from the native salaciousness of the sparrow. (Poliziano, *Miscellanea* 1.6)

Poliziano's interpretation became far more famous than Pontano's, no doubt because of its much wider circulation (Poliziano's *Miscellanea* was printed in hundreds of copies, while Pontano's poems were known only in manuscript until the end of the fifteenth century). It immediately provoked a storm of criticism, but less from moralists than from other humanists. Poliziano was a polemical man with many enemies, and many people considered his interpretation an assault on Catullus himself. Feeling was still running high thirty years later, when Pierio Valeriano broached the matter in his lectures on Catullus at the University of Rome in 1522.

> Good god! Had Catullus' body not been treated cruelly enough without their planning to quench his spirit? . . . We know that sparrows are so salacious that they mate seven times an hour; we know from medical writings that eating sparrows (or even their eggs) has an aphrodisiac effect. We know what filth the term *strouthoi* (that is, "sparrows") signifies in mimes; . . . we know from the writings of the Egyptian priests that human lust is symbolized by the picture of a sparrow. . . . We know these things, I say, but we neither know nor wish to know that in Catullus or perhaps even in Martial the male genitals (if you'll pardon the expression) ought to be understood under the word "sparrow."[33]

Catullus in the Sixteenth Century

The fifteenth-century Catullus was a blend of Pontano's sensibility and sensuality with Martial's brevity and polish. He could be romantic or erotic or obscene, and his poems were often laced with intertexts from Renaissance contemporaries as well as from Catullus, Martial, and other ancient poets. This Catullus was Pontano's creation, but he was taken up by other poets, as well as by scholars and commentators. All of these readers concentrated on Catullus' polymetrics and epigrams. Poets generally ignored the longer poems (61–68) and neither imitated nor discussed Catullus' passionate emotion.[34] Commentators took little notice of his Alexandrian learning, which was largely invisible to them in any case, given the fragmentary survival of Catullus' Greek models and their own limited knowledge of Greek. Only Angelo Poliziano, the greatest philologist of the age, took a real interest in matching Catullus with his Alexandrian sources, and he too was frustrated by lack of material.

Pontano's Catullus survived well into the sixteenth century, but now he was being read in a world whose religious, cultural, and literary landscape was very different from that of the previous century. Three changes most affected Catullus: the growth of classical studies in France, an increasing interest in Greek, and the hardening of sectarian religious fervor. The reception of Catullus greatly benefitted from the first two changes; not surprisingly, it was limited and threatened by the third. We will begin with Catullus' fortunes in France.

In the middle of the sixteenth century Paris was the scene of two literary events that would be of great importance to Catullus: the emergence of a group of young French poets who wanted to integrate the French and classical literary traditions, and the arrival of a young professor deeply interested in both Greek and Latin poetry. The poets would later be called the Pléiade, and they were led by Pierre de Ronsard, who became one of the greatest poets of the age. The professor was Marc-Antoine de Muret. Muret came to Paris in 1551 and spent two years there lecturing to enthusiastic crowds of students, working on a Catullan commentary, and in literary collaboration with Ronsard and his friends.

One of the most important products of this collaboration was Ronsard's *Livret de Folastries*, published anonymously in 1553. The *Folastries* ("Little Follies") were conceived as French counterparts of the Catullan hendecasyllable; their title recalls Catullus' names for his own verses: *nugae, ineptiae, lusus* ("trifles," "foolishness," "play"). Ronsard used the poet's excuse of Catullus' poem 16.5–6 as the epigraph for his collection, and his dedication to his friend Janot (the poet Jean-Antoine de Baïf) has a Catullan flavor:[35]

> To whom do I give these trifles
> and these dainty little verses?
> To you, my friend Janot . . .
>
> . . .
>
> Take it then, Janot, such as it is
>
> . . .
>
> so that you and I and my book
> may live more than a single age.
>   (Ronsard, *A Janot Parisien*,
>   1–3, 23, 29–30)

Inspired by both Muret and the Pléiade, others in Paris also wrote Catullan poetry, imitating Catullus in both Latin and French and drawing on Italian Neo-Latin poetry as well. Soon the influence went both ways, so that we find French and Latin poetry borrowing from each other.[36]

Near the end of 1553 Muret was forced out of Paris by charges of heresy and sexual immorality and fled to Venice. There he published his commentary on Catullus in 1554. Muret's work shows the influence of his new home, for it often reflects the polemic of contemporary Italian philological debates. One activity of his philological zeal has proved troublesome for readers of Catullus ever since. In an attempt to outdo an Italian rival who thought he had discovered two lost poems by Catullus, Muret discovered another—and printed all three after poem 17 in his text.[37] Later editors numbered the three poems 18, 19, and 20. They were banished in the nineteenth century by the famous German editor Lachmann, but by then the numbering had become canonical. Modern readers can thank Muret's vanity for the anomalous gap between poems 17 and 21 in their texts. Fortunately, however, the Italian philological polemic of Muret's commentary is offset by its French origins. It is steeped in the poetic interests and theory of Paris, and it is here that it is most important and innovative.

Muret and the French poets saw a different Catullus from that of Pontano and the fifteenth century. This French Catullus was less like Martial and more like the Greek Alexandrians. The French poets distinguished the epigram style of Catullus from that of Martial, admiring the one as much as they disdained the other.[38] Muret is of the same opinion. He remarks in his commentary:

> I think there is as much difference between the writings of Martial and Catullus as between the words of some wag on the street-corner and the well-bred jests of a gentleman, seasoned with sophisticated wit.[39]

Muret and his French colleagues also shared an admiration for both archaic and Alexandrian Greek poetry. In his commentary Muret regrets the loss of Callimachus' *Lock of Berenice* (translated by Catullus in poem 66) and admires Catullus' Alexandrian poems for their learning and emotion. His particular favorite is poem 68, but he also pays attention to poem 63, prefacing his commentary on it with a poem of his own in galliambics.[40] More important, however, is the fact that Muret was the first to identify Sappho 31 as the model for poem 51, publishing the two poems side by side for comparison.[41]

The reading and understanding of Catullus benefitted from the scholarly and literary advances of the sixteenth century. The greater knowledge of Greek and the rise of poetry in the modern languages brought him readers who could look at him in new ways and make creative use of his poetry, not only in Latin but in their own languages. But the sixteenth century was also an age of religious strife and a resulting hardening of religious positions all over Europe, developments that made Catullus's poetry more problematic for readers of all religious persuasions.

Catullus' obscenity provided much of the difficulty. The fifteenth century had been fairly tolerant, although reactions to obscenity varied from decade to decade and city to city, and even from one person to another, as we saw in the previous section. Some of Catullus' readers embraced it enthusiastically (the obscene passages in his poetry were explained more frankly and explicitly in the period from 1450 to 1520 than they would be for the next 450 years); but others wanted their poetry chaste even when they could not agree on what "chaste" meant. For Marullo it meant merely "not obscene or sexually explicit"; Mantuan insisted that chastity in poetry as in life required total abstinence from even purely romantic love.

Discomfort with Catullus and what he represented intensified throughout the sixteenth century, and humanists began to feel it increasingly necessary to find excuses for studying him. Thus, in his lectures at the University of Rome in 1521–2 the Italian humanist, Pierio Valeriano, tried, perhaps not very seriously, to replace the image of Catullus the sensualist with that of Catullus the teacher. Like Catullus' other interpreters, Valeriano created a Catullus in his own image. Valeriano saw himself as a teacher with a fatherly concern for his charges, in whom he wanted to instil both literary ambition and moral excellence. His Catullus had a similar beneficial purpose:

> The poet is certainly useful when he celebrates virtues and does not allow the achievements of illustrious men to perish, by whose example others

might be kindled to a desire for glory. He is useful when he chastises vice, criticizes evil ways, and attempts to deter mankind from imitating the wicked men he chastises in his poetry.[42]

Valeriano rejected Poliziano's interpretation of Catullus' sparrow, but he was willing to give frank, although not prurient, explanations of Catullus' sexual language. His lectures exist only in manuscript, and in an incomplete one at that, so that we cannot be sure how he dealt with Catullus' most obscene poetry. He began his lectures under the tolerant Medici pope, Leo X, but the straitlaced and censorious Adrian VI was in office by the time he came to 15, the first wholly truly obscene poem in the collection. We have the beginning of the lecture in which he debates about whether to omit it. He claims that his students objected to such censorship, comparing it to the barbarity of the Vandals and Goths: "Just as they used to cut off the genitals of all the statues, so now anything titillating is taken out of books, too."[43] Valeriano's tone suggests that he gave his lecture, but we will never be sure, since he (or someone else) cut out all the pages that would have contained it.

Justifying Catullus became more difficult as the century wore on. The Portuguese humanist Achilles Statius was a papal secretary in Counter-Reformation Rome. In the preface to his commentary on Catullus (1566), he claimed to have studied classical poetry in order to master lyric metres in preparation for his own Latin verse translation of the *Psalms*. After his friends urged him to use his notes to write commentaries on the poets, he began with Catullus on the grounds that "it was the verdict of every earlier age that he surpassed all poets in elegance." And he continues:

> as to the fact that he wrote somewhat racily and effeminately, this was the habit of those times, or rather the license and defect, although he says of himself as if in embarrassment: "For it is right for the true poet to be chaste himself, but not necessary for his verses to be so [poem 16.5–6]."[44]

Statius' language exactly (and no doubt deliberately) reflects the terms in which the Council of Trent had excluded ancient authors from its general ban on obscene literature: elegance of style and the acknowledged licentiousness of paganism.[45]

But if Catullus could be embarrassing to a papal secretary in Rome, he required still more care from a northern Protestant. Joseph Scaliger, Catullus' most famous Renaissance editor, claimed in his commentary (1577) to have begun work on Catullus, Tibullus, and Propertius ("the triumvirate of Love," as he called them) as a diversion after an illness, drawn by their elegance of style, while hating the lasciviousness characteristic of their age. "I compare the reading of poets to the sea," he says:

> There are reefs in it, but the experienced sailor never runs his ship aground on them. In poetry there are some indecent words on which the virtuous mind does not stumble, but briskly sails past unconcerned.[46]

Statius and Scaliger both studied Catullus, especially his text, but neither ever expresses any affection for his poetry. I suspect that they liked it, but were embarrassed to say so, for even when Catullus' poetry was not obscene it was uncongenial to the general spirit of the age, which was increasingly concerned with serious moral, philosophical, and theological issues. Catullus' subjects are poetry and personal emotions. The poet places himself in the center of a world of friends, enemies, lovers, and other poets, where the highest values are personal and aesthetic: the bonds of trust and obligation between individuals, and a poetic credo founded on learning, craftsmanship, and—above all—on charm and wit. There is no room in his poetic landscape for large moral or national themes, no reference to ideals or claims beyond those of the individual. The times demanded poetry with a serious purpose, but Catullus' poetry could not be recruited to the cause of moral utility. The only utilitarian value that his admirers could claim for him was that of teaching elegant Latin style.

Notes

1. Greene, *The Light in Troy*, 20.
2. Ibid., 11.
3. Martindale, *Redeeming the Text*, 7.
4. Ibid., 3.
5. For detailed studies of Catullus' reception by the Augustan poets, see McNeill, "Catullus and Horace"; Nappa, "Catullus and Vergil"; Miller, "Catullus and Roman Love Elegy."
6. Vergil also drew on significant passages from poems 66 and 101. See chapter 6 n. 40 and p. 138 above.
7. For Catullus' reception in the Silver Age, see Gaisser, *Catullus and his Renaissance Readers*, 7–12. Ancient quotations and mentions of Catullus have been collected by Wiseman in *Catullus and His World*, 246–62.

8   For Martial and Catullus, see Gaisser, *Catullus and His Renaissance Readers*, 200–11, 233–41. See also Swann, *Martial's Catullus*; Lorenz, "Catullus and Martial."

9   For a more detailed discussion of epigram 11.6 and his other epigrams on the sparrow, see Gaisser, *Catullus and His Renaissance Readers*, 238–42.

10 The interpretation is vigorously discussed by Hooper, "In Defence of Catullus' Dirty Sparrow"; Jocelyn, "On Some Unnecessarily Indecent Interpretations of Catullus 2 and 3."

11 For *mentula* as "prick," see chapter 1, note 2.

12 The verb *prurio*, according to the *Oxford Latin Dictionary*, means "to *feel* sexual excitement"—not, as most Martial translators would have it, "to *cause* sexual excitement." Richlin gets it right: "itch with lust" (*Garden of Priapus*, 10).

13 See Gaisser, *Catullus and His Renaissance Readers* 12–15, with earlier bibliography. The epitaph, preserved in an inscription from Auch (*Corpus Inscriptionum Latinarum* 1512), is a very close imitation of poem 3. See Walters, "Catullan Echoes in the Second Century A.D."; Goold, "Catullus 3.16."

14 See Gaisser, *Catullus and His Renaissance Readers* 12–15: Butrica, "History and Transmission of the Text," 24–8. For ancient citations of Catullus, see Wiseman, *Catullus and His World*, 246–61.

15 The ninth-century manuscript containing poem 62 (Paris, Bibliothèque Nationale lat. 8071, called T) belongs to the same tradition as V. See Butrica, "History and Transmission of the Text," 26.

16 *Versus domini Benevenuti de Campexanis de Vicencia de resurrectione Catulli poete Veronensis*

>   Ad patriam venio longis a finibus exsul;
>   causa mei reditus compatriota fuit,
>   scilicet a calamis tribuit cui Francia nomen
>   quique notat turbe praetereuntis iter.
>   quo licet ingenio vestrum celebrate Catullum,
>   cuius sub modio clausa papirus erat.

17 The material in this section is treated in detail in Gaisser, *Catullus and His Renaissance Readers*, 211–54. See also Gaisser, "Catullus in the Renaissance."

18 The manuscripts are listed in Thomson, ed., *Catullus*, 72–92.

19 Hankins, "The Latin Poetry of Leonardo Bruni"; Gaisser, *Catullus and His Renaissance Readers*, 211–15.

20 Ludwig, "The Origin and Development of the Catullan Style in Neo-Latin Poetry," 188–9.

21 Ludwig, "The Origin and Development of the Catullan Style in Neo-Latin Poetry," 189–97.

22 See, esp., Sullivan, *Martial: The Unexpected Classic*, 253–70; Swann, *Martial's Catullus*, 89–91.
23 *Pruritus* in its original form has been lost. It was reconstructed by Ludwig; see "The Origin and Development of the Catullan Style in Neo-Latin Poetry," 189–90.
24 The Latin texts of all three works are printed in *Ioannis Ioviani Pontani Carmina*, Soldati, ed. For the *Hendecasyllabi* (also called *Baiae*), see *Ioannis Ioviani Pontani Hendecasyllaborum Libri*, Monti Sabia, ed. The Latin text and English translation are printed in *Giovanni Gioviano Pontano: Baiae*, Dennis, trans.
25 Pontano, *Carmina*, ed. Soldati, 2:406.
26 Pontano, *Carmina*, ed. Soldati, 1.50, 2:406.
27 The seductions of Baiae were notorious in antiquity, as Martial noted in his comment on the wife who went to Baiae: "She came a Penelope, departed a Helen" (*Penelope venit, abit Helene, Epigram* 1.62.6)
28 Pontano would have seen poems 2 and 3 as a single poem in his manuscript, for the division between them had been lost in the course of transmission. They were first separated in the Aldine edition of 1502.
29 See Gaisser, *Catullus and His Renaissance Readers*, 233–54.
30 *Casta dei genetrix, castus regnator Olympi, / Mens capit ambrosias non nisi casta dapes.* Mantuan, *Contra poetas* 35–6.
31 Marullo's poem is discussed in detail in Gaisser, *Catullus and His Renaissance Readers*, 231–3.
32 *Quo intellectu Catullianus passer accipiendus, locusque etiam apud Martialem indicatus.*

> Passer ille Catullianus allegoricôs, ut arbitror, obscoeniorem quempiam celat intellectum, quam salva verecundia, nequimus enunciare. Quod ut credam, Martialis epigrammate illo persuadet, cuius hi sunt extremi versiculi:
>
>> Da mihi basia, sed Catulliana:
>> Quae si tot fuerint, quot ille dixit,
>> Donabo tibi passerem Catulli. [Mart. 11.6.14–17]
>
> Nimis enim foret insubidus poeta (quod nefas credere) si Catulli passerem denique ac non aliud quidpiam, quod suspicor, magis donaturum se puero post oscula diceret. Hoc quid sit, equidem pro styli pudore suae cuiusque coniecturae, de passeris nativa salacitate relinquo. (Poliziano, *Opera Omnia* 1:230–1)

33 For the Latin text, see Gaisser, *Catullus and His Renaissance Readers*, 350 n. 115.
34 Some poets, however, did imitate the galliambic meter of poem 63. See note 40 below.

35 Pierre de Ronsard, *A Janot Parisien*, 1–3, 23, 29–30; quoted from Ronsard, *Oeuvres complètes*, Laumonier, ed. 5:3–5.

> A qui donnai-je ces sornettes,
> Et ces mignardes chansonnettes?
> A toy mon Janot, . . .
> . . .
> Pren le donc, Janot, tel qu'il est,
> . . .
> Afin que toy, moy, et mon livre,
> Plus d'un siècle puissions revivre.

36 Morrison, "Catullus and the Poetry of the Renaissance in France"; Ginsberg, "Peregrinations of the Kiss."
37 The additional poems, like poem 17, are in the priapean meter. Two are from the *Appendix Vergiliana* (*Priapea* 2 and 3); the third is printed in modern editions of Catullus as fragment 1.
38 Hutton, *The Greek Anthology in France*, 51–3.
39 For the Latin text, see Gaisser, *Catullus and His Renaissance Readers*, 360 n. 40.
40 Here Muret was doing nothing new, for Catullus' galliambics had inspired imitation since the fifteenth century. See Campbell, "Galliambic Poems of the 15th and 16th Centuries."
41 Muret, *Catullus et in eum commentarius*, 56v–58r. The first detailed comparison of the two poems, however, appeared not in Muret, but nearly forty years later, in the 1592 discussion of Janus Dousa the younger (Gaisser, *Catullus and His Renaissance Readers*, 165).
42 For the Latin text, see Gaisser, *Catullus and His Renaissance Readers*, 337 n. 31.
43 For the Latin text, see ibid., 353 n. 139.
44 For the Latin text, see ibid., 369 n. 113.
45 Ibid., 170–1.
46 For the Latin text, see ibid., 378 n. 199.

8

Receiving Catullus 2: England and America

> It is the spectator, and not life, that art really mirrors.
> Oscar Wilde (*The Picture of Dorian Gray*)

Catullus' works slipped into England at an unknown date sometime in the late fifteenth or early sixteenth century.[1] English poets soon began reading and imitating his poetry, but texts had to be imported from the continent and were not always easy to find. The first text printed in England was the 1684 edition by the Dutch scholar Isaac Voss, which made Catullus generally available for the first time and opened a new era for English readers, poets, and translators.

Puritan strictures against erotic and frivolous poetry probably helped to delay the publication of Catullus, but lack of demand must have been the deciding factor. A comparison with the publication history of Martial is instructive. By 1700 Catullus had only the Voss edition of 1684, but there had been at least eight printings of Martial in England (three for use in Westminster School), and at least nine printings of translations of the *Epigrams*. It was Catullus' lack of moral utility, even more than his obscenity, that limited his popularity. Martial, after all, is often much more obscene than Catullus, but his epigrams (with some judicious surgery) were regarded as suitable school texts. The difference is that Martial is a satirist interested not in his own emotions but in the foibles of society. Suitably censored and selected, his epigrams have interesting and amusing moral—or at least, social—lessons to teach. His popularity in England during the sixteenth and seventeenth centuries was further assured by the contemporary taste for wit and a general enthusiasm for both Latin and English epigrams.[2] Catullus, with none of these factors to recommend him, was destined to move in much narrower circles.

From the beginning, Catullus' reception in England was very different from his reception in Italy. Catullus appeared in Italy in a period receptive to erotic and personal poetry; by the time he arrived in England, such poetry was becoming suspect even on the continent. This change in attitudes ensured that English Catullan poetry would be less overtly sensual than its continental counterpart. Poem 16, for example, is no longer used as a blanket excuse for obscenity or explicit sexual references. Instead, the principles culled from it by the continental poets are generally reversed or rejected. Thus, Abraham Cowley (1618–67) refuses to separate the character of the poet from that of his verse, proclaiming " 'tis just / The Author blush, there where the Reader must" (*On Wit*). Cowley presents poetry as an aphrodisiac for his readers ("My Lines of amorous desire / I wrote to kindle and blow others fire")—but in a poem lamenting that he has succumbed to the very emotions he counterfeited (*The Dissembler*). Sparrows and other birds abound, beginning with John Skelton (1460?-1529) and his *Boke of Phyllyp Sparowe* (c. 1505), but their lives and deaths have no obscene overtones. The many kiss poems deriving from poems 5 and 7 now tend less to assume consummation than to argue for it, and take as their subject seduction, not the intensification of an existing sexual affair.[3]

A second difference is still more important. Catullus appeared in Italy virtually out of nowhere, with no baggage of recent imitation, interpretation, or scholarship; and the Italian humanists first interpreted him through Martial's imitations. He arrived in England surrounded by generations of European (predominantly Italian) literary and scholarly interpretation, and there was no possibility for English readers and poets to have an unmediated encounter with him. They came to him with their minds full not only of Martial, but of a hundred and fifty years of European poetry from Pontano, Sannazaro, and Marullo to Tasso, Ronsard, and Johannes Secundus, and many more besides. The plethora of modern imitations, both in Latin and in the modern languages, both lessened the importance of Martial for Catullus and complicated the English tradition of Catullan poetry. Modern Catullan poets imitated each other as well as Catullus; by now many of Catullus' themes had been treated so often that they had become part of a general poetic currency. As a consequence, when we find them in English poems, it is not always possible to identify Catullus as the primary model, or even as a model at all. The English poems in turn became part of the stock for other imitations and translations.

A striking example of this process is John Skelton's *Boke of Phyllyp Sparowe*. Skelton identified himself as "the British Catullus"[4] and wrote on the death of a young woman's sparrow, but it is not clear that he had actually read Catullus himself or that anything in his 1380-verse lament owes a direct debt to his poetry. He comes closest in these verses, often compared with Catullus' poem 2.1–2 ("Sparrow, the darling of my girl, with which she plays, which she holds in her lap"):

> It had a velvet cap,
> And wold syt upon my lap,
> And seke after small wormes,
> And somtyme white bred crommes;
> And many tymes and ofte
> Betwene my brestes softe
> It wolde lye and rest—
> It was propre and prest.[5]
> (*Boke of Phyllyp Sparowe*, 120–7)[6]

But the parallel is not striking. Skelton is probably thinking not of Catullus, but of something in one of Catullus' many European imitators. The interesting point, however, as McPeek observed long ago, is that Skelton's Phyllyp Sparowe soon became elided with Catullus' sparrow, so that for several decades the mention of the one evoked the other.[7]

Before the middle of the seventeenth century we find a relatively small number of actual translations, and these of a rather small number of poems: poems 5 and 7 (on kisses), 8 (Catullus' renunciation of Lesbia), 51 (the translation of Sappho), portions of 61 and 62 (the epithalamia), and snippets of other poems probably taken from commonplace books. This last category deserves some explanation. Renaissance readers enjoyed classical authors for their own sake, but also as ornaments for their own speech and writing. As they read, they copied into their commonplace books useful phrases, memorable lines, and, above all, pithy sentiments and aphorisms. Although Catullus lent himself to this treatment less well than poets like Martial or Horace or Virgil, even his earliest Renaissance readers found and collected quotable verses. The process began in Italy within a few years of the discovery of Catullus when the Paduan judge, Geremia da Montagnone, excerpted seven Catullan passages for the commonplace book that he compiled around 1300.[8] Readers might make collections for themselves or supplement their own reading by borrowing from anthologies already in circulation.

Two of the earliest English translations were probably drawn from commonplace books: Sir Philip Sidney's translation of poem 70 (printed in 1598) and Sir Walter Ralegh's translation of 5.4–6 (printed in 1614).[9]

Here is Sidney (if you read the poem aloud you will see that he has brought the Latin elegiac couplet into English):

Out of Catullus
Unto no body my woman saith she had rather a wife be,
  Than to my selfe, not though *Jove* grew a suter of hers.
These be her words, but a woman's words to a love that is eager,
  In wind or water streame do require to be writ.

Ralegh embedded his translation in a prose work called *The History of the World*, which he wrote and published anonymously while he was imprisoned in the Tower of London.

That Man is (as it were) a little world: with a digression touching our mortalitie.... For this tide of mans life, after it once turneth and declineth, ever runneth with a perpetuall ebbe and falling streame, but never floweth againe: our leafe once fallen, springeth no more, neither doth the Sunne or the Summer adorne us againe, with the garments of new leaves and flowers.... of which Catullus:
              The Sunne may set and rise:
              But we contrariwise
              Sleepe after our short light
              One everlasting night.

The number of translated poems increased by the middle of the seventeenth century, with the largest contribution being that of Richard Lovelace (1618–57), who wrote literal translations of 13 poems, only one of which (poem 70) had been translated before.[10] The publication of Voss's edition in 1684 inspired still more translations and imitations; and by 1750 around half of Catullus' 116 poems had been translated or closely imitated.[11] Apart from Lovelace, however, no single poet before the end of the eighteenth century translated more than one or two poems. The first collection of translations was published in 1707, in the anonymous *Adventures of Catullus*, which contained 46 poems in renderings by an unknown number of different translators. The first complete translation appeared only in 1795. It was printed anonymously, but is generally acknowledged to be the work of a physician and scholar named John Nott.

Catullus' obscenity partly explains the very late appearance of a complete translation, but the diversity of his poetry must bear equal responsibility. Not only does his work fall into three distinct categories (lyrics,

Alexandrian set-pieces, and epigrams), but the poems within each category vary widely in subject, tone, and diction. By contrast, Martial's poetry, which was translated so much earlier, belongs to the single genre of epigram. To translate all of Catullus, a poet must command a wide range of genres and diction; to wish to translate him requires an even greater range of tastes, interests, and sympathies.

From the beginning, English-speaking poets and readers, like their European counterparts, brought their own interests and concerns to Catullus, creating a Catullus who fitted into their views of themselves and their world. In the next sections we will look at several aspects of the reception of Catullus in Britain from the eighteenth to the early twentieth century: the appeal of particular poems over time, the treatment of the poems as a narrative, the reception of obscenity and homoerotic themes, and the changing picture of the poet. The final section will consider some themes in the reception of Catullus in the twentieth century.

Favorite Poems

The sparrow poems and the kiss poems to Lesbia were perennial favorites in England as on the continent, but others varied in their appeal. The explanation for such shifts in taste is not always obvious. A reader coming from Catullan poetry in Europe to that of the early English tradition finds some surprising omissions. Catullus' dedication (poem 1) was a favorite model for imitation both in antiquity and in the Italian and French Renaissance; English poets before the eighteenth century virtually ignored it. Poem 4 (on Catullus' yacht) inspired the only parody of a whole poem that has survived from antiquity, *Catalepton 10*, generally attributed to Vergil in the Renaissance. On the continent original and parody alike inspired dozens of Latin imitations and parodies, and whole books were devoted to them from the end of the sixteenth to the middle of the seventeenth century.[12] The English poets were apparently not interested. Later poets produced imitations of both poems, but neither ever became a favorite in the English tradition. A few of Catullus' epigrams were translated early and more than once, but most did not receive any attention before the eighteenth century. Epigrams were undoubtedly in vogue, but their model was Martial rather than Catullus. Martial's epigrams were witty, pointed, and satirical. Catullus', by contrast, were emotional and personal. For the most part they lacked both general applicability and epigrammatic "point"—the witty surprise or "sting in the tail" that so endeared Martial to his many imitators.

The long poems, 61 to 68, experienced various fates. The wedding poems, 61 and 62, were imitated by writers of epithalamia in the sixteenth and seventeenth centuries, but their importance declined along with interest in the English epithalamium. Poem 67 (a conversation with the door of an adulterous household) was generally ignored, as were poems 65, 66, and 68. All four poems were probably too inaccessible—67 because its gossipy story seemed both uninteresting and hard to follow, and the others because of their Alexandrian learning and complexity (but poem 66 did inspire Alexander Pope's *Rape of the Lock*). Catullus' neoteric masterpiece, poem 64, also suffered from neglect. A poet named William Bowles (d. 1705) presented a substantial portion of it in *The Complaint of Ariadna*, but without success. As McPeek aptly remarks after quoting part of it: "Such lines witness the fascination of evil."[13] But better poets did appropriate shorter passages from 64. Walter Savage Landor (1775–1864) translated verses 269–75, a simile describing the departure of the wedding guests from the marriage of Peleus and Thetis. In an essay on Catullus published in 1842 Landor compares the passage favorably to a description of morning in Milton and appends the following, describing it as "a very inadequate translation":[14]

> As, by the Zephyr wakened, underneath
> The sun's expansive gaze the waves move on
> Slowly and placidly, with gentle plash
> Against each other, and light laugh; but soon,
> The breezes freshening, rough and huge they swell,
> Afar refulgent in the crimson east.
>   (Walter Savage Landor)

Of all the long poems, however, it was 63 (the Attis poem) that caught the English imagination. Latin poets on the continent had been imitating its galliambic meter since the late 1400s, but the poem began to attract serious attention in England only at the end of the eighteenth century. It is tempting to attribute the origin of this interest to Edward Gibbon, since the first English translators claim the authority of his praise.[15] Gibbon mentions Catullus in a footnote to his discussion of neo-Platonic interpretations of myths, including the story of Attis:

> But all the allegories which ever issued from the Platonic school are not worth the short poem of Catullus on the same extraordinary subject. The

transition of Atys from the wildest enthusiasm to sober pathetic complaint for his irretrievable loss, must inspire a man with pity, an eunuch with despair. (*Decline and Fall of the Roman Empire*, chapter 23, note 18)

Leigh Hunt (1784–1859) published an important translation of the poem in 1810. Fifteen years later he wrote a remarkable poem on a modern Attis, the *castrato* singer Velluti, who had been reviled for his condition when he appeared on the London stage. Here is a selection (the speaker is Velluti):

> Was I the cause of what I mourn? Did I
> Unmake myself, and hug deformity?   10
> Did I, a smiling and a trusting child,
> See the curst blow, to which I was beguil'd?
> Call for the knife? and not resist in vain,
> With shrieks convulsive and a fiery pain,
> That second baptism? bloody and profane?   15
> . . .
> How often have I wept the dreadful wrong,   143
> Told by the poet in as pale a song,
> Which the poor bigot did himself, who spoke   145
> Such piteous passion when his reason woke!—
> To the sea-shore he came, and look'd across,
> Mourning his native land and miserable loss.—
> Oh worse than wits that never must return,
> To act with madness, and with reason mourn!   150
> I see him, hear him, I myself am he,
> Cut off from thy sweet shores, Humanity!
>   (Leigh Hunt, *Velluti to his Revilers*,
>   9–15, 143–52)

Landor admired 63 extravagantly in his 1842 essay on Catullus, and his disciple, Algernon Charles Swinburne, shared his enthusiasm. In his strange poem *Dolores* (1866) Swinburne evokes both 63 and other poems of Catullus, to contrast present-day weakness symbolized by the castrated worshippers of Cybele with the full-blooded male sexuality of antiquity. Wiseman calls his verses an "intoxicating chant of studied impropriety," and so they are.[16] Tennyson and Meredith later imitated the galliambic meter (Tennyson in *Boädicéa* and Meredith in *Phaéthôn*). Swinburne does not attempt galliambics, but his verses have a strange and hypnotic effect of their own. Here are two of its 55 stanzas:

Cry aloud; for the old world is broken:
   Cry out; for the Phrygian is priest,
And rears not the bountiful token
   And spreads not the fatherly feast.
From the midmost of Ida, from shady
   Recesses that murmur at morn,
They have brought and baptized her, Our Lady,
   A goddess new-born.

And the chaplets of old are above us,
   And the oyster-bed[17] teems out of reach;
Old poets outsing and outlove us,
   And Catullus makes mouths at our speech.
Who shall kiss, in thy father's own city,
   With such lips as he sang with, again?
Intercede for us all of thy pity,
   Our Lady of Pain.
                    (Algernon Charles Swinburne,
                       Dolores, stanzas 42–3)

Other poems also came into their own in the nineteenth century. Poems 31 (Catullus' return to Sirmio), 46 (his departure from Bithynia), and 101 (his lament for his brother), all of little interest before 1800, received great attention in the nineteenth century that continued into the twentieth. But 101 achieved the greatest popularity. Landor in 1842 admired its "sorrowful but . . . quiet solemnity," but it was the next generation of poets who took it to heart. Swinburne both imitated it and used it to celebrate his "brother poet," Charles Baudelaire.[18] Tennyson combined it with poem 31 to lament the death of his own brother. Arthur Symons and Aubrey Beardsley translated it at the turn of the century, and it has received scores of translations since.

Story Telling

Catullus' poetry lends itself to the construction of a narrative. It is set in an exciting period with plenty of interesting historical characters, treats an ill-fated love affair with a desirable but faithless woman, and—best of all—features a multi-faceted and tortured hero who dies young. Readers have found it irresistible to make a story of all this, but only since the end of the seventeenth century. The idea was born in France, its genesis coinciding with the rise of the novel. At a time and place where romances were sweeping the country, what could seem more obvious than a

Figure 3. Title page of Jean de Lachapelle's *Les Amours de Catulle* (1713).

romance of Catullus? In 1680 a French dramatist and diplomat named Jean de Lachapelle published *Les Amours de Catulle*, a fanciful history (he refused to call it a "romance") constructed from hints in Catullus and interspersed with translations of his poems. The work went through several reprintings. Figure 3 shows the title page of the 1713 edition. Lachapelle wanted to rescue Catullus from the pedantry of scholars, as he says in his preface:

> I had a long time lamented the want of Skill, in most of those, that have undertaken to explain the Gallant Poets of Antiquity. They give us long and

tiresome Dissertations upon every Verse, which might be explained with less pains, and much more pleasure to those that wou'd understand these fine wits. . . . I had a mind then, to give the Sense of Catullus, in a manner, that shou'd not smell of the School, or the Commentary: And in Reading over his Works with some Thought and Application, I have endeavour'd to give a Guess at all his Intrigues and Galantries. Perhaps I have hit right; however it be, I have found out a Link, and by it a certain Chain of Adventures, which gives a very fair connexion to all the amorous Sonnets, that lie scatter'd without order or design, amidst his other Works.[19]

Lachapelle's work was published in London in 1707 in a translation entitled *The Adventures of Catullus and History of his Amours with Lesbia*. The English version, like its model, treats Catullus and his friends as if they were characters in a novel about seventeenth-century courtiers and their ladies. Its anonymous translations, from various sources and variable in quality, are notable for their frankness. Here is poem 58:

> That *Lesbia*, *Caelius*, that dear faithless she;
> That *Lesbia*, who was all in all to me;
> That *Lesbia*, whom alone *Catullus* priz'd
> Above himself, and Friends, for whom he all despis'd;
> False to her Vows, to her attested Flame,
> Forgetful of her Love, and of her Fame,
> Now upon Bulks,[20] in every Alley, lies,
> And in the Arms of Brawny Porters dies.

Lachapelle was scornful of scholars and their "tiresome dissertations," but not even scholars were immune to the Catullus narrative. In 1862 the German scholar Ludwig Schwabe reconstructed Catullus' biography from his poetry and evidence from Cicero about Clodia and Caelius. His reconstruction, as Wiseman observes, offered "a coherent and dramatic story of love and jealousy."[21] Schwabe's work inaugurated a new age of story telling. Translators and editors began to rearrange the poems to suit the narrative, and novelists, most of whom had never heard of *The Adventures of Catullus*, retold the tale, often interspersing it with their own translations of the appropriate poems.[22]

Delicate Subjects

Catullus' obscenity and pederastic themes have been major stumbling blocks for English readers from his first appearance on English soil until almost yesterday. In this section we will see what they did with these subjects from the eighteenth to the beginning of the twentieth century. Our case histories will be translations of the obscene poems 32 and 16 and the treatment of Catullus' boy Juventius.

Concern about obscenity undoubtedly affected the reception of poems 16 and 32. In the early tradition English poets neglected 32, no doubt appalled by Catullus' invitation of Ipsitilla to "nine fuckings one after the other" (32.8). They avoided 16, not only because it separated the poet's character from his verses, but for its explicit threats of oral and anal rape against Furius and Aurelius. But both poems were translated, although with some euphemism, in the eighteenth century. The earliest English translation of 32 that I have been able to find is from *The Adventures of Catullus* (1707), where Ipsitilla is instructed, unambiguously, but without obscenity: "prepare to meet repeated Joy, continued bliss without Alloy."[23] The earliest translation of 16 seems to be the 1795 rendition of John Nott, who softens Catullus' obscene threat. Catullus says, "I'll bugger you and stuff it down your throats, / queer Aurelius and faggot Furius!" (16.1–2). Nott translates:

> I'll treat you as 'tis meet, I swear,
> Lascivious monsters as ye are![24]

In 1821, a generation after Nott, George Lamb simply *rewrote* both poems, expunging the threat of the one and the sexual invitation of the other. His excuse in each case was that a literal translation "could not be tolerated."[25]

The change between Nott and Lamb reflects not only an increasing moral conservatism around the turn of the eighteenth century but also a difference in their approaches to translation.[26] Lamb wished to make the poet elegant and charming to his own readers and was willing to rewrite his poetry to secure the desired effect. Nott, by contrast, argued for the necessity of presenting Catullus as he was in his own time:

> When an ancient classic is translated, and explained, the work may be considered as forming a link in the chain of history: history should not be falsified, we ought therefore to translate him somewhat fairly; and when he gives us the manners of his own day, however disgusting to our sensations, and repugnant to our natures they may oftentimes prove, we must not in translation suppress, or even too much gloss them over, through a fastidious regard to delicacy.[27]

Lamb's method had more adherents in the nineteenth century than Nott's, but with two interesting exceptions: James Cranstoun (1867) and Sir Richard Burton (1894). Cranstoun, a Scottish schoolmaster, allowed himself some departures from strict verbal accuracy for what he termed "obvious reasons," but argued against rewritings and omissions:

> His expressions, it is true, are often intensely sensuous, sometimes even grossly licentious, but to obliterate these and to clothe him in the garb of purity would be to misrepresent him entirely. He would be Atys, not Catullus.[28]

Burton, whose purpose was to produce a literal and completely unexpurgated translation, made an even stronger case for historical honesty than Nott:

> A Scholar lively, remembered to me, that *Catullus* translated word for word, is an anachronism, and that a literal English rendering in the nineteenth century could be true to the poet's letter, but false to his spirit. I was compelled to admit that something of this is true; but it is not the whole truth. "Consulting modern taste" means really a mere imitation, a re-cast of the ancient past in modern material. It is presenting the toga'd citizen, rough, haughty, and careless of any approbation not his own, in the costume of to-day,—boiled shirt, dove-tailed coat, black-cloth clothes, white pocket-handkerchief, and diamond ring. Moreover, of these transmogrifications we have already enough and to spare. But we have not, as far as I know, any version of Catullus which can transport the English reader from the teachings of our century to that preceding the Christian Era.[29]

But neither Cranstoun nor Burton lived up to his promise. In Cranstoun the threat of poem 16 is reduced to "Base Furius and Aurelius! hence, away!"; and Catullus' obscene request to Ipsitilla becomes: "Caresses rare for me prepare, / Be three times three the number."[30] Burton, on the other hand, was thwarted by his wife. He died before his manuscript was sent to press, and his wife deleted the obscenities from his text, leaving dots of omission in their place.[31] Ipsitilla apparently survived unscathed ("for us prepare / Nine-fold continuous love-delights"), but only dots were left for Furius and Aurelius:[32]

> I'll . . . you twain and . . .
> Pathic Aurélius! Fúrius, libertines!

Catullus' boy Juventius was problematic for translators in a different way. Obscenity could be euphemized, glossed over, or even omitted, but how could they handle pederasty? The answer, almost universally, was to change his sex—a practice that as far as I know, begins only at the end of the seventeenth century. *The Adventures of Catullus*, generally so frank, argues that "Juventius" was really the nickname given to a woman named Crastinia, who just happened to resemble a young man named Juventius. "Catullus call'd her nothing but the *Lovely Juventius*," the author explains: "The verses that he made upon her were inscribed to *Juventius*, and there were but very few that understood the Mystery."[33]

Nott entitles each of the four Juventius poems (24, 48, 81, 99) "To his Favourite" and avoids any reference to gender. Lamb depicts Juventius as merely a friend in 24 and 81, but suppresses his name and changes his sex in 48 and 99, both on the subject of kisses. (In 99 Lamb's Juventius becomes "dearest maid of my soul.")[34] Cranstoun, for all his avowed honesty, follows Lamb, although he is at least consistent: he depicts Catullus' darling as always anonymous and always female (in 99 she is 'fair honey'd maid').[35] Burton alone is honest about the gender and the situation; his collaborator Leonard Smithers clarifies matters still further with his note on poem 99: "This poem shews beyond contradiction that Catullus himself was not free from the vice of paederasty, so universal amongst the Roman youth."[36]

Thus, apart from Burton, even translators who could treat obscenity and homosexuality frankly according to the standards of their time, could not stomach Juventius. They could render the homosexual invective Catullus hurled against his enemies, but they could not allow a homosexual romance to the poet himself. The reason is to be sought in the vividness and immediacy of Catullus' persona and the way in which readers identified with it. Like both Martial and the readers of the Italian Renaissance before them, they created a Catullus like themselves. They saw in Catullus someone with their own emotions and moral values—or perhaps one should say that they saw in Catullus someone with the emotions and moral values *they professed* in accordance with the standards of their time. Before the end of the nineteenth century (and well into the twentieth), this Catullus, whatever else he did, could not possibly indulge in homosexual love, and he most certainly could not plead with a young boy for kisses, as the poet does in poems 48 and 99.

Picturing Catullus

The picture of Catullus created by his English readers changed over time, along with the readers themselves. In *The Adventures of Catullus* he was a seventeenth-century French courtier in English translation. In Lamb he appeared to be a man of aristocratic manners and temperament living in an uncongenial age, as if he were a high-minded English gentleman transplanted into a somewhat unsavory period:

> we may fairly describe him as irascible but forgiving; careless and imprudent; affectionate to his kindred, warm in friendship, but contemptuous and offensive to those whom he disliked; grateful, but not cringing, to his patrons; and inclined to constancy in love, had his constancy met with return. He seems to have been as little sullied by the grossness of the age, as was possible for one invited to the pleasures of the times by the patronage of his superiors: as far as we know, he gave into no vice which was then stigmatized as disgraceful; and pure indeed must that mind naturally have been, which, amidst such coarseness of manners, could preserve so much expressive delicacy and elevated refinement.[37]

Other nineteenth-century poets and translators pictured their Catullus in similar terms, although he became somewhat more sentimental as the century progressed—more Victorian, one might say. In 1861 Theodore Martin criticized Lamb for presenting "not Catullus, but the graceful sarcasms of a well-bred gentleman of the days of the Regency," and depicted an equally anachronistic Catullus of his own.[38] Martin's Catullus was an embodiment of "manliness," a strange conglomerate of Public School virtues that attained almost the status of a cult in England from about 1860 to 1900:

> Impulsive, irascible, intense, wayward, and hasty, but at all times hearty, frankly spoken, generous, and manly, it is impossible not to be drawn towards him, and to forget his faults in our sympathy with his warm heart and thoroughly genial temperament.[39]

Only Burton saw that Catullus was not a nineteenth-century English gentleman complete with "boiled shirt, dove-tailed coat, black-cloth clothes, white pocket-handkerchief, and diamond ring."

Burton's own picture of Catullus ("the toga'd citizen, rough, haughty, and careless of any approbation not his own") seems a lot like what is known of Burton himself.[40] But Burton's rugged figure also has something in common with the far more famous portrait of Catullus created twenty years later by William Butler Yeats in his poem, "The Scholars" (1915).[41] Yeats' scholars are unimaginative conformists ("All think what other people think; / All know the man their neighbour knows"). They are elderly pedants, picking over the verses "rhymed out in love's despair" by young men they cannot possibly understand—young men like Catullus, and like Yeats and his friends. The Catulluses of Burton and Yeats are different (we might consider Burton's more rugged, Yeats' more romantic), but both, like their creators, are rebellious, anti-bourgeois, out of tune with conventional Victorian or Edwardian morality. The similarity is not surprising, for Burton and Yeats moved in some of the same literary and aesthetic circles, where new ideas were in the air and eagerness to flout traditional morality was *de rigueur*.[42]

One link between them is the slightly unsavory figure of Burton's collaborator, Leonard Smithers, who specialized in privately-printed pornography. Smithers published not only Burton, but also a group of younger poets associated with *The Savoy*, a short-lived but important avant-garde periodical of the 1890s[43] Their numbers included three figures of importance to Catullus: Aubrey Beardsley, Arthur Symons, and Yeats himself. Aubrey Beardsley, better known as an artist than a writer, translated poem 101 in *The Savoy* of 1896. He illustrated it with a portrait of Catullus headed "Ave atque Vale" (Figure 4).[44] Even more than most, Beardley pictured himself in Catullus, for the nude torso of Catullus in his drawing is outlined by black draperies that form a profile of Beardsley, his eye sketched in the navel and his characteristically beaky features and prominent nose outlined by the lower folds of the garment.[45] Arthur Symons translated and imitated Catullus and visualized his own relations with a London chorus girl as a reenactment of Catullus' life with Lesbia.[46] "Catullus loved passion for Passion's sake," he says in his memoirs. "I have loved Passion . . . as passionately as Catullus."[47] Symons, a close friend of Yeats, could certainly have been one of the young men in Yeats's poem, "tossing on their sleepless beds," making lines "rhymed out in love's despair."[48]

Catullus in the Twentieth Century

In the twentieth century the reception of Catullus no longer lends itself to a single coherent narrative.[49] From the first years of the century on the poet was read in more places and by a more diverse audience than at any time in his history. Even in the English-speaking world his readership was no longer homogeneous ethnically, culturally, or socially. He was even being read by women, some of whom went so far as to translate or write about his work. (He had undoubtedly had women readers before, but their names and opinions are unrecorded.) By mid-century

Figure 4. *Ave atque Vale*, portrait of Catullus by Aubrey Beardsley. Reprinted from *The Savoy*, no. 8 (1896): 53, with permission of the Bryn Mawr College Library.

this diverse audience included yet another new category of readers: classical scholars. This comment is not so outrageous as it seems. Scholars had been among Catullus' most important readers from the Renaissance on, but by the nineteenth century if not before, they were studying not Catullus' *poetry*, but his text, language, and historical period, leaving the literary aspects of his work to poets and other non-professionals.[50] But by 1950 or so, the study of classics itself began to change, and a new generation of scholars began to insist on reading the works of Catullus *as poetry*.[51] The ideas of twentieth-century classicists, then, constitute an important strain in Catullus' reception in a way that the ideas of their nineteenth-century predecessors did not. In the nineteenth century only Ludwig Schwabe, with his biographical reconstruction, had a significant influence on Catullus' literary reception.

A definitive account of Catullus' reception in English in the twentieth century would require (and repay) a long and detailed study ranging over several countries and three continents. It would consider not only poetry and other creative works, but also the demographic makeup of readers, changes in the nature of classical scholarship, shifts in sexual attitudes, new styles of writing poetry, and the influence of literary theory. What follows is much more modest: a brief consideration of three aspects of Catullan reception in English between around 1915 and 2000: the treatment of obscenity, the Catullan narrative, and the idea of Catullus as a misfit in his own time.

Obscenity, so long a barrier to the full reception of Catullus' poetry, began to be treated with more openness and tolerance in the early decades of the century. An early landmark is the appearance in 1929 of two translations. The translators were F.W.C. Hiley and Jack Lindsay.[52] Both translations were privately printed in London and illustrated by contemporary artists. Figure 5 shows the illustration to poem 37 by Véra Willoughby in Hiley. Both poets translated Catullus' poems honestly but without using English obscenities. Hiley apologized, not for Catullus' obscenity, but for the prudishness of his readers. Lindsay made no apologies at all. Hiley was English, an assistant keeper in the Department of Printed Books in the British Museum, Lindsay an Australian poet living in England.[53] Here is each poet's rendition of the opening verses of poem 16 (for a literal translation see pages 170–1 above):

First Hiley:

> I'll show you my manhood,—I'll give you both beans,
> Aurelius and Furius—you couple of queans!
> (16.1–2, translated by F.W.C. Hiley)

Now Lindsay:

> Guard both the ventholes of your dirt,
> slanderous and excrementious, both!
> pathic Aurelius, Furius you
> at bottom filthy fellow too.
> (16.1–2, translated by Jack Lindsay)

Figure 5. Lesbia and a Satyr by Véra Willoughby. Reprinted from F.W.C. Hiley, trans., *Catulli Carmina: The Poems of Catullus* (London, 1929).

Both poets treat the pederastic poems frankly, and neither gives Juventius a sex-change operation. Two years later, an American, Horace Gregory, published another translation in the same spirit as those of Hiley and Lindsay: printed by a small press, honest, but avoiding English obscenities.[54] These three early collections, little known at the time and far from being full-throated translations of Catullus' language, were harbingers of a new and enthusiastic reception of Catullus' obscenity by translators. Here is the English poet and translator James Michie in 1969:

> I'll have you by the short and curly hair,
> Furius and Aurelius, horrible pair,
> Bugger and bum-boy!
> (16.1–2, translated by James Michie)

And the American classicist Dorothea Wender in 1980:

> I'll bugger you, Aurelius Swishy-tail,
> I'll shove it down your throat, Queen Furius.
> (16.1–2, translated by Dorothea Wender)

Classical scholarship was much slower to come to grips with obscenity. C. J. Fordyce's otherwise excellent commentary (1961) simply omitted 32 poems, apparently because Oxford University Press wanted to market his work to schools. Kenneth Quinn in 1970 included the obscene poems and explained them, but in Latin. But by the 1970s scholars were beginning not only to see that obscenity played an important *literary* function in Catullus' poetry, but to study and compare the meanings of sexual acts and sexual roles in ancient and modern society.[55]

The idea of finding a narrative in Catullus' poetry goes back to a seventeenth-century work of fiction, Jean de Lachapelle's *Les Amours de Catulle*. But it became important only around 175 years later, in 1862, when Ludwig Schwabe presented a narrative of Catullus' biography as historical fact. After Schwabe, creative writers and scholars alike believed that they had a firm biographical foundation for their own work, whether they were producing fiction or serious scholarship. The basic story in both cases was the same, a picture drawn primarily from the poems, but fleshed out by Cicero's vicious depiction of Clodia in *Pro Caelio* and stretched over an armature of contemporary historical information. It goes something like this.

> A talented young provincial of good family comes to Rome and makes friends with other gifted young poets like himself, but also falls in love with an aristocratic woman who is both charming and depraved. He expresses his love in his poetry, but she can never understand or truly reciprocate his feelings since she is by nature fickle and promiscuous. The young poet becomes disillusioned and angry but cannot free himself of her since he loves her "more than himself and everyone dear to him" (58.3).

The other great event of his life is the death of his brother, whose loss brings him inconsolable grief. He dies young.

From the end of the nineteenth century on, novelists built on these "facts" not only to reconstruct Catullus' life but to find meaning in it—to write his emotional as well as his physical biography.[56] Narratives of Catullus' story still continue to appear. Among the most recent are Benita Jaro's *The Key* (1988) and Helen Dunmore's *Counting the Stars* (2008). Scholars created similar narratives, but thinking of their work as fact and not considering just how flimsy and circular their reconstructions were. They used the poems to construct a narrative that they equated with the life of the historical Catullus, and then used this "biography" to interpret the poetry. The habit of writing full-scale biographies from the poems began to disappear about mid-century, but scholars still constructed mini-narratives to link and interpret poems and to understand the mind behind them.

Two examples will suffice. Each has a different basis, but each is derived from the poems (or from the poems together with Cicero's *Pro Caelio*) rather than from our scanty information about the historical Catullus.

The first example is the narrative constructed from poems 51 and 11. Poems 51 and 11 are the only poems in the collection in the sapphic meter (the poems are discussed on pages 140–44 above). Poem 51, a translation from Sappho, celebrates Lesbia; poem 11 contemptuously dismisses her. The narrative constructed from these facts is that the young Catullus, perhaps only just arrived in Rome, used 51 to approach the dazzling Lesbia, introducing himself with a translation because he was too shy to speak to her directly. After the affair soured he remembered the beautiful poem he had written at the beginning and chose the same meter to reject her. The earliest instance of this narrative I have been able to find is the work of a poet rather than a scholar. In 1929 Jack Lindsay had this to say about poem 51 in the essay accompanying his translation of the poems:

> It pleases me to think that Catullus first met Clodia in the fitting splendours of Metellus' palace on the Palatine. . . . He sat in the same room with her. He came away, and of course wrote a poem. Perhaps because he felt that he could not trust the incoherencies of his emotion when approacht too directly and personally, and perhaps because this was the way his mind flew, like a homing dove, through the hubbub of cadences the experience

sent thrilling along his blood, he turned to Sappho. . . . In the violence of an emotion which half lost sight of its object in its dogged contemplation of itself also with a halfsense that he must mask an emotion to which he had yet no proprietary right, he addressed the poem to Lesbia, mingling Sappho and Clodia.[57]

Lindsay's discussion of poem 11, equally effusive, sees Catullus as deliberately evoking 51 in a final rejection of Lesbia. The earliest classical scholar to tell the story seems to have been L. P. Wilkinson in a discussion at Fondation Hardt in 1953. I do not know if Wilkinson was aware of Lindsay's idea, but he does not claim any originality:

I believe, with others, that this [51] was the first poem Catullus sent to Clodia. . . . It was intended as a test, a "feeler." If she were in love with him, she would understand what he meant; if not—after all, it was only a translation. . . . Further evidence: for the 11th poem, in which he finally broke with her, with devastating irony he used this same metre. . . . The poem has double force if it is thus a reminder of the first poem he ever sent to her in the dawning of their love.[58]

Wilkinson's remarks were decisive: the story is repeated in the commentaries of Fordyce (1961), Quinn (1970), and Thomson (1997), as well as in numerous books and articles.

The second example is a psycho-biography of Catullus derived from a twentieth-century characterization of Lesbia. This characterization is a compound of three ingredients used in equal measure: Catullus' poetry, the portrait of Clodia in Cicero's *Pro Caelio*, and modern misogynist sentiment. It has its basis in poem 11. There we see Lesbia as a woman of voracious sexual appetite. She crushes the virility of her lovers, and she has destroyed the poet's love—"which has fallen . . . by her fault like a flower / on the edge of a meadow after it has been touched / by a plow going by" (11.21–24). Cicero's portrait of Clodia adds historical verisimilitude: phrases from *Pro Caelio* like "this Medea of the Palatine," and "a woman not only noble but notorious" suggest a woman both deadly and promiscuous.[59] Misogyny does the rest, turning Lesbia into an obscene castrating monster and the historical Catullus into her unsexed and unhappy victim.[60] From there it is only a small step to seeing poem 63 as an autobiographical allegory, with Cybele as Lesbia and Catullus as Attis.[61]

The narrative of the castrating destroyer and her victim has also appealed to poets. It was surely the basis of Swinburne's *Dolores*, "Our

Lady of Pain," in the nineteenth century (discussed earlier in this chapter). It was also used by James Baxter (1926–72), often called New Zealand's most famous poet, in his fourteen-poem sequence entitled *Words to Lay a Strong Ghost: After Catullus* (1973). In *The Wound* Baxter reminds his lover Pyrrha of how Attis, "ruled by Cybele," castrated himself and "became a girl." He continues:

> So it was for me, Pyrrha,
> And the wound will ache, aches now.
> (James Baxter, *The Wound*, 7–8)

The idea of Catullus as a misfit in his own time appeared at least once in the early nineteenth century. For Charles Lamb (1821) Catullus was a gentleman of delicate sensibilities managing as well as he could in an immoral age. He belonged in a better place and time, say in England in the time of the Regency. But for the most part the idea is a twentieth-century phenomenon. From at least the 1930s on, there has been a tendency for readers to think of Catullus as better than the times he lived in, and really much more suited to their own. Eric Havelock (1939) and R.G.C. Levens (1954) both saw Catullus as "modern," like themselves and out of tune with his age. But they did not mean the same thing by "modern." Here is Havelock:

> Catullus paid the price to Roman posterity of defying the unromantic Roman temper. He wrote love lyrics which his countrymen proved incompetent to classify and enjoy as modern taste may enjoy them. We have cleared a dignified space in literature for sexual passion. That is the difference.[62]

Now Levens:

> The present age is all the more at home with Catullus because the feelings he expressed were those of an individualist clinging, in a disintegrating society, to the one standard which he could feel was secure, that of personal integrity.[63]

For Havelock, Catullus is modern in his sexual passion, for Levens, in his individualism. The idea of Catullus' modernity persists, whatever the criteria or the period of the writer. In 2007, generations after Havelock and Levens, Brian Arkins still calls Catullus "a modern poet":

> Catullus appears to be modern because he is an advocate of sexual love (despite its pain), because his approach to everything is highly individualistic, because he was devoted to the art of poetry, because he employs a brief, lucid, hard style.[64]

Catullus' modernity often has a moral dimension that makes him superior to the society he lived in. In 1923 the English poet and editor J. C. Squire (1884–1958) published a poem to Catullus he called, "To a Roman."[65] In section II he addresses Catullus, imagining him in a group of "gross companions":

> Amusing them, one of them, seeming with them:
>   They are pleased to find Catullus of their kind,
> They sprawl and drink and sneer and jest of wenches,
>   Pose to you: but they do not hear your mind.
>   J. C. Squire, "To a Roman," II. 5–8.

In section III he sees Catullus as misunderstood by Lesbia, who wanted to degrade him and failed, unable to do more than wound his "love of fineness, sweetness, loyalty, candor" ("To a Roman," III.15). In section IV he calls Catullus "an alien / Who was born to cherish all his world forgot" (IV.7–8). For Squire, Catullus' superiority to his contemporaries consisted in the purity of his nature, unsullied either by the coarseness around him or by his own participation in it. For later readers—after 1970 or so—Catullus has often seemed superior to, or at least critical of, the actions of his whole society.[66] This Catullus, like his forebears from Martial to Burton and Yeats, has the features of his creators, in this case a late-twentieth-century and largely American sensibility influenced by the 1960s and Vietnam.

Epilogue

Catullus—the real, historical Catullus—is long dead and inaccessible to us. His poems are all we have. They are unchanging in that their words remain—for the most part, anyway—as Catullus left them, although we must always allow for errors and corruptions befalling the text in its mysterious passage from antiquity to the Renaissance. But if the words are the same, the poems, paradoxically, are not. The words on the pages of my text in 2008 may be, for the most part, the same ones that appeared in the text of Martial or Pontano or Sir Walter Ralegh or Aubrey Beardsley or any reader of the twentieth century. But the poems are different, and speak to each of us differently.

At the beginning of the last chapter, I noted that "the words may remain, but their meaning and context change—subtly or drastically—depending on the degree of alteration in the world they describe." This much is true of any work of literature and its reception over time. But it is true in a special way of Catullus because of the nature of his persona. The Catullus we meet in the poems is so realistic, sympathetic, and apparently sincere that readers of almost every era have identified it with themselves and then read that self-portrait back into the poetry. As a consequence, both the sensibility of the poet and the meaning of his words become those of the reader; and the poetry is doubly anchored in the reader's own time. I cannot predict what Catullus will look like ten years from now (he already has many different aspects depending on the gender, nation, and interests of his readers), but I am confident that the process will continue—or to put it another way, that Catullus' poems will "remain enduring for more than a single age" (1.10) as long as readers find interest and meaning in his words.

Notes

1 The indispensable guide to Catullus' early reception in England is McPeek, *Catullus in Strange and Distant Britain*. See also Duckett, *Catullus in English Poetry*. Unless otherwise indicated, all poems in this chapter have been quoted from Gaisser, ed., *Catullus in English*.
2 See Boyle and Sullivan, eds., *Martial in English*, xx-xxx; Sullivan, *Martial: The Unexpected Classic*, 282–95.
3 Braden, "*Vivamus, mea Lesbia* in the English Renaissance."
4 McPeek, *Catullus in Strange and Distant Britain*, 95.
5 *propre and prest*: "pretty and neat."
6 Skelton, *The Complete English Poems*, 74–5.
7 McPeek, *Catullus in Strange and Distant Britain*, 56–67. A pleasant offshoot of this tradition is Thomas Campion's Latin epitaph for Sir Philip Sidney, whom he mourns in an imitation of Catullus' lament for Lesbia's sparrow (poem 3); the name Philip provides the link. McPeek, 296.
8 See Gaisser, *Catullus and His Renaissance Readers*, 19, with earlier bibliography.
9 Sidney also translated poem 51.5–12, but he was probably also thinking of Sappho; Gaisser, ed., *Catullus in English* 4.

10 Lovelace's translations are printed in Gaisser, ed. *Catullus in English*, 26–31.
11 McPeek, *Catullus in Strange and Distant Britain*, 288.
12 See Gaisser, *Catullus and His Renaissance Readers*, 255–71.
13 McPeek, *Catullus in Strange and Distant Britain*, 245.
14 Landor, "The Poems of Catullus," 192.
15 John Nott (1751–1825) and Leigh Hunt (1784–1859). See Gaisser, ed., *Catullus in English*, xxxiv n. 29.
16 Wiseman, *Catullus and His World*, 215.
17 The "oyster-bed" of Lampsacus, the home of Priapus, is a reference to Catullus, fragment 1, which was printed in Swinburne's text as poem 18. For "poem 18," see p. 187 above.
18 The poems of Swinburne and Tennyson are printed in Gaisser, ed., *Catullus in English*, 285–6, and 282.
19 The translation of Lachapelle is from the English version of his work published in 1707. It is quoted from Gaisser, ed., *Catullus in English*, 62.
20 *Bulks*: frameworks or stalls projecting from fronts of shops, notoriously frequented by prostitutes and thieves.
21 Wiseman, *Catullus and His World*, 217.
22 Ibid., 217–25.
23 *The Adventures of Catullus* (London, 1707) 71.
24 [Nott], *The Poems of Caius Valerius Catullus in English Verse*, 1:51.
25 Lamb, *The Poems of Caius Valerius Catullus*, 1:141, 1:154.
26 Venuti, *The Translator's Invisibility: A History of Translation*, 81–98.
27 [Nott], *The Poems of Caius Valerius Catullus* 1:xi.
28 Cranstoun, *The Poems of Valerius Catullus*, vi. For Cranstoun, see Wiseman, *Catullus and His World*, 216–18.
29 Burton and Smithers, *The Carmina of Caius Valerius Catullus*, ix.
30 Cranstoun, *The Poems of Valerius Catullus*, 42 and 58.
31 As Burton's collaborator Smithers strongly implies in his introduction: "With respect to the occasional lacunae which appear, I can merely state that Lady Burton has repeatedly assured me that she has furnished me with a faithful copy of her husband's translation, and that the words omitted (which are here indicated by full points, not asterisks) were *not* filled in by him, because he was first awaiting my translation with the view of our not using similar expressions. However, Lady Burton has without any reason consistently refused me even a glance at his MS.; and in our previous work from the Latin I did not find Sir Richard trouble himself in the least concerning our using like expressions." Burton and Smithers, *The Carmina of Caius Valerius Catullus*, xvii. For more on Burton's translation and its fate, see Brodie, *The Devil Drives: A Biography of Sir Richard Burton*, 320–41, 367 nn. 26 and 27.

32 Burton and Smithers, *The Carmina of Caius Valerius Catullus*, 60 and 31. Burton's translation of poem 16 is reprinted in Gaisser, ed., *Catullus in English*, 137.
33 *The Adventures of Catullus*, 122.
34 Lamb, *The Poems of Caius Valerius Catullus*, 2.92.
35 Cranstoun, *The Poems of Valerius Catullus*, 163. Cranstoun's translation of poem 99 is reprinted in Gaisser, ed., *Catullus in English*, 143.
36 Burton and Smithers, *The Carmina of Caius Valerius Catullus*, 313. Burton calls Catullus' darling "honied Juventius" (p. 281).
37 Lamb, *The Poems of Caius Valerius Catullus*, 1.xliii.
38 Martin, *The Poems of Catullus Translated into English Verse*, xxx.
39 Ibid., xxvi. For more on manliness, see Newsome, "Godliness and Manliness."
40 For Burton's life, see *Dictionary of National Biography* Supplement; Brodie, *The Devil Drives*.
41 Yeats' poem is reprinted in Gaisser, ed., *Catullus in English*, 287–8.
42 Of himself and his circle, Yeats says, "The critic might well reply that certain of my generation delighted in writing with an unscientific partiality for subjects long forbidden. Yet is it not most important to explore especially what has been long forbidden, and to do this not only 'with the highest moral purpose', like the followers of Ibsen, but gaily, out of sheer mischief, or sheer delight in that play of the mind?" *The Autobiography of William Butler Yeats*, 277–8.
43 According to Yeats, the poets of *The Savoy* despised Smithers. He says, "I considered the publisher a scandalous person, and had refused to meet him; we were all agreed as to his character, and only differed as to the distance that should lie between him and us." *The Autobiography of William Butler Yeats*, 279–80.
44 Beardsley's translation is reprinted in Gaisser, *Catullus in English*, 156. Figure 4 is reproduced from *The Savoy* no. 8 (1896): 53, with permission of the Bryn Mawr College Library.
45 Snodgrass, *Aubrey Beardsley: Dandy of the Grotesque*, 160. Beardsley's drawing is shown on 159; a photograph of him in profile appears on 162.
46 For Symons' translations, see his *Knave of Hearts: 1894–1908*. For his Catullan affair, see "Lydia," in *The Memoirs of Arthur Symons: Life and Art in the 1890s*, 156–69.
47 It is worth quoting the passage in full. "I have loved Passion—in my own way—as passionately as Catullus and Villon and Verlaine. And yet there are such infinite ways as well as entanglements by which one apprehends Passion. Verlaine was more passionately in love with life than any man I ever knew and yet I do not imagine that he loved Passion for Passion's sake—nor as amorously as Villon and Catullus loved Passion for Passion's sake." Symons, *The Memoirs of Arthur Symons*, 141.

48 For Yeats' friendship with Symons, see *The Autobiography of William Butler Yeats*, 271–8.
49 For discussions, see Wiseman, *Catullus and His World*, 211–45; Fitzgerald, *Catullan Provocations*, 19–33, 212–35; Arkins, "The Modern Reception of Catullus."
50 In the nineteenth century talented schoolmasters like James Cranstoun and Hugh Vibart Macmaghtan translated or wrote on Catullus (see Wiseman, *Catullus and His World*, 216–21). Because of their broader interests I have put them in a different category from the professional scholars.
51 Gaisser, "Introduction: Themes in Catullan Criticism (c. 1950–2000)."
52 Hiley, *Catulli Carmina: The Poems of Catullus*; Lindsay, *The Complete Poetry of Gaius Catullus*. See Wiseman, *Catullus and His World*, 229–30.
53 Lindsay was a prolific novelist and translator. He later published a second, revised (and slightly less frank) translation of Catullus (1948). Hiley's literary career was less distinguished than Lindsay's, but his works include a wonderful epitaph for a cat owned by the famous Egyptologist, Sir Ernest Wallis Budge. The epitaph concludes with these lines: "Old Mike! Farewell! We all regret you, / Although, you would not let us pet you; / Of cats the wisest, oldest best cat,/ This be your motto—Requiescat."
54 Gregory, *The Poems of Catullus*. See Wiseman, *Catullus and His World*, 230–31.
55 See Lateiner, "Obscenity in Catullus"; Richlin, *The Garden of Priapus*; Wiseman, *Catullus and His World*, 10–14.
56 Examples in English include a short story by Anne Emery Allinson entitled "L'Estranger" (1913) and Thornton Wilder's *Ides of March* (1948). See Wiseman, *Catullus and His World*, 221–3, 233–41.
57 Lindsay, *The Complete Poems of Gaius Catullus*. (The volume has no page numbers.)
58 Wilkinson, in discussion of Jean Bayet's paper, "Catulle: La Grèce et Rome," 47–8.
59 "hanc Palatinam Medeam," Cicero, *Pro Caelio* 18; "muliere non solum nobili verum etiam nota," *Pro Caelio* 31.
60 An extreme example can be found in a paper published in 1983 by Ernst Fredricksmeyer, "The Beginning and the End of Catullus' *Longus Amor*," 71: "Like some huge, obscene monster, Lesbia wraps her thighs about the middles of her countless lovers simultaneously. . . . By her insatiable sexual rapacity she crushes their manhood and thus renders them limp, useless, and impotent." The passage is quoted by Fitzgerald (*Catullan Provocations*, 12).
61 But the autobiographical argument is usually made in a more nuanced way. For a good example, see Putnam (1974), "Catullus 11: The Ironies of Integrity," esp. 75–80 (=93–100 in Gaisser, ed., *Catullus*). Putnam's

argument is picked up by Janan (1994), *When the Lamp Is Shattered*, 103–7.
62 Havelock, *The Lyric Genius of Catullus*, 92.
63 Levens, "Catullus," 284.
64 Arkins, "The Modern Reception of Catullus," 462.
65 Squire, "To a Roman."
66 One of the most important examples of this view is Konstan, *Catullus' Indictment of Rome* (1977).

Appendix I
Catullus' Meters

Dactylic Hexameter   62, 64

Elegiac Couplet   65–116

Galliambic   63

Glyconic and Pherecratean Stanza   34, 61

Greater Asclepiad   30

Iambic
  pure iambic   4, 29
  choliamb   8, 22, 31, 37, 39, 44, 59, 60
  iambic trimeter   52
  iambic septenarius   25

Phalaecean hendecasyllable   1, 2, 3, 5, 6, 7, 9, 10, 12, 13, 14, 15, 16, 21, 23, 24, 26, 27, 28, 32, 33, 35, 36, 38, 40, 41, 42, 43, 45, 46, 47, 48, 49, 50, 53, 54, 56, 57 58

Phalaecean hendecasyllable (variant)   55, 58b

Priapean   17

Sapphic Strophe   11, 51

Appendix 2

Glossary of Metrical and Rhetorical Terms

alliteration: repetition of the same sound at the beginning of consecutive or nearby words. The title of the American national anthem uses alliteration: *The Star Spangled Banner* (and compare the phrases: "**r**ockets' **r**ed glare" and "**b**ombs **b**ursting in air").

anaphora: repetition of the same word or sound at the beginning of one or more phrases or clauses. In the *Gettysburg Address*, Lincoln used anaphora when he said: "We cannot dedicate, we cannot consecrate, we cannot hallow this ground."

antepenult: the third to last syllable in a word. In the word *syllable*, *syl-* is the antepenult.

apostrophe: turning aside from a third-person narration to address a character in the second person.

assonance: repetition of the same vowel sound in consecutive or nearby words. In Byron's line, "So, we'll go no more a roving," there is assonance of *o*.

caesura: "cutting." a regular word break within a foot or metron.

diaeresis: a word break between feet or metra.

diphthong: two adjacent vowels sounded as one. In the word *sounded*, *ou* is a diphthong.

ecphrasis: description, often of a work of art. The story of Ariadne in poem 64 is told in an ecphrasis, the description of the coverlet on the marriage bed of Peleus and Thetis.

elide: suppress a vowel to avoid hiatus.

elision: the suppression of a vowel.

epanalepsis: the repetition of an important word near the end of one verse in the beginning of the next.

hiatus: "gaping," the effect produced when a word ending in a vowel is followed by a word beginning with a vowel. The phrase *a infant* would be an example of hiatus. English avoids it by adding the consonant *-n* to the end of the first word: *an infant*.

ictus: metrical emphasis. It falls on the first long syllable of the foot.

penult: the next to last syllable in a word. In the word *Latin*, *La-* is the penult.

prodelision: the suppression of *e* in *es* or *est* after a word ending with a vowel. In poetry the phrase *Lesbia mea est* ("Lesbia is mine") would be pronounced *Lesbia mea –st* with the prodelision of *e*.

Bibliography

Editions, Commentaries, and Translations of Catullus

The Adventures of Catullus and History of His Amours with Lesbia. London, 1707.

Burton, Richard Francis, and Leonard C. Smithers. *The Carmina of Caius Valerius Catullus. Now first completely Englished into Verse and Prose.* London, 1894.

Cranstoun, James. *The Poems of Valerius Catullus.* Edinburgh, 1867.

Fordyce, C. J., ed. and comm. *Catullus: A Commentary.* Oxford, 1961.

Gaisser, Julia Haig, ed. *Catullus in English.* London, 2001.

Godwin, John, ed. and trans. *Catullus: The Shorter Poems.* Warminster, 1999.

Goold, G. P., ed. and trans. *Catullus.* London, 1983.

Green, Peter, trans. *The Poems of Catullus.* Berkeley, 2005.

Gregory, Horace, trans. *The Poems of Catullus.* New York, 1931. Reprint, New York and London, 1956.

Hiley, F.W.C., trans. *Catulli Carmina: The Poems of Catullus.* London, 1929.

Lachapelle, Jean de. *Les Amours de catulle.* Paris, 1713.

Lamb, George, trans. *The Poems of Caius Valerius Catullus.* 2 vols. London, 1821.

Lindsay, Jack, trans. *The Complete Poetry of Gaius Catullus.* London, 1929.

Martin, Theodore, trans. *The Poems of Catullus Translated into English Verse.* London, 1861.

Michie, James, trans. *The Poems of Catullus.* London, 1969.

Muret, Marc-Antoine de. *Catullus et in eum commentarius.* Venice, 1554.

Mynors, R.A.B., ed. *C. Valerii Catulli Carmina.* Oxford, 1958.

[Nott, John.] *The Poems of Caius Valerius Catullus in English Verse.* 2 vols. London, 1795.

Quinn, Kenneth, ed. and comm. *Catullus: The Poems.* London, 1970.

Thomson, D.F.S., ed. and comm. *Catullus: Edited with a Textual and Interpretative Commentary.* Toronto, 1997.

Wender, Dorothea, trans. *Roman Poetry: From the Republic to the Silver Age.* Carbondale, Illinois, 1980.

Other Primary Sources

Callimachus. *Callimachus Hecale*. A. S. Hollis, ed. Oxford, 1990.
—. *The Poems of Callimachus*. Frank Nisetich, trans. Oxford, 2001.
Courtney, Edward, ed. and comm. *The Fragmentary Latin Poets*. Oxford, 1993, 2003 (with additions).
Ennius. *The Tragedies of Ennius: Edited with an Introduction and Commentary*. H. D. Jocelyn, ed. Cambridge, 1967.
Homer. *Odyssey*, Richmond Lattimore, trans. New York, 1975.
Landor, Walter Savage. "The Poems of Catullus." In *The Complete Works of Walter Savage Landor*. T. Earle Welby, ed. vol. 11. London, 1930. Pp. 177–225.
Martial. *Martial in English*. A. J. Boyle and J. P. Sullivan, eds. Penguin. 1996.
Page, Denys, ed. *Sappho and Alcaeus*. Oxford, 1955.
Parthenius. *The Love Romances of Parthenius and Other Fragments*. S. Gaselee, ed. and trans. Loeb edition. Cambridge, Mass., and London, 1962.
—. *Parthenius of Nicaea: Extant Works Edited with Introduction and Commentary*. J.L. Lightfoot, ed. Oxford, 1999.
Pliny. *Letters of the Younger Pliny*. Betty Radice, trans. Penguin Books, 1985.
Poliziano, Angelo. *Opera Omnia*. I. Maïer, ed. 3 vols. Turin.
Pontano, Giovanni Gioviano. *Ioannis Ioviani Pontani Carmina*. B. Soldati, ed. 2 vols. Florence, 1902.
—. *Ioannis Ioviani Pontani Hendecasyllaborum Libri*. Liliana Monti Sabia, ed. Naples, 1978.
—. *Giovanni Gioviano Pontano: Baiae*. Rodney Dennis, trans. I Tatti Renaissance Library 22. Cambridge, Mass., and London, 2006.
Pound, Ezra. *The Translations of Ezra Pound*. London, 1970.
Ronsard, Pierre de. *Oeuvres complètes*. Paul Laumonier, ed. vol. 5. Paris, 1928.
Skelton, John. *The Complete English Poems*. John Scattergood, ed. New Haven and London, 1983.
Snell, Bruno, ed. *Tragicorum Graecorum Fragmenta*. Vol. 4. Göttingen, 1977.
Squire, J. C. "To a Roman." In *The Living Age*, Vol. 317, 28 April 1923, pp. 228–9.
Symons, Arthur. *Knave of Hearts: 1894–1908*. London, 1913.
—. *The Memoirs of Arthur Symons: Life and Art in the 1890s*. Karl Beckson, ed. University Park and London, 1977.
Yeats, William Butler. *The Autobiography of William Butler Yeats*. New York, 1938.

Secondary Sources

Adams, J. N. *The Latin Sexual Vocabulary*. London, 1982.
Adams, J. N., and R. G. Mayer, eds. *Aspects of the Language of Latin Poetry*. Proceedings of the British Academy 93. Oxford, 1999.

Allen, W. Sidney. *Vox Latina: The Pronunciation of Classical Latin.* Cambridge, 1970.
Anderson, R. D., P. J. Parsons, and R.G.M. Nisbet, "Elegiacs by Gallus from Qaṣr Îbrim." *Journal of Roman Studies* 69 (1979): 125–55.
Arkins, Brian. "The Modern Reception of Catullus." In Skinner, ed., *A Companion to Catullus*, 461–78.
Barchiesi, Alessandro, "The Search for the Perfect Book: A PS to the New Posidippus." In Gutzwiller, ed., *The New Posidippus*, 320–42.
Batstone, William. "Logic, Rhetoric, and Poesis." *Helios* 20 (1993): 143–72.
Biondi, Giuseppe Gilberto. "Poem 101." In Gaisser, ed., *Catullus*, 177–97. Translated and reprinted from "Il carme 101 di Catullo," *Lingua e stile* 11 (1976): 409–25.
Braden, Gordon. "*Vivamus, mea Lesbia* in the English Renaissance." *English Literary Renaissance* 9 (1979): 199–204.
Bramble, J. C. "Structure and Ambiguity in Catullus LXIV." *Proceedings of the Cambridge Philological Society* 16 (1970): 22–41.
Braund, David. "The Politics of Catullus 10: Memmius, Caesar and the Bithynians." *Hermathena* 160 (1996): 46–67.
Bright, David F. "*Confectum Carmine Munus*: Catullus 68." *Illinois Classical Studies* 1 (1976): 86–112.
Brodie, Fawn M. *The Devil Drives: A Biography of Sir Richard Burton.* New York, 1967.
Burgess, Dana L. "Catullus c. 50: The Exchange of Poetry." *American Journal of Philology* 107 (1987): 576–86.
Butrica, J. L. "History and Transmission of the Text." In Skinner, ed., *A Companion to Catullus*, 13–34.
Campbell, D. "Galliambic Poems of the 15th and 16th Centuries: Sources of the Bacchic Odes of the Pléiade School." *Bibliothèque d'humanisme et renaissance* 22 (1960): 490–510.
Clare, R. J. "Catullus and the *Argonautica* of Apollonius Rhodius: Allusion and Exemplarity." *Proceedings of the Cambridge Philological Society* 42 (1996): 60–88.
Clausen, Wendell. "Ariadne's Leave-taking: Catullus 64. 116–20." *Illinois Classical Studies* 2 (1977): 219–23.
—. "Callimachus and Latin Poetry." *Greek, Roman, and Byzantine Studies* 5 (1964): 181–96.
—. "Catullus and Callimachus." *Harvard Studies in Classical Philology* 74 (1970): 85–94.
Coleman, R.G.G. "Poetic Diction, Poetic Discourse and the Poetic Register." In Adams and Mayer, eds., *Aspects of the Language of Latin Poetry.* Proceedings of the British Academy 93. Oxford, 1999. Pp. 21–93.
Commager, Steele. "Notes on Some Poems of Catullus." *Harvard Studies in Classical Philology* 70 (1965): 83–110.

Conte, Gian Biagio. "Poetic Memory and the Art of Allusion." In Gaisser, ed., *Catullus*, 167–76. Translated from "Memoria dei poeti e arte allusiva," *Strumenti critici* 16 (1971): 325–33.
—. *The Rhetoric of Imitation: Genre and Memory in Virgil and Other Latin Poets*. Ithaca, N.Y., 1986.
Courtney, Edward. "Three Poems of Catullus." *Bulletin of the Institute of Classical Studies* 32 (1985): 85–100.
DeBrohun, Jeri Blair. "Catullan Intertextuality: Apollonius and the Allusive Plot of Catullus 64." In Skinner, ed., *A Companion to Catullus*, 293–313.
Duckett, Eleanor Shipley. *Catullus in English Poetry*. Smith College Classical Studies 6. Northampton, Mass., 1925.
Duckworth, George E. *The Nature of Roman Comedy: A Study in Popular Entertainment*. Princeton, 1952.
Edmunds, Lowell. *Intertextuality and the Reading of Roman Poetry*. Baltimore and London, 2001.
Edwards, Catherine. *The Politics of Immorality in Ancient Rome*. Cambridge, 1993.
Edwards, M. J. "Apples, Blood, and Flowers: Sapphic Bridal Imagery in Catullus." In Carl Deroux, ed., *Studies in Latin Literature and Roman History* 6. Brussels, 1992. Pp. 181–203.
Elder, John Petersen. "Notes on Some Conscious and Subconscious Elements in Catullus' Poetry." *Harvard Studies in Classical Philology* 60 (1951): 101–36.
Elliott, Robert C. *The Literary Persona*. Chicago, 1982.
Fantham, Elaine. "*Stuprum*: Public Attitudes and Penalties for Sexual Offences in Republican Rome." *Echos du Monde Classique* 35 (1991): 267–91.
Fantuzzi, Marco, and Richard Hunter. *Tradition and Innovation in Hellenistic Poetry*. Cambridge, 2004.
Feeney, D. C. "'Shall I compare thee . . . ?' Catullus 68b and the Limits of Analogy." In Tony Woodman and Jonathan Powell, eds., *Author and Audience in Latin Literature*. Cambridge, 1992. Pp. 33–44 and 220–4. Reprinted in Gaisser, ed., *Catullus*, 429–46.
Feldherr, Andrew. "*Non inter nota sepulcra*: Catullus 101 and Roman Funerary Ritual," *Classical Antiquity* 19 (2000): 209–31. Reprinted in Gaisser, ed., *Catullus*, 399–426.
Fitzgerald, William. *Catullan Provocations: Lyric Poetry and the Drama of Position*. Berkeley, 1995.
Forsyth, P. Y. "Catullus 64: Dionysus Reconsidered." In Carl Deroux, ed., *Studies in Latin Literature and Roman History* 2 (1980): 98–105.
Fowler, Don. "On the Shoulders of Giants: Intertextuality and Classical Studies." *Materiali e discussioni* 39 (1997): 13–34. Reprinted in Fowler, *Roman Constructions: Readings in Postmodern Latin* (Oxford, 2000), Pp. 115–37.

—. "First Thoughts on Closure: Problems and Prospects." *Materiali e discussioni* 22 (1989): 75–122. Reprinted in Fowler, *Roman Constructions: Readings in Postmodern Latin* (Oxford, 2000), 239–83.
Fraistat, Neil, ed. *Poems in Their Place: The Intertextuality and Order of Poetic Collections.* Chapel Hill, 1986.
Fredrick, David. "Beyond the Atrium to Ariadne: Erotic Painting and Visual Pleasure in the Roman House." *Classical Antiquity* 14 (1995): 267–87.
Fredricksmeyer, Ernst. "The Beginning and the End of Catullus' *Longus Amor*." *Symbolae Osloenses* 58 (1983): 63–88.
Gaisser, Julia Haig. *Catullus and His Renaissance Readers.* Oxford, 1993.
—. "Catullus in the Renaissance." In Skinner, ed., *A Companion to Catullus*, 439–60.
—. "Introduction: Themes in Catullan Criticism (c. 1950–2000)." In Gaisser, ed., *Catullus,* 1–24.
—. "Threads in the Labyrinth: Competing Views and Voices in Catullus 64." *American Journal of Philology* 116 (1995): 579–616. Reprinted in Gaisser, ed., *Catullus,* 217–58.
Gaisser, Julia Haig, ed. *Catullus in English.* Penguin, 2001.
—. *Catullus.* Oxford Readings in Classical Studies. Oxford, 2007.
Ginsberg, E. S. "Peregrinations of the Kiss: Thematic Relationships between Neo-Latin and French Poetry in the Sixteenth Century." *Acta Conventus Neo-Latini Sanctandreani.* Binghamton, N.Y. Pp. 331–42.
Goold, G. P. "Catullus 3.16." *Phoenix* 23 (1969): 186–203.
Grant, Michael. *The Art and Life of Pompei and Herculaneum.* New York, 1979.
Gratwick, A. S. "Those Sneezes: Catullus 45.8–9, 17–18." *Classical Philology* 87 (1992): 234–40.
—. "*Vale, Patrona Virgo*: The Text of Catullus 1.9." *Classical Quarterly* 52 (1997): 305–20.
Greene, Ellen. "Re-figuring the Feminine Voice: Catullus Translating Sappho." *Arethusa* 32 (1999): 1–18.
Greene, Thomas M. *The Light in Troy: Imitation and Discovery in Renaissance Poetry.* New Haven, Conn., 1980.
Gruen, Erich. "Cicero and Licinius Calvus." *Harvard Studies in Classical Philology* 71 (1967): 215–33.
Gutzwiller, Kathryn. "Callimachus' *Lock of Berenice*: Fantasy, Romance, and Propaganda." *American Journal of Philology* 113 (1992): 359–85.
—. "The Literariness of the Milan Papyrus, or 'What Difference a Book?'" In Kathryn Gutzwiller, ed. *The New Posidippus: A Hellenistic Poetry Book.* Oxford, 2005. Pp. 287–319.
Hankins, James. "The Latin Poetry of Leonardo Bruni." *Humanistica lovaniensia* 39 (1990): 1–39.
Havelock, E. A. *The Lyric Genius of Catullus.* Oxford, 1939.

Hinds, Stephen. *Allusion and Intertext: Dynamics of Appropriation in Roman Poetry.* Cambridge, 1998.

Hooper, R. W. "In Defence of Catullus' Dirty Sparrow." *Greece and Rome* 32 (1985): 162–78. Reprinted in Gaisser, ed., *Catullus,* 318–40.

Horsfall, Nicholas. "Cornelius Nepos." In E. J. Kenney, ed. *The Cambridge History of Classical Literature,* vol. 2: *Latin Literature.* Cambridge, 1983. Pp. 116–18.

Hubbard, Thomas K. "The Catullan *Libellus.*" *Philologus* 127 (1983): 218–37.

—. "The Catullan *Libelli* Revisited." *Philologus* 149 (2005): 253–77.

Hunter, Richard. "Callimachean Echoes in Catullus 65." *Zeitschrift für Papyrologie und Epigraphik* 96 (1993): 179–82.

Hutchinson, G. O. "The Catullan Corpus, Greek Epigram, and the Poetry of Objects." *Classical Quarterly* 53 (2003): 206–21.

Hutton, James. *The Greek Anthology in France.* Ithaca, N.Y., 1946.

Iser, Wolfgang. "The Reading Process." In Jane P. Tomkins, ed. *Reader-Response Criticism: From Formalism to Post-Structuralism.* Baltimore, 1992. Pp. 50–69.

Janan, Micaela. *When the Lamp Is Shattered: Desire and Narrative in Catullus.* Carbondale and Edwardsville, 1994.

Jenkyns, Richard. "Catullus and the Idea of a Masterpiece." In *Three Classical Poets: Sappho, Catullus, and Juvenal.* Pp. 85–150.

—. *Three Classical Poets: Sappho, Catullus, and Juvenal.* Cambridge, Mass., 1982.

Jocelyn, H. J. "On Some Unnecessarily Indecent Interpretations of Catullus 2 and 3." *American Journal of Philology* 101 (1980): 421–41.

Johnson, William A. *Bookrolls and Scribes in Oxyrhynchus.* Toronto, 2004.

—. "Pliny the Elder and Standardized Roll Heights in the Manufacture of Papyrus." *Classical Philology* 88 (1993): 46–50.

—. "Toward a Sociology of Reading in Classical Antiquity." *American Journal of Philology* 121 (2000): 593–627.

Kenyon, F. G. *Books and Readers in Ancient Greece and Rome.* Oxford, 1951.

Knox, Bernard. "Silent Reading in Antiquity." *Greek, Roman, and Byzantine Studies* 9 (1968): 421–35.

Konstan, David. *Catullus' Indictment of Rome: The Meaning of Catullus 64.* Amsterdam, 1977.

Krostenko, Brian A. *Cicero, Catullus, and the Language of Social Performance.* Chicago and London, 2001.

—. "Elite Republican Social Discourse." In Skinner, ed., *A Companion to Catullus,* 212–32.

Kubiak, David. "The Orion Episode of Cicero's *Aratea.*" *Classical Journal* 77 (1981): 12–22.

Lateiner, Donald. "Obscenity in Catullus." *Ramus* 6 (1977): 15–32. Reprinted in Gaisser, ed., *Catullus*, 261–81.
Levens, R.G.C. "Catullus." In Maurice Platnauer, ed. *Fifty Years of Classical Scholarship.* Oxford, 1954. Pp. 284–305.
Lorenz, Sven. "Catullus and Martial." In Skinner, ed., *A Companion to Catullus*, 418–38.
Lowe, E. A., ed. *Codices latini antiquiores: A Palaeographical Guide to Latin Manuscripts Prior to the Ninth Century.* 11 vols. Oxford. 1934–66.
Ludwig, Walther. "The Origin and Development of the Catullan Style in Neo-Latin Poetry." In Oswyn Murray and Peter Godman, eds., *Latin Poetry and the Classical Tradition. Essays in Medieval and Renaissance Literature.* Oxford, 1990. Pp. 183–97.
Lyne, R.O.A.M. *The Latin Love Poets from Catullus to Horace.* Oxford, 1980.
—. "The Neoteric Poets." *Classical Quarterly* 28 (1978): 167–87. Reprinted in Gaisser, ed., *Catullus*, 109–40.
Macleod, C. W. "Parody and Personalities in Catullus." *Classical Quarterly* 23 (1973): 294–303.
Martindale, Charles. *Redeeming the Text: Latin Poetry and the Hermeneutics of Reception.* Cambridge, 1993.
McNeill, Randall L. B. "Catullus and Horace." In Skinner, ed., *A Companion to Catullus*, 357–76.
McPeek, James A. S. *Catullus in Strange and Distant Britain.* Cambridge, Mass., 1939.
Miller, Paul Allen. "Catullus and Roman Love Elegy." In Skinner, ed., *A Companion to Catullus*, 399–417.
—. *Lyric Texts and Lyric Consciousness. The Birth of a Genre from Archaic Greece to Augustan Rome.* London and New York, 1994.
—. "Sappho 31 and Catullus, C. 51: The Dialogism of Lyric." *Arethusa* 26 (1993): 183–99. Reprinted in Gaisser, ed., *Catullus*, 476–98.
Moreland, Floyd L., and Rita M. Fleischer. *Latin: An Intensive Course.* Berkeley and Los Angeles, 1977.
Morrison, Mary. "Catullus and the Poetry of the Renaissance in France." *Bibliothèque d'humanisme et renaissance* 25 (1963): 25–56.
Nappa, Christopher. *Aspects of Catullus' Social Fiction.* Frankfurt am Main, 2001.
—. "Catullus and Vergil." In Skinner, ed., *A Companion to Catullus*, 377–98.
Neudling, C. L. *A Prosopography to Catullus.* Iowa Studies in Classical Philology 12. Oxford, 1955.
Newman, John Kevin. *Roman Catullus and the Modification of the Alexandrian Sensibility.* Hildesheim, 1990.
Newsome, D. "Godliness and Manliness." In *Godliness and Good Learning.* London, 1961. Pp. 195–239.

O'Bryhim, Shawn. "Catullus 23 as a Roman Comedy." *Transactions of the American Philological Association* 137 (2007): 133–46.
Pedrick, Victoria. "*Qui potis est, inquis?* Audience Roles in Catullus." *Arethusa* 19 (1986): 187–207.
Putnam, M.C.J. "Catullus 11: The Ironies of Integrity." *Ramus* 3 (1974): 70–86. Reprinted in Gaisser, ed., *Catullus*, 87–106.
Quinn, Kenneth. *The Catullan Revolution*. Carlton, The Melbourne University Press, 1959. Second ed. Cambridge, 1969. Reprint, Ann Arbor, 1971; Bristol, 1999.
—. "Poet and Audience in the Augustan Age." *Aufstieg und Niedergang der römischen Welt*. Berlin and New York, 1982. II.30.1: 75–180.
Richardson, Lawrence, Jr. "*Furi et Aureli, comites Catulli*." *Classical Philology* 58 (1963): 93–106.
Richlin, Amy. *The Garden of Priapus: Sexuality and Aggression in Roman Humor*. Revised ed. Oxford, 1992. First published in New Haven and London, 1983.
—. "Not before Homosexuality: The Materiality of the Cinaedus and the Roman Law against Love between Men." *Journal of the History of Sexuality* 3 (1993): 523–73.
Roberts, Colin H., and T. C. Skeat. *The Birth of the Codex*. London, 1983.
Rosenmeyer, Thomas G., Martin Ostwald, and James W. Halporn. *The Meters of Greek and Latin Poetry*. Indianapolis and New York, 1963.
Ross, David O. *Style and Tradition in Catullus*. Cambridge, Mass., 1969.
—. *Virgil's Aeneid: A Reader's Guide*. Malden, Mass., Oxford, and Carlton, Victoria, Australia, 2007.
Roux Aîné, H., and M.L. Barré. *Herculaneum et Pompéi: Receuil Général des Peintures, Bronzes, Mosaïques, etc*. Paris, 1861.
Santirocco, Matthew S. *Unity and Design in Horace's Odes*. Chapel Hill, 1986.
Schmiel, Robert. "The Structure of Catullus 8: A History of Interpretation." *Classical Journal* 86 (1990–1):158–66.
Scott, W. *Fragmenta Herculanensia*. Oxford, 1885.
Segal, Charles. "Catullan 'Otiosi': The Lover and the Poet." *Greece and Rome* 17 (1970): 25–31. Reprinted in Gaisser, ed., *Catullus*, 77–86.
—. "Catullus 5 and 7: A Study in Complementaries." *American Journal of Philology* 89 (1968): 284–301.
—. "The Order of Catullus, Poems 2–11." *Latomus* 27 (1968): 305–21.
Seidel, Frederick. "Interview with Robert Lowell." *Paris Review* 25 (1961–2):1–41.
Sheets, George A. "Elements of Style in Catullus." In Skinner, ed., *A Companion to Catullus*, 190–211.
Skinner, Marilyn B. "Authorial Arrangement of the Collection: Debate Past and Present." In Skinner, ed., *A Companion to Catullus*, 35–53.

—. "Catullus 8: The Comic 'Amator' as 'Eiron'." *Classical Journal* 66 (1971): 298–305.
—. *Catullus in Verona: A Reading of the Elegiac Libellus, Poems 65–116.* Columbus, 2003.
—. "Clodia Metelli." *Transactions of the American Philological Association* 113 (1983): 273–87.
—. *Sexuality in Greek and Roman Culture.* Blackwell Publishing, 2005.
—. "*Ut Decuit Cinaediorem*: Power, Gender, and Urbanity in Catullus 10." *Helios* 16 (1989): 7–23.
Skinner, Marilyn B., ed. *A Companion to Catullus.* Malden, Mass., Oxford, and Carlton, Victoria, Australia, 2007.
Smith, Barbara Herrnstein. *Poetic Closure: A Study of How Poems End.* Chicago and London, 1968.
Snodgrass, Chris. *Aubrey Beardsley: Dandy of the Grotesque.* Oxford and New York, 1995.
Solodow, Joseph. "On Catullus 95." *Classical Philology* 82 (1987): 141–5.
Starr, Raymond J. "The Circulation of Literary Texts in the Roman World." *Classical Quarterly* 37 (1987): 213–23.
Sullivan, J. P. *Martial, The Unexpected Classic: A Literary and Historical Study.* Cambridge, 1991.
Swann, Bruce W. *Martial's Catullus. The Reception of an Epigrammatic Rival.* Hildesheim, Zürich, New York, 1994.
Tatum, W. Jeffrey. "Friendship, Politics, and Literature in Catullus: Poems 1, 65 and 66, 116." *Classical Quarterly* 47 (1997): 482–500. Reprinted in Gaisser, ed., *Catullus,* 369–98.
—. *The Patrician Tribune: Publius Clodius Pulcher.* Chapel Hill and London, 1999.
Thomas, Richard F. "Catullus and the Polemics of Poetic Reference." *American Journal of Philology* 103 (1982): 144–64.
—. "Menander and Catullus 8." *Rheinisches Museum* 127 (1984): 308–16.
Tracy, Stephen V. "*Argutatiinambulatioque* (Catullus 6,11)." *Classical Philology* 64 (1969): 234–5.
Tuplin, C. J. "Catullus 68." *Classical Quarterly* 31 (1981): 113–39.
Van Sickle, John. "The Book-Roll and Some Conventions of the Poetic Book." *Arethusa* 13 (1980): 5–42.
Vendler, Helen. *Our Secret Discipline: Yeats and Lyric Form.* Cambridge, Mass., 2007.
Venuti, Lawrence. *The Translator's Invisibility: A History of Translation.* London and New York, 1995.
Veyne, Paul. *Roman Erotic Elegy: Love, Poetry, and the West.* David Pellauer, trans. Chicago, 1988.
Walters, K. R. "Catullan Echoes in the Second Century A.D." *Classical World* 69 (1976): 353–60.

Ward-Perkins, John, and Amanda Claridge. *Pompeii A.D. 79*. New York, 1978.
Watson, Lindsay C. "Epigram." In Stephen Harrison, ed., *A Companion to Latin Literature*. Malden, Mass., Oxford, Carlton, Victoria, Australia, 2005. Pp. 201–12.
Weber, Clifford. "Two Chronological Contradictions in Catullus 64." *Transactions of the American Philological Association* 113 (1983): 263–71.
Wender, Dorothea. *Roman Poetry: From the Republic to the Silver Age*. Carbondale, Ill., 1980.
Wheeler, Arthur Leslie. *Catullus and the Traditions of Ancient Poetry*. Berkeley, 1934. Reprint, 1964.
Wheelock, Frederic M. *Wheelock's Latin*. 6th ed. Revised by Richard A. LaFleur. New York, 2006.
Wilkinson, L. P. Discussion of Jean Bayet, "Catulle: La Grèce et Rome." In *L'Influence grecque sur la poésie latine de Catulle à Ovide*. Geneva, 1953. Pp. 47–8.
—. *Golden Latin Artistry*. Cambridge, 1970.
Williams, Craig A. *Roman Homosexuality: Ideologies of Masculinity in Classical Antiquity*. Oxford, 1999.
Wills, Jeffrey. *Repetition in Latin Poetry: Figures of Allusion*. Oxford, 1996.
Winterbottom, M. Review of E. S. Ramage, *Urbanitas. Ancient Sophistication and Refinement. Classical Review* 26 (1976): 59–60.
Wiseman T. P. *Catullan Questions*. Leicester, 1969.
—. "Catullus 16." *Liverpool Classical Monthly* 1 (1976): 14–17. Reprinted in *Roman Studies*, Liverpool, 1987, Pp. 222–4.
—. "Catullus 68." In *Cinna the Poet*, 77–103.
—. *Catullus and His World*. Cambridge, 1985.
—. "Catullus, His Life and Times." *Journal of Roman Studies* 69 (1979): 161–8.
—. "Catullus' Iacchus and Ariadne." *Liverpool Classical Monthly* 2 (1977): 177–80.
—. *Cinna the Poet*. Leicester, 1974.
—. *Clio's Cosmetics: Three Studies in Greco-Roman Literature*. Leicester, 1979.
—. "Looking for Camerius." *Papers of the British School at Rome* 48 (1980): 6–16.
—. "The Masters of Sirmio." In *Roman Studies*, 309–70.
—. "Structural Patterns in Catullus." In *Cinna the Poet*, 59–76.
Wormell, D. E. "Catullus as Translator." In L. Wallach, ed., *The Classical Tradition: Literary and Historical Studies in Honor of Harry Caplan*. Ithaca, 1966. Pp. 187–201.
Wray, David. *Catullus and the Poetics of Roman Manhood*. Cambridge, 2001.
Zetzel, James E. G. "Catullus and the Poetics of Allusion." *Illinois Classical Studies* 8 (1983): 251–86. Reprinted in Gaisser, ed., *Catullus*, 198–216.

General Index

Note: Poem numbers are in italics.

Adventures of Catullus: 197; on
 Juventius, 206; as translation of
 Les Amours de Catulle, 203;
 translation of *poem 32* in, 204;
 translation of *poem 58* in, 203;
 see also Catullus, reception of;
 Catullus, translation of
allusion. *See* intertextuality
Les Amours de Catulle, 201–3,
 212; *see also Adventures of
 Catullus*
Apollonius Rhodius and *poem 64*,
 151, 153, 154, 158
Ariadne: description of, 115–18,
 128; lament of, 86, 158–9; and
 Medea, 150–61; in Roman wall
 painting, 155–7, Figures 1 and
 2
Arkins, Brian, 215–16
arrangement: ancient principles of,
 40; of Catullus' poems, 27–8, 31,
 40, 61, 100; of personal
 anthologies, 30–1; *see also*
 collection of poems; opening
 sequence
Auden, W. H., 100
Aurelius: in *poem 11*, 39, 50, 143; in
 poem 15, 50, 62, 63, 66; in *poem*
 16, 12, 48–50; in *poem 21*, 50, 62,
 63

Batstone, William, 50
Baxter, James, 215
Beardsley, Aubrey: as illustrator of
 poem 101, 208, 209, Figure 4; as
 translator of *poem 101*, 201,
 208
bellus (nice). *See* language of social
 performance
Berenice in *poem 66*, 147–50
books, ancient: circulation of, 24–7;
 production of, 30–1; promotion of,
 26–7; stages in composition of,
 23–5, 31; *see also* arrangement;
 collection of poems; tablets
Burton, Sir Richard: character
 of Catullus in, 206, 207, 208,
 216; theory of translation of,
 205; *see also* Catullus,
 translation of

Caecilius, 24–5
Caesar, Gaius Julius: and Catullus'
 father, 2; Catullus' invectives
 against, 2–3, 6, 31, 89; and
 Pompey, 6–7

Callimachus: influence of on neoteric poets, 14, 161; in *poem 7*, 112; and *poem 64*, 159–60; and *poem 65*, 146–7; and *poem 66*, 139, 147–50, 161, 176, 188; and *poem 70*, 33, 135–6, 161

Calvus, Gaius Licinius: as a friend of Catullus, 8; as a neoteric poet, 14–15, 17; in *poem 14*, 10–11, 14, 30–1, 37, 39; in *poem 50*, 24, 139–40, 142; in *poem 96*, 15

Campesani, Benvenuto, 166, 175

castus (chaste): in Catullus, 49–50; in Mantuan, 183–4, 188; in Marullo, 184, 188; *see also* language of aristocratic obligation

Catullus, biography of: 2–6, 7–9, 18; Apuleius as source for, 3; evidence in his poetry for, 4–5; Jerome as source for, 2; Suetonius as source for, 2–3

Catullus, brother of: 5, 118–21, 124–6, 138, 144–8, 150

Catullus in feminine role: in *poem 11*, 141, 143, 144, 161; in *poem 51*, 141, 144, 161; in *poem 65*, 144, 161; in *poem 66*, 148, 161; in *poem 68*, 124, 127–8, 136, 141, 144; in *poem 70*, 136, 141, 144, 161

Catullus, persona of: believability of, 1, 45–7, 67–8, 167, 206, 217; in Juventius poems, 60–7; in *poem 8*, 55–60; in *poem 10*, 51–5; in *poem 16*, 47–51; *see also* Catullus, reception of

Catullus, present text of: assembled from several bookrolls, 29–30, 40; length and contents of, 28; *see also* opening sequence

Catullus, reception of: contrasted with that of Martial, 194, 198–9; in fifteenth century, 176–85; by Martial, 169–74; in Middle Ages, 175; as narrative, 68, 143, 201–3, 212–15; persona, 68, 167–8, 174, 206–8, 215–17; in sixteenth century, 185–90; in twentieth century, 208–16; *see also* Catullus, translation of; Muret; Poliziano; Pontano; Ronsard; Scaliger; Statius; Valeriano

Catullus, style of. *See* meter, sound, structure, word order

Catullus, translation of: in eighteenth and nineteenth centuries, 204–6; favorite poems for, 198–201; first phases of, 196–7; Juventius as a problem for, 205–6; of *poem 5*, 196–7; of *poem 16*, 204–5, 210; of *poem 32*, 204, 205; of *poem 58*, 203; of *poem 64*, 199; of *poem 70*, 196–7; of *poem 101*, 201; in twentieth century, 210–12; *see also* obscenity

Cicero: 7, 9, 11, 14, 27, 53; *Pro Caelio* of, 4, 8, 10, 13, 212, 213, 214

Cinna, Gaius Helvius: as a neoteric poet, 14–17, 93; in *poem 10*, 54; his *Zmyrna* praised by Catullus, 16–17, 27

Clodia. *See* Lesbia

Clodia Metelli attacked by Cicero, 4, 8, 13, 212, 214

Clodius (Publius Clodius Pulcher): as brother of Lesbia, 3–4; as a political figure, 7

collection of poems: as an ensemble, 31–2; reading of, 32–6, 38; *see also* shared patterns of meaning

comic elements: in *poem 8*, 57, 60; in *poem 10*, 51–2, 54–5, 57; in *poem 24*, 63
Conte, Gian Biagio, 136–8
Cornelius Nepos, 22–3, 25–7, 29, 30, 31, 38
Cranstoun, James, theory of translation of, 205; *see also* Catullus, translation of

dactylic hexameter, description of, 84–6
decet (it is fitting). *See* language of aristocratic obligation
diction, Catullan coinage of, 52, 153, 78, 88, 89, 91, 112
diction, distribution of: 88; in epigrams (*69–116*), 94–7; in long poems (*61–68*), 91–4; in polymetrics (*1–60*), 88–91
diction, registers of: diminutives, 76–7, 88–9, 92–4; Grecisms, 88, 91–2, 94; neutral language, 88, 94–5; obscenity and vulgarisms, 88, 89, 91, 95–6; *see also* language of aristocratic obligation; language of social performance
Dryden, John, 93
Dunmore, Helen, 213

Elder, J. P., 114
elegans (tasteful). *See* language of social performance
elegiac couplet, description of, 86–7
elision: description of, 75–6; effects of, 76–7, 78–9, 89, 91, 95
Ennius' *Medea exul* and *poem 64*, 151, 152, 159
epigrams (*poems 65–116*); as a part of the collection, 28; structure of, 103, 109–11; *see also* diction, distribution of; *poem 101*
epyllion: Cinna's *Zmyrna*, 16–17; *poem 64*, 17, 29–30, 91, 108, 115–18, 150–61
Euripides' *Medea* and *poem 64*, 151, 152, 158, 159

facetus (witty). *See* language of social performance
false closure, 113, 128
Feeney, Denis, 126
festivus (humorous). *See* language of social performance
fides (fidelity). *See* language of aristocratic obligation
foedus (compact). *See* language of aristocratic obligation
Fordyce, C. J., 112, 212, 214
Fowler, Don, 133, 134
Furius: in *poem 11*, 39, 50, 143; in *poem 16*, 12, 48–50; in *poem 23*, 50, 62; in *poem 24*, 50, 62–3; in *poem 26*, 50
futuere (to penetrate vaginally): 11; words related to, 78, 91

galliambics, description of, 82–3
Gibbon, Edward, 199–200
Greene, Thomas, 166–7
Gregory, Horace, 211

Havelock, Eric, 215
hendecasyllables. *See* phalaecean hendecasyllables
Hesiod, 46
Hiley, F. W. C., 210–11
Homer as an intertext: in *poem 11*, 143–4; in *poem 65*, 144–6; in *poem 101*, 136–8, 161
Hunt, Leigh, 200

iambics description of, 80–2
intertextuality: in *poem 11*, 143–44; in *poem 51*, 140–1; in *poem 65*, 145–6; in *poem 64*, 150–61; in *poem 65*, 144–7; in *poem 66*, 147–50; in *poem 70*, 33, 134–6, 161; in *poem 101*, 136–8, 161; signposts of allusion in, 33, 134–5, 136–7, 152; theory of, 133–4; *see also* Vergil and *poem 101*
irrumare (to penetrate orally), 11, 12, 48, 96

Jaro, Benita, 213
Juventius: as a counterpart of Lesbia, 61, 64, 66; not mentioned by name, 50, 59, 61–2; in *poem 24*, 50, 62–3, 88–9; in *poem 48*, 49, 63–4; in *poem 81*, 63: in *poem 99*, 64–6; sex change of by translators, 205–6, 211

Lachapelle, Jean de. *See Les Amours de Catulle*
Lachmann, Karl, 187
Lamb, George: character of Catullus in, 207, 215; theory of translation of, 204; *see also* Catullus, translation of
Landor, Walter Savage: on *poem 63*, 200; on *poem 101*, 201; as translator, 199
language of aristocratic obligation: *bene velle* (to wish well) in, 96; *castus* in, 50, 51; *decet* in, 51; *fides* in, 58, 96, 97; *foedus* in, 58, 67, 96; *officium* in, 96, 97, 122; *pietas* (sense of obligation) or *pius* in, 51, 96, 97
language of social performance: *bellus* in, 9, 10, 89; *elegans* or *inelegans* in, 9, 89; *ineptiae* in, 90; *facetus* in, 9, 89; *festivus* in, 9; *insulsus* in, 54;

lepidus or *illepidus* in, 9, 52, 54, 89–91; in polymetrics, 88–91; *urbanitas* in, 9–10; *venustus* or *invenustus* in, 9, 10, 52, 54, 89
Laodamia and Protesilaus, 121–8
lepidus (charming). *See* language of social performance
Lesbia: affair of with Catullus, 3, 7, 68, 123; contrast of with Juventius, 64, 66–7; not mentioned by name, 32, 37–8, 55, 61, 121, 123, 135, 136, 150; in *poem 68*, 121–8; promiscuity of, 34, 55, 58–60, 66, 80, 126–7, 144; reception of, 214–15; and Sappho, 142; as sister of Clodius, 3–4; social position of, 3, 8
Levens, R. G. C., 215
libellus given to Cornelius Nepos: contents and arrangement of, 27–30; as subject of *poem 1*, 22–3, 25; *see also* arrangement; books; papyrus roll
Lindsay, Jack: and narrative from *poems 11* and *51*, 213–4; as translator of Catullus, 210
Longinus, 141
long poems (*poems 61–68*), 28; *see also* diction, distribution of
love, Catullus' conception of: as a compact, 58, 60, 66–7, 96–7; familial, 5, 34–5, 59, 60, 126, 127, 147–50, 161; *see also* language of aristocratic obligation
Lovelace, Richard, 197
Lowell, Robert, 46

Macleod, C. W., 63
McPeek, James A. S., 199

Mamurra, Catullus' invectives against, 2–3, 31, 89
Mantuan, 183–4
Martial: persona of, 169–70, 216; and *poems 2 and 3*, 170; and *poem 5*, 170; and *poem 16*, 170–3; and reception of Catullus, 170, 174, 177–8, 182, 187, 194–5, 197–8, 217; *see also* poet's excuse; sparrow
Martin, Theodore, character of Catullus in, 207
Martindale, Charles, 167
Marullo, Michele, 183, 184
masculinity associated with penetration, 11–12, 48
Memmius: Catullus in entourage of, 4–5, 52, 113; in *poem 28*, 12
Meredith, George, 200
meter: long and short syllables in, 73, 77–8; types used by Catullus, 222; *see also* dactylic hexameter, elegiac couplet, galliambics, iambics, phalaecean hendecasyllable, sapphic strophe
Michie, James, 212
mollis and *mollitia* as sexual terms, 11–12, 48–50
Muret, Marc-Antoine de: and Pléiade poets, 186; commentary on Catullus, 187–8

negotium. *See otium*
neoteric poetry: Calvus as a practitioner of, 14–15; Cinna as a practitioner of, 14–16; importance of style in, 17, 72, 116–18; influenced by Callimachus, 14; learning as a feature of, 161; *see also* epyllion, word order
Nepos. *See* Cornelius Nepos.

Nott, John, theory of translation of, 204; *see also* Catullus, translation of

obscenity: as a barrier to reception, 188–90, 197, 203–5, 210; in epigrams, 94–6; greater openness to in twentieth century, 210, 212; in polymetrics, 88–91
officium (duty). *See* language of aristocratic obligation
opening sequence: *poems 1–11* as, 36, 39; *poems 1–14* as, 36–9
ordering: by blocks of text, 101, 104–7; by question and answer, 101, 108–11; by repetition, 101–4; by sequencing, 101, 107–8
otium (leisure): contrasted with *negotium* (duty), 10–11, 51; in *poem 50*, 11, 142–3; in *poem 51*, 142–3
Ovid: description of elegiacs by, 87; *see also* poet's excuse

papyrus roll: length and capacity of, 28–9; reading of, 36, 38, 39, 41
Parthenius of Nicaea, 16
Peleus and Thetis, 151–4, 155, 160, 161
persona: and performance, 45, 55; *see also* Catullus, persona of; poet's excuse
pedicare (to penetrate anally), 11, 12, 48
phalaecean hendecasyllable: description of, 78–9; in Martial, 169; in Pontano, 181
pius (dutiful). *See* language of aristocratic obligation
Pliny the younger: as an admirer of Catullus, 169; editing method of, 25; *see also* poet's excuse

poems 2 and *3*, reception of. *See* sparrow
poem 5, reception of, 170, 195
poems 11 and *51*, narrative constructed from, 213–14
poem 16, reception of: by Martial, 170–2; by Pliny, 173–4; by Pontano, 178–80, 183; by Ronsard, 186–7; *see also* Catullus, translation of
poem 63, reception of, 188, 199–201, 214–15
poem 66, reception of, 199
poem 101: and funeral epigram, 118–19; reception of, 201; *see also* Catullus, translation of
poetry, exchange of: in *poem 45*, 106–7, 141; in *poem 50*, 139–40, 141–3; in *poem 62*, 105–6, 141
poet's excuse: in Catullus, 47, 173; in England, 195; in Martial, 47, 173–4, 184; in Ovid, 47, 173; in Pliny, 173–4; in Renaissance, 182–4
Poliziano, Angelo. *See* sparrow
polymetrics (*poems 1–60*), 27, 29; *see also* diction, distribution of
Pope, Alexander, 199
Pompey, 6–7
Pontano, Gioviano Giovano: *Hendecasyllabi* of, 177, 178, 180–1; *Parthenopaeus* of, 177, 179–80; *Pruritus* of, 177, 178–9; treatment of hendecasyllables by, 181; *see also poem 16*, reception of; sparrow
Pound, Ezra, 46, 95
pronunciation: of consonants, 73–4; of vowels, 73, 74–5; word accent in, 74–5; *see also* elision

Quinn, Kenneth, 57, 104, 212, 214

Ralegh, Sir Walter, 196–7
reading aloud: in antiquity, 41–2, 45, 46, 55, 72, 101; value of for modern readers, 72–3, 76–7, 82–3, 87, 114–15, 181, 197
reception, theory of, 166–7
Ronsard, Pierre de, 186–7
Ross, David, 85, 93, 112

sapphic strophe: description of, 79–80; in *poem 11*, 80, 141, 143; in *poem 51*, 79–80, 141, 142
Sappho; and *poem 11*, 143–4; and *poem 51*, 138, 139, 140–2, 188
Scaliger, Joseph, 189–90
Schwabe, Ludwig, 203, 210, 212
sexual partners allowed and illicit, 12–13, 61, 66
shared patterns of meaning, 32–6, 38, 57–60, 100–1, 133–4, 136
Sheets, George, 92
Sidney, Sir Philip, 196–7
Skelton, John, 195, 196
Smithers, Leonard, 208
song, exchange of. *See* poetry, exchange of
sound. *See* elision, meter, pronunciation, reading aloud
Spagnoli, Battista. *See* Mantuan
sparrow: in Martial, 170; in *poems 2 and 3*, 37–8; in Poliziano, 184–5; in Pontano, 181–3; in Skelton, 195–6; in Valeriano, 185
Squire, J. C., 216
Statius, Achilles, 189–90
status in Roman society, 8–9; *see also* masculinity; *urbanitas*
structure: of *poem 1*, 23, 108; of *poem 4*, 107–8; of *poem 7*, 111–13; of *poem 8*, 102, 104; of *poem 13*, 102–3; of *poem 16*, 48, 102, 171;

of *poem 17*, 102; of *poem 36*, 102; of *poem 42*, 103–4; of *poem 45*, 106–7; of *poem 52*, 102; of *poem 57*, 102, 108–9; of *poem 46*, 113–15; of *poem 61*, 103, 104; of *poem 62*, 103, 105–6; of *poem 63*, 104; of *poem 64*, 103, 104–5, 108, 115–18; of *poem 65*, 144; of *poem 68b*, 102, 121–8; of *poem 69*, 109; of *poem 78*, 103; of *poem 79*, 110; of *poem 80*, 109; of *poem 86*, 103; of *poem 87*, 58; of *poem 89*, 110; of *poem 92*, 110–11; of *poem 97*, 109–10; of *poem 99*, 65, 102; of *poem 101*, 118–21; *see also* ordering

Suffenus, bad poetry of, 9–10, 18, 30, 68

Swinburne, Algernon Charles: as imitator of Catullus, 200, 201; misogyny of, 214–15

Symons, Arthur: identification with Catullus by, 208; as translator of *poem 101*, 201

tablets as vehicles for writing, 24

Tennyson, Alfred Lord, as imitator of Catullus, 200–1

Thomson, D. S. F., 214

Tracy, Stephen V., 91

translation, by Catullus: *poem 51* as, 138, 139, 140–1; *poem 66* as, 91–2, 138–9, 147; *see also* intertextuality

urbanitas as a marker of status, 9–10, 51; *see also* language of social performance

Valeriano, Pierio: Catullan lectures of, 188–9; *see also* sparrow

Vendler, Helen, 97, 104

venustus (attractive). *See* language of social performance

Vergil and *poem 101*, 137–8

Veyne, Paul, 45

Volusius, bad poetry of, 17–18

Wender, Dorothea, 212

Wilde, Oscar, 194

Wilkinson, L. P., 214

Willoughby, Véra, 210, 211, Figure 5; *see also* Hiley

Winterbottom, Michael, 9

Wiseman, T. P., 12, 200, 203

word order, 93–4

Yeats, William Butler: character of Catullus in, 207–8, 216

Index of Catullus' Poems

Note: Pages where poems or passages are discussed in some detail are printed in boldface.

1: **22–3**, **26–7**, 37, 38, 39, 88, **108**, 166, 168, 198
2: 37–8, 40, 61, 169, 170, 182, 196
3: 37–8, 40, 61, 77, 78, 133, 169, 170, 182
4: 37, 38, 39, 80–1, **107–8**, 198
5: 37, 38, 40, 49, 57, 61, 64, 75–6, 77, 78, 79, 113, 128, 169, 170, 195, **196–7**
6: 37, 39, 40, **89–91**
7: 37, 38, 40, 49, 64, 101, **111–13**, 128, 169, 195, 196
8: 36, 37, 38, 40, **55–60**, 57, 63, 67, **81–2**, 102, **104** 176, 196
9: 37, 39, 40
10: 4–5, 8, 16, 37, 39, 40, **51–55**, 57, 63, 67, 68, 78
11: 7, 37, 38, 39, 40, 50, **80**, 141, **143–4**, 161, 176, **213–14**
12: 4, 8, 37, 39, 40
13: 37, 38, 39, 40, **102–3**
14: 10–11, 14, **30–1**, 37, 39
15: 50, 59, 61–2, 63, 66, 189
16: **12**, **47–51**, 54, 67, 88, 102, 169, **170–4**, **178–80**, **182–4**, 186, 195, **204–5**, 210, 212

17: 102, 187
"18–20": 187
21: 50, 61–2, 63, 187
22: 9–10, 11, 18, **68**
23: 50, 62
24: 50, 61, **62–3**, 67, 88–9, 206
26: 50
27: 77, 78, 79
28: 4, **12**
29: 2, 6, 7, 31, 80–1, 91, 168
30: 67
31: 3, 201
32: 60, 78, **204–5**
35: 11, 24–5
36: 18, 102
37: 36, **58–60**, **91**, 210–11
38: 11
41: 60–1, 91
41–43: 176
42: 24, **103–4**
43: 38
45: **106–7**, 141
46: 4, 101, 103, **113–15**, 128, 201
47: 4
48: 49, 61, **63–4**, **65**, 169, 206
49: 7

50: 11, 14, **24**, **139–43**, 140, 144, 147
51: **79–80**, 134, 138, 139, **140–44**, 147, 161, 188, 196, **213–14**
52: 102
53: 14
54: 7
57: 2–3, 7, 31, **89**, 91, 102, **108–9**
58: 36, 58, **59–60**, 76–7, 78, 133, **203**
61: 103, 104, 196, 199
62: 29, 31, 103, **105–6**, 141, 176, 196, 199
63: **82–3**, 91, **94**, 104, 150, 188, **199–201**, 214–15
64: 17, 29–30, 31, **84–6**, 91, **92**, **93**, 101, 103, 104–5, **108**, **115–18**, 128, 134, 148, **150–61**, 199
65: 5, 91, 92, **93–4**, 118, 134, 138, 139, **144–7**, **149**, 161, 199
66: 91, 92, 134, 138, 144, **147–50**, 161, 176, 199
67: 91, **93**, 150, 199
68: 5–6, 91, **92**, 101, 102, 118, **121–8**, 136, 138, 141, 144, 145, 150, 188, 199
69: 109
70: **32–3**, 34, 35, 37, **134–6**, 138, 141, 144, 161, **196–7**
72: 32, **33–5**, 87

73: 67, 97
74: **95–6**
75: 36
77: 67
78: **103**
79: 4, 7, 110
80: 95, 109
81: 61, **63**, 206
84: 8
85: 32, **35**, **95**, 109
86: **103**
87: **58**, 59, 60, 76, 101
88: 95
89: 95, 110
90: 95
91: 95
92: **110–11**
93: 7
95: **16–17**, **27**
96: **14–15**
97: **109–10**
99: 61, **64–66**, 67, 102, 206
101: 5, 76, 101, **118–21**, 128, 134, **136–8**, 145, 150, 161, 201, **208–9**
102: 97
109: 36, **66–7**
110: 61, 97
113: 7
116: 95